Developmental Psychology

INTRODUCTORY PSYCHOLOGY

This series of titles is aimed at introductory level psychology students in sixth forms, further education colleges and on degree courses and those wishing to obtain an overview of psychology. The books are easy to use, with comprehensive notes written in coherent language; clear flagging of key concepts; relevant and interesting illustrations; well-defined objectives and further reading sections to each chapter; and self-assessment questions at regular intervals throughout the text.

Published

DEVELOPMENTAL PSYCHOLOGY (Second Edition)
Ann Birch

INDIVIDUAL DIFFERENCES
Ann Birch and Sheila Hayward

BIOPSYCHOLOGY
Sheila Hayward

COGNITIVE PROCESSES
Tony Malim

SOCIAL PSYCHOLOGY (Second Edition)
Tony Malim

RESEARCH METHODS AND STATISTICS
Tony Malim and Ann Birch

COMPARATIVE PSYCHOLOGY
Tony Malim, Ann Birch and Sheila Hayward

PERSPECTIVES IN PSYCHOLOGY (Second Edition)
Alison Wadeley, Ann Birch and Tony Malim

DEVELOPMENTAL PSYCHOLOGY

From Infancy to Adulthood

Second Edition

Ann Birch

MACMILLAN

First edition 1988
Second edition 1997

Published by
MACMILLAN PRESS LTD
Houndmills, Basingstoke, Hampshire RG21 6XS
and London
Companies and representatives
throughout the world

ISBN 0-333-66959-2

A catalogue record for this book is available
from the British Library.

This book is printed on paper suitable for recycling and
made from fully managed and sustained forest sources.

10   9   8   7   6   5   4   3   2   1
06   05   04   03   02   01   00   99   98   97

Copy-edited and typeset by Povey–Edmondson
Tavistock and Rochdale, England

Printed in Hong Kong

Contents

List of Figures and Boxes

FIGURES

BOXES

Preface

Like the first edition of this book, the second edition aims to provide an introduction to Developmental Psychology. It takes the form of comprehensive notes which may be used as a basis for further study.

The book is aimed primarily at those who are studying psychology at GCE A level or GCSE. However, it should also be a useful starting point for students encountering Developmental Psychology for the first time at degree level or on other courses, such as Access to Higher Education, GNVQ and those in education and nursing.

Since the first edition was published, research in Developmental Psychology has burgeoned and there have been some exciting new developments. Also, new modular syllabuses have appeared at A level; the AEB have modified their A level syllabus, which will be examined from 1998 on. This new edition aims to accommodate all these changes. As well as bringing the original material up to date, a number of new topics have been added.

Chapter 1 has been expanded to examine influences on development, the ecology of development and cultural variations, as well as ethical considerations in developmental research.

Chapter 2 has an additional section which examines early social interactions with parents (including special consideration of fathers), grandparents and siblings. The material on attachment contains more recent research, including that into cross-cultural differences in child-rearing; the topics of childminding and day care have been added.

Chapter 3 is expanded to include sections on the measurement of intelligence and cognitive development in a social context. The latter includes coverage of the work of Bruner and Vygotsky.

In **Chapter 4**, the section on the cognitive-developmental approach contains additional material on social cognition.

Chapter 5 now contains the section on moral development, which includes coverage of additional theories and up-to-date research findings; the section on gender includes further material on the cognitive-developmental approach; in the last section, recent work is examined on 'theory of mind' and the proposed deficits in sufferers from autism.

Chapter 6 is not substantially different, though, as with the rest of the book, the material has been brought up to date.

In line with the other books in the series, every effort has been made to offer a readable, 'user-friendly' style. Key concepts are clearly highlighted through the use of bold type, insets and sub-headings. Each chapter begins with objectives to be met and at the end of each section there are self-assessment questions to help independent students to test their understanding. A list of recommended further readings appears at the end of each chapter. Readers are advised to work carefully through the text, section by section, considering the self-assessment questions at the end of each one. These may be reconsidered later when further reading has been undertaken.

I am confident that this book will prove as useful and popular as the first edition and the other books in the series. I hope very much that you will enjoy it.

ANN BIRCH

*" I TRIED OBSERVATIONAL TECHNIQUES
— WAS JUST ABOUT TO MOVE
INTO INTERVIEWS..."*

The Study of Development 1

At the end of this chapter, you should be able to:

1. appreciate some approaches to the study of human development;
2. discuss some of the conceptual issues relevant to the study of human development, including the interaction of biological and social factors, cross-cultural influences and ethical issues;
3. describe a range of research designs and methods used in developmental psychology;
4. discuss the strengths and limitations of each design or method.

WHAT IS DEVELOPMENTAL PSYCHOLOGY?

Developmental psychology is the study of the psychological changes that take place between birth and old age. The most dramatic changes occur in childhood. Therefore, most research has focused upon childhood and adolescence. This is also, in part, because the two most significant theorists to influence our thinking about development, Freud and Piaget, concentrated on the period up to adolescence. The study of adults did not emerge to any great extent until after the Second World War. Even today there are relatively few psychologists who study adulthood *per se*, and only the study of the aged has received substantial attention from researchers. Nonetheless, research interest in adult development is growing and that interest will be reflected in this book.

INFLUENCES IN DEVELOPMENT

Traditionally, psychologists have related developmental processes to age. For example, the reasoning ability of a typical five-year-old is very different from that of a nine-year-old. A developmental psychologist may wish to investigate the processes involved in this progression. What experiences and interactions have influenced the child's development? However, in 1980, Baltes, a German psychologist, wrote an influential paper emphasising the lifespan nature of development and pointing out that factors other than age influence the developmental process.

Baltes *et al.* (1980) proposed that there are three important influences on development. He called these influences **normative age-graded**, **normative history-graded** and **non-normative** life events:

- **Normative age-graded** influences are those which are strongly related to chronological age. For example, the way in which children develop language ability is very closely linked to their age, a two-year-old having far less mastery of language than a five-year-old.
- **Normative history-graded** influences are those related to events happening at a particular time and affecting most members of a given generation (or 'cohort'). Examples might be the civil war in the former Yugoslavia or the famine in Rwanda.
- **Non-normative life events** are those which may influence the development of individuals at particular times and at different ages. Examples might be the effects of divorce in a family or a severe accident resulting in physical disability.

Baltes pointed out that each influence is determined by an interaction of biological and environmental factors (see Box 1.1), though one or the other may be the more dominant in particular circumstances.

THE ECOLOGY OF DEVELOPMENT

Recent researchers into human development have emphasised the importance of studying the **ecology** of development – or development in context. By 'ecology' is meant the environmental conditions which a person experiences or is affected by, directly or indirectly. This is an approach based on the work of the American psychologist Urie Bronfenbrenner (1979).

BOX 1.1
The interaction of biological and social factors

It has been said that development is about how the 'biological' infant turns into the 'social' adult. Throughout the history of psychology, there has been a tradition of separating out 'heredity' and 'environment', 'nature and nurture', 'biology' and 'society' in attempts to explain how a child develops particular qualities and capacities. It is now generally accepted that development occurs through an interaction of biological factors (genetic programming) and social factors (the quality of the environment). This is by no means a simple proposition. There are two ways in which this interaction could be considered:

On the one hand, we could look at the skills a child is born with and watch how these skills develop and are influenced by particular experiences as the child matures. This is the general approach taken by those who have studied perceptual development and language development.

Alternatively, we could look for ways in which the same environment might have different effects on children who are born with different characteristics. An important approach of this kind has involved the study of 'vulnerable' and 'resilient' children.

Horowitz (1987; 1990) sees the 'vulnerable' child as starting life with a particular handicap, such as premature birth or 'difficult' temperament. The 'resilient' child will start life with a particular advantage, such as a sunny disposition. Horowitz proposes that a child's inborn vulnerability or resilience interacts with the 'facilitativeness' of the environment. A highly facilitative environment is one where the child has loving and sensitive parents and is provided with rich and stimulating experiences.

It might be supposed that the most favourable consequences would occur for resilient infants brought up in highly facilitative environments, the least favourable for vulnerable infants in unsatisfactory environments, with other combinations falling somewhere in between. However, Horowitz suggests that a resilient child may do quite well in a poor environment. Similarly, a vulnerable child might do quite well in a highly facilitative environment. According to Horowitz's model, it is only the vulnerable child in a poor environment that experiences extreme disadvantage.

Horowitz' model of development is receiving support from a growing body of research. For example, low-birth-weight children brought up in middle-class homes tend to have normal IQs, as do normal-weight children reared in poverty-level homes. However, children who are low-birth-weight *and* reared in poverty-level homes are most likely to have very low IQs (Werner, 1986). Psychologists are beginning to realise that the same environment can have very different effects on development, depending upon the inborn characteristics of the child.

(See also a discussion of the heredity/environment issue in Chapter 3, Section IV.)

Bronfenbrenner believed that the environment within which an individual develops is much more complex than was originally thought. It is much more than just 'the immediate concrete setting containing the living creature', though this may be an appropriate way to think of it in relation to animal behaviour. Bronfenbrenner proposes that the ecological environment consists of a set of four nested systems (see Figure 1.1).

FIGURE 1.1

The ecology of development: 'development in context'

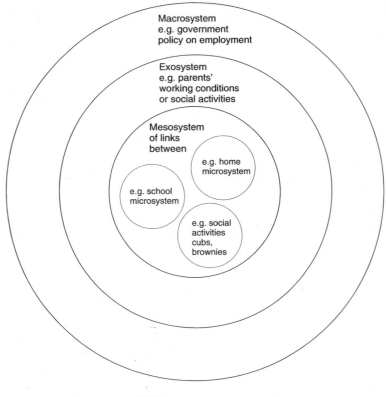

Source: Bronfenbrenner (1979).

1. At the heart is the microsystem, stemming from an individual's experiences in a particular setting. For example, one system a young child experiences is the pattern of activities and interactions in the home environment with parents and siblings. As the child grows older, he or she is influenced by other microsystems, in settings such as playgroup, school, church, and so on. Most psychological research has been carried out from the perspective of the microsystem, for example patterns of play in the nursery school or interactions between mother and child in the home.

2. At the next level is the mesosystem. This involves the relationships between the various settings the developing individual participates in. For example, for a child, this might be the links between the home and school environments; for an adult those between family and work settings.

3. The third level, the exosystem, refers to settings in which children do not actively participate, but which do affect them. For example, the parents' work or their social activities may influence the kind of care given to children.

4. The final level, the macrosystem, consists of the organisation of the social institutions and the ideologies that exist in the society of which the individual is a part. Factors such as generally accepted working hours, rates of unemployment, social mores about working mothers or the availability of child care may affect parents' well-being in the work situation which in turn will affect a child's microsystems and mesosystems.

The value of Bronfenbrenner's model lies in showing us the importance of recognising *all* these systems *as well as* the links between them, when we conceptualise and design psychological investigations – not just the microsystems which have most commonly been studied.

Bronfenbrenner suggests that developmental psychologists should strive to understand the ecological environment as it influences the child's development. For example, events such as starting nursery school, having a new sibling, going to university and, more indirectly, factors such as parental unemployment or divorce, present individuals with challenges to which they must adapt. In this way, development takes place. Bronfenbrenner believes that the best way to understand people is to look at how they cope with and adapt to change.

Criticisms of ecological theory

Thomas (1992) has argued that Bronfenbrenner's theory does not lead to very precise and testable hypotheses. This may in part reflect the fact that existing developmental research had tended to neglect the role played by ecological factors as represented by Bronfenbrenner. However, Thomas holds that, notwithstanding this point, the theory is imprecise about important factors such as the relationships between microsystems. (For example, how does involvement in the family relate to involvement at school?) Thomas concludes that though there has been insufficient research carried out to test and develop the theory, it remains a very important framework for developmental psychology since, unlike some theories, it attempts to address the real world directly.

In studying the ecology of development, Bronfenbrenner does not examine the concept of culture. However, if we are to understand development we must examine cultural influences as part of the environment in which the child is growing up (see Box 1.2).

RESEARCH DESIGNS AND METHODS

In order to study human behaviour scientifically, developmental psychologists use a number of different research designs and methods. Those most commonly used are summarised below.

Research designs

Where the aim is to observe age-related changes in some area of psychological functioning, two principal designs are used to gather information about individuals at different points in their development: **cross-sectional** and **longitudinal**.

Cross-sectional design

In a cross-sectional design, groups of individuals of different ages are compared at the same point of time. For example, researchers who wish to compare moral values held during early adulthood with those held during middle age will make observations or carry out tests on groups of both young and middle-aged adults moral values at these two age levels. The strengths and limitations of cross-sectional design include:

BOX 1.2

Cultural influences on development

While there is no generally agreed definition of the term, culture basically refers to a system of meanings and customs, including values, attitudes, goals, laws, beliefs, morals, physical artefacts such as tools, kinds of dwellings, and so on (Bee, 1995). In order to be called a culture, this system of meanings and customs must be shared by some identifiable group and transmitted from one generation of that group to the next (Betancourt and Lopez, 1993).

Culture clearly impacts upon the way families socialise their off-springs. It is important to realise that actions or events that appear to be the same on the surface may have totally different meanings in different cultural contexts (see Chapter 2, Section II). For example, smacking a child might be acceptable in one culture but be considered a brutal form of abuse in another.

Bee (1995) argues that there are two main reasons why studying culture is important to the understanding of development.

1. If we are to discover those aspects of development which are truly universal, it is not sufficient to study white, middle-class children from Western cultures and assume that what is observed applies to all children.
2. If we are to understand fully how the environment influences a child's development, it is important to understand culture as part of that environment. We need to consider how different cultural beliefs influence the way people experience their lives. For example, it has been argued that the heavy emphasis in Western cultures on independence, achievement and freedom of the individual leads to a higher level of tolerance of aggression and violence than is true in other cultures (Lore and Schultz, 1993). This could be one explana-tion for the growing violence in Western cultures.

So far in developmental psychology, there has been insufficient truly cross-cultural research to draw on, with most studies restricted to just a few cultures which have much in common, such as European and North American. However, the database is expanding and this book will refer to the findings from cross-cultural research wherever possible.

Strengths

- It is quick and relatively inexpensive.
- It can be easily replicated.
- It can identify differences between age groups and general trends in development which may then be studied more intensively.

Limitations
- Because behaviour is observed at only one time, it tells us nothing about development *within* individuals.
- People of widely differing age groups will have received different social and cultural experiences. Observations might reflect these differences rather than differences due to age.

Longitudinal design

In a longitudinal study, a single group of individuals will be studied over a period of time, usually a number of years. Observations and tests will be carried out at various time intervals. Thus, a study of moral values during adulthood might involve testing one group of adults every ten years between the ages of 20 and 60. The strengths and limitations of this design include:

Strengths
- It provides a view of the development of individuals over time.
- Questions can be answered about the stability of behaviour
- It may be possible to determine some of the effects of earlier experience and conditions on later development.

Limitations
- It requires a very large investment of time and money.
- Participants may be lost or drop out. Those who remain may form a biased group.
- Changes in societal influences at different points in time may result in some rather dated conclusions being drawn. When the study was originally designed, it may have asked research questions that are no longer relevant or interesting. For example, the effects of divorce on a child's psychological adjustment might be very different now that divorce is more socially acceptable than it was, say, 30 years ago.

Cohort design

Baltes' model of three major kinds of influence on development, referred to earlier, led to other kinds of research design for studying development, in addition to the cross-sectional and longitudinal ones already considered. One of these is **cohort design**, in which different samples of children born in different years are compared at the same ages. This, of course, involves studying the samples at different points in time. It therefore combines some of the features of cross-sectional design with some of longitudinal design. An extension of this is **cohort-sequential design**. Here, it would be possible to study, say, the effects of particular educational policies on children born in 1985, 1990 and 1995. Each cohort would be followed through longitudinally from, say, age 3 to age 16. This would provide both cross-sectional and longitudinal data and would allow researchers also to assess the impact of historical changes over a period of time.

Because of their complexity and the time involved, cohort-sequential designs have not yet become widely used except as small scale studies. One example is a study by Olweus (1989) into the problems of school bullying in Norway.

Methods of study

Within the overall research designs discussed above, a wide range of different methods can be used to make observations and collect data. These are discussed below.

Experiments

Manipulation and control are key features of the experimental method. The investigator **manipulates** one variable – called the **independent variable** – and observes its effect on another variable – called the **dependent variable**. At the same time, all other factors which might affect the dependent variable are controlled. Experiments are usually carried out in a laboratory, though they may take place in a more natural setting.

The study by Bandura, Ross and Ross (1963) described in Chapter 4 is an example of a strictly controlled laboratory experiment. The aim was to investigate how far models influence aggressive behaviour in children. Exposure to an aggressive model was the independent variable and the number of aggressive acts reproduced by the children was the dependent variable. Strengths and limitations include the following.

Strengths
- Because unwanted variables are strictly controlled, it is possible to draw firm conclusions about whether the independent variable affected the dependent variable, that is, whether there was a **cause–effect** relationship between the two.
- Experiments provide precise and objective information about human behaviour. Because of this precision, they can usually be easily **replicated**.

Limitations
- Most experiments are short-term. One therefore cannot be sure that the behaviour observed would be the same in the longer-term 'real world' situation.
- Subjects observed under relatively restricted laboratory conditions may not behave as they would in a more natural setting.
- For ethical and practical reasons some kinds of behaviour cannot be experimentally manipulated. For example, children cannot be deliberately exposed to deprivation or abuse in order to examine the effects on their development.

Observational techniques

The natural behaviour of individuals is observed and recorded with as little intervention from the observer as possible. The following two main observational techniques are used.

(i) Naturalistic observation   Spontaneous, ongoing behaviour is observed in a natural setting. An example is the study of children's play activities by Sylva *et al.* (1980) described in Chapter 2.

Strength
- Observational techniques give a more realistic picture of how people function in their everyday world.

Limitations
- Because of the lack of strict control, it is not possible to be sure whether or not unwanted variables are affecting the behaviour studied. One cannot therefore infer cause-and-effect relationships.

- Observational techniques are more open to potential observer bias than are other methods, since they rely more heavily upon the observer's subjective interpretation of events.

(ii) Controlled observation Spontaneous behaviour is observed, but in a situation which has to some extent been manipulated and controlled by the observer.

Ainsworth's studies of infants' reactions to a strange situation referred to in Chapter 2 are examples of controlled observation. Typically, a mother and infant interact in an observation room equipped with a one-way mirror. The baby's reactions to different events are recorded by the investigator. For example, the mother may leave the room or a stranger may approach either during the mother's presence or when she has left the room.

Strengths
- This method has much in common with naturalistic observation, with its emphasis on observing spontaneous behaviour.
- Since the environment in which the behaviour occurs has to some extent been controlled, the investigator can be more confident about which variables are influencing subjects' behaviour.

Limitation
- As the settings in which the observations are made are often unfamiliar to the subjects, the behaviour observed may not be typical of that which would occur in a more natural setting.

Interview techniques

These usually involve one-to-one interchanges between the investigator and the subjects. Initially questions may be asked in a relatively standard way. Subsequent questions may vary in the light of subjects' answers.

Piaget's **clinical interview** method is one example of this technique (see Chapter 3).

Strength
- It is a flexible and effective means of gaining a detailed picture of a person's thought processes, attitudes, fantasies, etc. which are not usually available for direct observation.

Limitations

- The lack of standardisation results in questions varying slightly from one person to another. The interviewer may 'lead' the subject to views she/he does not possess.
- The reliance placed on language as a means of communication limits this method to subjects whose own understanding and use of language is well-developed. It may not, therefore, be a suitable method to use with young children or retarded people.

Correlational techniques

This statistical technique is used in many studies to discover whether or not there is a relationship between two variables. For example, the amount of violent TV watched by a group of primary school-children has been recorded. The level of aggressive behaviour displayed by the children at school was also recorded. The data were correlated to determine whether those children who watched the most violence on TV also displayed the most aggressive behaviour. Findings revealed a positive correlation between the two variables.

Strength

- This technique allows an investigator to measure relationships between naturally occurring variables, without manipulating or controlling them.

Limitation

- The use of correlation does not permit an investigator to draw conclusions about **cause and effect**. Some other factor, unknown to the investigator, may be responsible for the findings. For example, children who display highly aggressive behaviour may have an innate pre-disposition to behave aggressively, which in turn may motivate them to watch more violent TV programmes.

Case study methods

A case study makes a detailed examination of a single individual or a small group. Typical data might include the individual's socio-economic background, family history, school experiences, relationships and details of any experiences which are relevant to the research situation. Information is likely to be gathered by observation or through interviews. In some situations, the participant may be required to take psychological tests.

Probably the best known exponent of the case study method is Freud (see Chapter 3). Detailed case histories of his patients were compiled and it was from these that his theories of the nature of personality were developed. Another well-known case study was conducted by Freud and Dann (1951), who studied a small group of children who had spent most of their lives in a German concentration camp (see Chapter 2). Strengths and limitations of the case study method are as follows:

Strengths
- It provides an opportunity to focus in depth on a particular individual or small group. Thus, there is a greater chance that the researcher might gain insights into the nature of behaviour which might be missed with other methods.
- Because it is generally based upon description and other qualitative data, rather than measurement and quantitative data, case study is not so likely as other methods to ignore those facets of behaviour which are not easily measured.

Limitations
- Case studies may be subjective. Since the researcher alone decides what to include and what to leave out and how to interpret what is observed, it may be very easy to select only those observations which support the theory or hypothesis put forward.
- Because case studies relate to a single or very few individuals, it is not possible to generalise the findings to other people. The results of a study are only valid when applied to that case.
- Because of the subjective nature of a case study and since no two people are the same, replication is not possible.

(A more detailed account of the strengths and limitations of research methods used in psychology can be found in Malim and Birch, 1997.)

Which method?

As we have seen, all the methods described have both strengths and weaknesses. The method chosen by an investigator will depend largely upon what aspect of development is being studied.

Ideally, a number of different methods should be used within one study. If these different methods produce similar findings, confidence can be placed in the conclusions drawn.

Ethical considerations

Any research into human behaviour raises some ethical questions. If we go into someone's home to observe parent–child interaction, we are invading their privacy. Parents may even feel that there is an implication that something is wrong with the way they are bringing up their children. If we test adults or children in a laboratory situation, some will perform worse than others; what is the risk that some participant may react badly to what he or she perceives as a poor performance? Some ethical issues are considered in Box 1.3.

Self-assessment questions

1. Describe the three main influences on development proposed by Baltes *et al* (1980).
2. Discuss Bronfenbrenner's (1979) theory relating to the ecology of development.
3. Why is it important to study cultural influences on development?
4. Which research design, cross-sectional, longitudinal or cohort sequential, do you consider would be the most appropriate for the study of children's patterns of play behaviour at different ages? Give reasons for your answers.
5. Evaluate the usefulness of experimental methods in developmental psychology compared with other methods. What might influence an investigator's choice of research method?
6. Discuss some ethical considerations that might arise in developmental research.

Further reading

Bee, H. (1995) *The Developing Child* (7th edn) (New York: HarperCollins).
Durkin, K. (1995) *Developmental Social Psychology: From Infancy to Old Age* (Cambridge, Mass.: Blackwell).
Malim, T. and Birch, A. (1997) *Research Methods and Statistics* (Basingstoke: Macmillan).
Meadows, S. (1986) *Understanding Child Development* (London: Routledge).
Smith, P. K. and Cowie, H. (1991) *Understanding Children's Development* (Oxford: Blackwell).

BOX 1.3
Ethical issues in developmental research

In the UK the British Psychological Society has issued guidelines on ethical questions in research (BPS, 1990). In the United States, similar guidance is offered by the US Department of Health and Human Services, which all recipients of grants must adhere to. In addition, papers have been written both here and in the US. In particular, Wadeley (1991) has highlighted some of the salient points. There is also a section on ethics in research in *Perspectives in Psychology* (Wadeley *et al.* (1997) to which the reader may refer.

The most fundamental guideline is that participants in research must be protected from possible mental or physical harm. More specific guidelines include the following:

Informed consent
Participants must agree in writing to take part in the investigation. In the case of research involving children, informed consent must be obtained from the parent or guardian. The procedures to be used and their possible consequences should be described. For example, if you intended to study relationships between adolescents and their parents, you might wish to observe individual families as they discussed some area of conflict between them. Before starting the study, it would be essential to explain to each family exactly what is involved and to point out that the scenarios to be observed might sometimes promote tension. After the procedure, you would need to debrief the families and offer support to any who found it particularly stressful.

Confidentiality
Participants must feel confident that any personal information they provide will be regarded as confidential. In reporting the research, no data should be associated with the name of an individual participant unless that participant gives written permission.

Research with children
Ethical guidelines are particularly important in research involving children. Any child who is reluctant to take part must not be tested or observed; any child who becomes distressed must be comforted; potential risks to a child's psychological well-being must be avoided.

" PERSONALLY, I THINK THAT
NURSERY SCHOOL PUTS **TOO** MUCH
EMPHASIS ON CREATIVE PLAY
WITH TOY MONEY ! "

Early Socialisation 2

At the end of this chapter, you should be able to:

1. understand the concept of socialisation;
2. describe some of the major milestones in the social and emotional development of infants and consider early social interactions both with parents and other family members;
3. describe the views of Bowlby and other researchers concerning the nature and significance of attachment;
4. describe and assess the importance of the Strange Situation procedure for measuring attachment in infancy and consider some measures of attachment in older children and adults;
5. critically evaluate Bowlby's views on 'maternal deprivation' in the light of subsequent reassessments of his work;
6. assess the importance of early experience for later social and emotional development in the light of the available evidence;
7. discuss the nature and functions of play in early childhood.

INTRODUCTION

Socialisation is a concept which is used to describe and explain how children acquire the behaviour necessary to enable them to fit in with their culture or society. It is the process by which someone acquires the rules of behaviour and the systems of beliefs and attitudes of a given society or social group, so that he or she can function within it.

In infancy, the socialisation process is influenced most by the parents who act as models for acceptable behaviour, provide loving support and decide on which behaviours to restrict and which to allow. However, increasingly, research findings indicate the importance also of a young child's relationships with people other than the parents, for example siblings and grandparents.

17

It is important not to think of socialisation as **unidirectional** (moving in one direction) – something which is imposed on children by other people. Babies are not passive beings waiting to be moulded into a particular kind of personality. They are active individuals, each with their own genetic potential, who are capable of influencing the way other people react to them. Most parents of more than one child will be able to testify to the differences between their infants – what was effective with one child did not necessarily work with another. Therefore, we should take a **bi-directional** (two-way) view of the socialisation process.

While the term 'socialisation' used to be applied exclusively to the developing behaviour of the child, it has over the past few years widened to consider the adjustments and changes which take place through life. This chapter will be concerned mainly with some of the processes which influence social and emotional development in infants and young children, and will consider in particular the development and significance of the intimate attachments which are formed between children and the adults who care for them. However, it will also briefly consider the attachment process in older children and adults.

SECTION 1   DEVELOPING SOCIAL RELATIONSHIPS

Before considering children's social development in detail, it is important to note a number of events – or milestones – which occur during the first year of life (Bornstein and Lamb, 1988).

Milestones in social and emotional development

Social smiling

A necessary precursor to the socialisation process is the existence of communication, or 'social signals', between child and adults. One such signal which has been investigated is social smiling.

Although newborn infants often produce facial expressions which look like smiling these expressions seem to represent involuntary reactions to the child's physical state, for example tiredness or discomfort. Voluntary smiling – often, smiling which occurs in response to overtures from an adult – usually starts when the infant is around four to six weeks old. Smiles are initially prompted by a variety of things, including faces, bells and bullseyes (Emde and Harmon, 1972). Gradually, however, they are reserved for *social* contexts, with the human face being the most likely stimulus to encourage smiles. From the second and third months, the child seems capable of recognising particular faces and thereafter is most likely to smile in response to familiar people, such as members of the family or regular visitors. Less familiar individuals will bring forth only weak smiles. Infant smiles appear to serve as a powerful mechanism which is designed to attract the attention of adults and encourage them to come closer.

Stranger anxiety or wariness

At about the age of eight to nine months, a child will often exhibit what Spitz (1965) has described as 'eight months anxiety'. This refers to the wariness or open distress which the young child displays when faced with a strange adult. The phenomenon of 'stranger anxiety' has been extensively studied by Ainsworth *et al.* (1969, 1974). It will be considered in greater detail later in this chapter.

Separation anxiety

In the early weeks of life, a baby will not discriminate between different people – if you pick her up she will respond no differently to you than she would to anyone else. At around 6–8 months, babies begin to protest if they are separated from specific people, usually the parent. If the separation continues, the reaction changes from distress and anger (Bowlby, 1973 and 1980, called this the '**protest**' stage) to apparent depression and dejection (the stage of '**despair**'). Finally, the child apparently recovers, adjusts to the situation and becomes responsive again to social overtures (the stage of **detachment**). A child under the age of six months who experiences a long-term separation from the parent may appear to be unsettled by new routines and approaches. However, this cannot be compared to the extreme distress and misery that has been observed in older infants who have experienced similar separations (Yarrow, 1964)

Social attachment

Attachment may be defined as a bond of affection directed towards a specific individual. In a young child, the first strong attachments appear to form around eight months and tend to coincide with the emergence of separation anxiety as described above. Once a baby becomes mobile, it is possible to observe the kinds of behaviour which signal that an attachment has been formed. These include:

● moving towards and staying close to the parent (or main care giver), particularly when distressed or afraid;
● protest when separated from the adult;
● clinging and using the adult as a 'secure base' from which to explore.

John Bowlby (1969), a key theorist in attachment research, believed that these behaviours have survival value and are designed to encourage physical (and later psychological) closeness to the mother. Bowlby's theories and research will be considered in more detail later in this and the following section.

EARLY SOCIAL INTERACTIONS

There have been a few rare instances where a child has been found in a state of extreme deprivation and has had little or no interaction with other human beings. For example, Davis (1947) described the case of a little girl, Anna, who was found at the age of six in an attic where she had been kept with no social contact since she was a baby. When she was discovered, Anna could not speak or feed herself and was totally apathetic. What she had in common with other children found in similar circumstances was that she was totally lacking in the normal skills of social interaction, in fact was considered to be 'barely human'.

What cases such as Anna's show is that children's development takes place to a large degree through social relationships. Other people's behaviour towards the child and the child's behaviour towards them influence the development of personality, cognition (perception, memory, thinking), language, emotion and, of course, social behaviour.

Schaffer (1977) drew attention to what was termed the 'mutual reciprocity' (giving and receiving) of the infant–mother relationship.

He described the sensitive and finely balanced patterns of interaction which occur as each responds to the activities of the other and each influences the behaviour of the other. So how do these crucial early social interactions take place and what are the factors which help the development of social interactions between an infant and other people?

Smith and Cowie (1991) describe a number of characteristics which can be observed in the young baby's repertoire of behaviour. These include the following.

(1) *The ability to learn*   From a very early age, babies pay attention to human faces and voices in preference to other stimuli. To the delight of parents, they learn to distinguish between the familiar voice of the mother or father and other less familiar voices (Mehler *et al.*, 1978). Behaviour such as this is likely to make parents feel 'special' and become even more responsive.

(2) *Behaviours which invite social responses*   For a very young baby, smiling or crying does not have any social meaning. She cries if hungry or uncomfortable and often seems to smile quite randomly. However, parents tend to respond to these signals as if the child were trying to initiate social interaction. If she cries, they are likely to pick her up and talk to her; if she smiles, they tend to smile back and talk to her. Gradually the baby learns the social consequences of crying and smiling because of the social importance parents attach to them. As Newson (1979) observed: 'Human babies become human beings because they are treated as if they already were human beings.' Lock (1980) suggests that a whole range of behaviours that initially do not have any social significance for the infant take on an intended social meaning through the child noting their effects on the mother and then deliberately using them to produce this effect.

(3) *Enjoyment of 'contingent responding' in others*   Contingent responding refers to the response made by a parent following quickly upon an action instigated by the baby – a sort of 'answer' to the baby's action. For example, with a very young baby, contingent responding is given when the parent reacts quickly and appropriately to the child's smiles or coos. Later, this enjoyment of contingent responding develops into games such as 'peek-a-boo' which are at first initiated by the adult and then later develop into genuine interactions which involve anticipation and turn-taking.

Social referencing   Studies have shown that babies of around one year old are actually quite good at gauging a parent's emotional response in a particular situation before deciding how to react themselves. This is known as **social referencing**. It seems to occur in situations which are ambiguous in some way and where the infant is not sure how to respond. The baby scrutinises the mother's face for emotional cues and if she is not there, will do the same with other adults. For example, Klinnert (1984) observed how infants reacted to some unfamiliar toys. They often turned to their mothers as if to gauge her reaction. Where the mother responded positively, so did the baby. If the mother's response was negative, so was the baby's. This early social referencing is thought to be the beginning of a baby's ability to empathise with others.

Parenting

What all this tells us is that these aspects of infant and parent behaviour help the child to develop appropriate skills of social interaction. Babies seem to be programmed to behave in certain ways, and parents, by their responses, provide frameworks for them to learn and develop. Kaye (1984) calls these frameworks '**scaffolding**' or '**framing**' and suggests that the infant is like an apprentice who is learning the skills of social interaction from an expert. (See also Chapter 3, Section III.) Kaye explains that good parents provide these frameworks in a number of different ways:

- They **nurture** children by providing for their physical and emotional needs. This paves the way for communication and a mutual understanding to develop.
- They **protect** children from danger, though allow them to try out things which they are not yet quite capable of.
- They act as **helpers** either by doing things for children that they cannot yet manage for themselves or adapt the particular activity or object so the child can cope with it.
- They give children **feedback** on their actions to help them to improve their performance or to avoid danger.
- They act as **models** by demonstrating skills and attitudes.
- They encourage **discourse** (talk or conversation) and this promotes understanding and sharing.
- They act as a **memory** for the child, which helps the child to organise information and accomplish plans.

Infant imitation

A very important way in which infants learn is through imitation. Many studies have shown that even newborn babies will imitate certain mouth movements like mouth opening or sticking out your tongue (Meltzoff, 1985). This is quite an amazing feat for a newborn, since not only must the baby pay attention to the other person's mouth movement, but must then match her own mouth movements to fit. This occurs simply through feedback from her own muscle movements, since she cannot see her own face.

Research by Kaye and Marcus (1981) showed that babies imitate social stimuli from around the age of six months. The researchers performed various actions such as clapping their hands in front of the child or adopting exaggerated facial expressions. The infants invariably tried to imitate the actions themselves, with their efforts improving as they got older.

Bremner (1988) argues that not only is imitation in infants an index of social awareness, it is an important source of information about the infant's understanding of the world. In particular, it demonstrates their understanding of the relationship between self and other people.

A large amount of research has been carried out into infant imitation. There have been some disagreements and discrepancies in the findings of different workers, some of which probably arise from methodological differences. Nonetheless, we can conclude that the existence of the ability to imitate has important implications for the infant's social development, since it provides a mechanism for learning human behaviour.

Fathers

Until relatively recently, most of the research into early relationships focused on the mother/infant relationship and parenting was assumed to be carried out by a female. But what of fathers? Over the last two decades or so, research has been carried out into infant/ father interactions and relationships.

In an early study carried out in a maternity ward, Parke showed that there was little difference between the reactions of mothers and fathers towards their babies (Parke and O'Leary, 1976). Kotelchuk (1976) demonstrated that infants were equally upset in the presence of a stranger whether mother or father left the room. Lamb (1977) detected few differences in signs of attachment when children played alone, first with one parent and then the other. However, when both parents were present, most children were likely to display stronger attachment to the mother.

As research interest in the role of the father grew, attention was given to the different *ways* in which mothers and fathers interact with children. Lamb (1977) found that, typically, fathers played more vigorously with their children than mothers did; they did not sit as close and they talked to them in more adult language. Mothers tended to interact with their infants in a gentler, more low-key fashion.

It is often suggested that the role of fathers has changed in recent years, with males becoming more involved in caring for their infants. Research carried out in a number of different societies has shown that fathers are as capable of performing the parenting role as are mothers. Typically, however, mothers tend to play a larger part in child-rearing and domestic tasks than do fathers (Lamb, 1987). Studies by Lewis and Cooper (1988) and Frankenhauser *et al.* (1991) show that where both parents go out to work, fathers generally take a greater responsibility for child-care. However, the mother usually takes the main responsibility. So perhaps the idea of the new, nurturant father is a little premature.

Siblings

The majority of children grow up in a family where there are other brothers and sisters. Usually the age difference between siblings is quite small, so they are usually similar enough in age and developmental stages to become important social companions for each other within the home environment. Unfortunately, there is only a limited amount of information available on sibling relationships or what effects interaction between siblings might have on the developmental process.

The most extensive research into sibling relationships within the home was carried out by Dunn and her colleagues (Dunn and Kendrick, 1982; Dunn, 1984) Initially, 40 firstborn children were observed in the home. In each family, a new baby was expected in about a month and in the majority of cases the first child was around 2 years old. After the birth of the new baby, visits were made to the home when the child was one month old and then eight months and 14 months. The natural behaviour between the siblings and with their parents was observed and parents were interviewed. Some of the findings are as follows:

- Inevitably, interaction between firstborns and their parents decreased when the new baby arrived. As might be expected, many older children showed signs of jealousy because the new arrival received more attention. Parents did usually try to include the firstborn in activities such as feeding sessions and sometimes fathers were able to pay more attention to the older child while the mother was involved in activities with the new baby.
- Few firstborns were overtly hostile towards the infant, though some were hostile, often through language – for example, 'Baby, baby. Monster, monster'. The large majority of the firstborns were affectionate towards and interested in the new sibling.
- There was a wide variety of responses from firstborns when the baby cried. Fourteen of them were usually concerned and anxious to help, 10 were ambivalent, 5 were sometimes gleeful and 10 actually tried to exacerbate the baby's distress.

Dunn and Kendrick concluded that:

- Sibling relationships involve deep emotions, both of love and envy.
- These deep and powerful relationships may be the means through which individuals may learn to understand and influence others. Even a child under two years old seems to be learning how to frustrate, tease, placate, comfort and influence the behaviour of their brother or sister. The same is true also of the younger ones as they grow up.

The behaviour geneticist, Sandra Scarr, points out that although siblings share around 50 per cent of their genetic inheritance and many similar experiences within the family, they differ in intelligence, personality and most kinds of mental disorder almost as much as unrelated people do (Scarr and Weinberg, 1976). This suggests that it is important to investigate how a 'family environment' may effect different family members in different ways and how siblings may influence each other's development. It is possible that siblings may often try to be as different as possible from each other (Lamb and Sutton-Smith, 1982). Schachter (1982) calls this 'sibling de-identification'. It may also be that siblings seek out different 'roles' for themselves within the family situation. What is needed is more data on family dynamics and on what actually happens in the home.

Studies of only children show that they generally do well in achievement and intelligence tests and do not appear to have any deficiencies in adjustment or sociability (Falbo and Polit, 1986). This and other studies into the effects of family size seem to suggest that relationships between children and adults are still the most important to many aspects of development.

Grandparents

Relatively few grandparents share the same home as their grandchildren, though many live fairly close, and those who live further away tend to keep in touch through letters, phonecalls and visits. In the 1930s and 1940s, there were many negative stereotypes of grandparents. In particular, some psychiatrists and social workers regarded grandmothers as too strict and punitive and likely to have a harmful effect on their grandchildren. At other times, grandparents were thought of as too lenient with their grandchildren (Townsend, 1957). More recently, the more positive aspects of child–grandparent relationships have been recognised. For example, a grandparent may act as a companion and become an important part of a child's social world. Many grandparents provide emotional support, particularly where a child is in conflict with the parents.

As with sibling relationships, there has not been a large amount of research into child–grandparent interactions and relationships. However, studies that have been carried out indicate that grandparents can considerably influence the behaviour of their grandchildren.

Tinsley and Parke (1984) examined both *direct* and *indirect* influences. Indirect influences are those which occur without there necessarily being any direct interaction. For example, the way parents interact with their children will be influenced by the way they themselves have been brought up by their parents, that is, the grandparents. Grandparents may also provide financial and emotional assistance to the parents which will be of great value at times of family stress.

Direct influences can vary in intensity. The strongest influences will occur in situations where a grandparent acts as a surrogate parent, perhaps looking after children while the parents work.

Usually, it is the maternal grandmother who performs this role. However, Radin, Oyserman and Benn (1991) suggest that grandfathers can also be influential. They found that grandfathers had a beneficial effect on young grandchildren of teenage mothers. This was particularly the case for grandsons.

Self-assessment questions

1. Outline some of the milestones in social and emotional development that occur during the first year of life.
2. Describe some of the mechanisms that contribute to the development of a young child's social relationships.
3. Discuss some research which has examined a child's relationships with parents, siblings and grandparents.

SECTION II THE DEVELOPMENT OF ATTACHMENT

As we saw in Section I (see page 20), attachment can be defined as an enduring bond of affection directed towards a specific individual. Traditionally, research into attachment has been heavily influenced by Freud's psychoanalytic theory (see Chapter 3) and has stressed the importance of the infant–mother relationship. Bowlby (1969) and other researchers influenced by the psychoanalytic tradition believed that the attachment bond which develops between an infant and its mother forms the basis of all interpersonal relationships in later years. More recent research, however, has also stressed the importance of attachments which form with other adults, particularly the father.

Some questions that have been tackled by researchers include:

- How is the relationship between a child and parent formed and maintained?
- Is continuity of care necessary for the formation of attachments or is the quality of the relationship the crucial feature?
- How do we distinguish between 'good' and 'bad' relationships? What features of the parent child interaction are important?

Running throughout most research is the question, what is the relationship between early attachment and later development? For example, what are the consequences for later social and emotional development if a bond does not form?

Interest in the last question was prompted in the 1940s and 1950s by evidence concerning the effects of institutionalisation on social and emotional development. Children who had grown up in institutions frequently seemed to display listlessness and troubled behaviour and showed no interest in social interaction (Bowlby, 1951).

Bowlby's theory

Many early theories explained attachment as operating to satisfy some kind of innate need or drive. Environmental-learning theorists favoured the explanation of secondary drive theory – the mother, as a source of food, satisfied the child's basic physiological needs. The primary drive was towards satisfaction of basic needs, the secondary drive was attachment to the mother in order to satisfy these needs. However, this theory was largely overturned by the work of Harry Harlow who investigated the effects of maternal deprivation on infant monkeys in the late 1950s and 1960s (see Box 2.1). Harlow showed that given the choice between an artificial wire 'mother' which offered milk and one covered with soft terry-towelling cloth which did not offer food, the young monkeys chose the cloth 'mother', and became attached to it rather than to the one which offered nourishment.

BOX 2.1
Harlow's studies of deprivation in monkeys

Harlow (1958), a prominent investigator of animal behaviour in the USA, carried out a series of controlled experiments with rhesus monkeys over a period of some 20 years. Harlow's experiments took several forms

(a)   Infant monkeys were removed from their mothers shortly after birth and were placed alone in a cage with a surrogate (substitute) mother. The surrogate mothers were of two kinds: either a 'cloth mother' which consisted of a cylinder of wood covered with soft, terry towelling material, or a 'wire mother', which was simply a wire cylinder. Both were of the same size and general shape as an adult monkey. Each 'mother' was equipped with a feeding bottle so that the infant could nurse from it. Each monkey had the opportunity to gain access to the other surrogate mother.

The finding was that, irrespective of which 'mother' provided the nourishment, each infant spent most of its time clinging to the cloth mother. Harlow concluded that baby primates need a source of warmth or '**contact comfort**', in addition to the source of food.

Observation of the monkeys' behaviour when they were later introduced to the company of other, normally reared monkeys revealed a bleak picture. Most could not interact adequately with other monkeys; many were either aggressive or indifferent; males were unable to mate successfully; those females who did mate and produce offspring were cruel and inadequate mothers. Harlow concluded that infant mothers cannot develop normal behaviour without the presence of a live mother. However, later experiments showed that brief exposure to other juvenile monkeys each day greatly reduced the abnormal behaviour of deprived monkeys. Could interaction with age-mates compensate for the lack of a mother?

(b) In an attempt to assess the total importance of a mother, whether real or surrogate, Harlow and Harlow (1969) raised infant monkeys in complete isolation from both humans or other monkeys. The later behaviour of these monkeys was even more bizarre than that of the surrogate-raised monkeys. They clutched their own bodies and rocked compulsively. When later they were exposed to other, normally reared monkeys, they were usually apathetic and often became aggressive towards both others and themselves, biting their own arms and legs. The extent of the abnormal behaviour reflected the length of the isolation.

As a result of these experiments, Harlow claimed in 1971 that mothering is crucial for normal development in *all* primates.

(c) Later research questioned Harlow's earlier claims. Novak and Harlow (1975) raised infant monkeys in total isolation for a year. When the monkeys were later introduced to younger, 'therapist' monkeys, who played and interacted with them, the behaviour of the deprived monkeys became much more normal and they were able to participate effectively in all social situations. It was concluded that the effects of deprivation are not irreversible.

Ethical issues

When these studies were conducted, it was felt that the distress and damage caused to the monkeys could be justified because of the important insights which were gained into human behaviour. However, critics questioned both the cruelty of the procedures and the relevance of the findings in relation to humans. Given the much stricter guidelines and regulations which now exist in relation to research with animals (see Malim *et al.* 1996), it is doubtful that the experiments would be carried out today.

Though Bowlby was influenced initially by psychoanalytic theory, he also become heavily influenced by **ethological** concepts (see Box 2.2) and particularly the work done by Tinbergen (1907–1988) and Lorenz (1903–1989) into imprinting in animals. Through imprinting, the young of many species form early attachments to parents. A manifestation of this attachment is the young animal's tendency to stay close to the parent whenever the parent moved. Remember that Bowbly believed that the various kinds of attachment behaviour shown by human babies (see page 20) are designed to maintain proximity between mother and baby.

BOX 2.2
Insights from studies of imprinting

Ethologists study the behaviour of animals in their natural habitat, from the standpoint of biology. Such naturalistic observations are considered crucial to the understanding of important behaviours such as aggression and sexual relations. Ethologists are guided by specific hypotheses in their work, and once their hypotheses have been tentatively supported from a study of the animals' natural behaviour, a specific experiment may be devised.

Konrad Lorenz (1935), an important figure in ethology, showed that young animals such as geese and ducks follow their mothers from an early age and become permanently bonded or **imprinted** on her. This 'attachment', he contended, is of crucial importance to the animals' later social and mating behaviour. Lorenz showed, during the course of his experiments, that if animals become imprinted upon a human or on some inanimate object instead of the parent, their later mating behaviour becomes seriously disrupted. He also suggested that such abnormal behaviour was irreversible.

In addition to studying the process and effects of imprinting, Lorenz also investigated the time during which imprinting behaviour emerged. He proposed that there was a **critical period** or fixed time, during the first three days of life, when imprinting must occur if a lasting attachment is to result.

Later researchers such as Sluckin (1965) and Bateson (1964) were less convinced of the existence of such a rigid critical period in the development of imprinting. They preferred to speak instead of a **sensitive period**, a more flexible time during which imprinting is most likely to occur

---

Bowlby's theory contained a number of concepts drawn from biology:

- Attachment behaviour was seen as a system which evolves in order to provide the infant with protection as occurs in other mammals – in other words, it is **adaptive** (has survival value). The tendency to remain close to adults offers protection against predators and reduces the likelihood that the child will become separated from the adult on whom he or she depends for survival. Bowlby suggests that this mechanism can only be understood in terms of the primeval human environment (the very early stages of human development). This is because changes in the fairly recent history of human development have been too rapid for evolutionary mechanisms to keep up.
- Bowlby stressed that attachment behaviours are not designed to maintain proximity with *any* adult. As the child develops, its attention becomes increasingly directed to one person in particular, the primary caregiver (usually the mother). Though the child may form other attachments, he believed that there is always one which is qualitatively different from the others. This aspect of Bowlby's theory is usually referred to as **monotropy**.

Bowlby's three publications (1969, 1973, 1980) revolutionised concepts on what is involved in the development of social relations and his ethological-based theory dominates this field of research (Rutter and Rutter, 1993).

Is monotropy correct?

Bowlby's views, particularly on monotropy – the idea of attachment to just one caregiver, usually female – have attracted controversy and criticism. A naturalistic study which provided contradictory evidence was carried out by Schaffer and Emerson in 1964.

Schaffer and Emerson observed the attachment behaviour of 60 babies in the home situation. They observed that:

- The first strong attachment to a particular person occurred around the age of 7 to 8 months.
- Most children formed attachments with many people in addition to the mother. Attachment figures included fathers, siblings, grandparents, family friends, etc. The researchers described a

small group of infants whose strongest attachments were with their fathers.

- By the age of 18 months, only 13 per cent of the babies had just one attachment figure. The remainder had formed multiple attachments.

Schaffer and Emerson concluded that 'mother' can be male or female and 'mothering' can be shared by several people. Any person who provides a great deal of stimulation and interaction can become an attachment figure, even if they are not providing food. These findings were supported in research carried out in the USA by Cohen and Campos (1974) and by studies of attachment in other cultures.

Cross-cultural studies of attachment

Ainsworth (1967) spent several months observing patterns of attachment in infants of the Ganda tribe in Uganda. Her study provided striking support for Bowlby's description of the course of attachment behaviour. Most of the babies were clearly attached to their mothers by around six months; most began to fear strangers during the last three months of their first year. However, the babies were cared for by several adults in addition to their mothers and most formed attachments simultaneously with several people.

In **Israeli kibbutzim**, from early infancy children spend most of their waking time being cared for in a children's house by a metapalet, or children's nurse. Research suggests that the infants appear to form strong attachments both to their mothers and to the metapalets (Fox, 1977). The babies also develop strong bonds with their own infant peers, which leads to much greater social involvement than is usually observed in such young children.

Security of attachment

Much research into attachment behaviour in babies has been carried out by Mary Ainsworth and her colleagues (1967, 1974). She has described behaviours such as smiling and vocalising preferentially to the mother, crying when the mother leaves the room, following the mother and lifting arms to her, using the mother as a secure base from which to explore in a strange situation and as a refuge to retreat to when frightened.

Ainsworth developed a method for observing and assessing the attachment behaviour babies display towards their mothers. This method is known as the **Strange Situation** and it has been widely used with 12- to 24-month-old babies in the UK, and in the USA, Germany, Holland, Israel and Japan. It is essentially a method for assessing how far a baby would use the mother as a secure base from which to explore and how the child would react to the mother's absence and return when placed in a slightly stressful situation (see Box 2.3).

BOX 2.3

The Strange Situation (Ainsworth *et al.* (1978))

The procedure is a kind of controlled observation (See Chapter 1) and is carried out in a comfortably equipped laboratory situation. It involves 8 short episodes, during which the child successively experiences playing in a strange room in their mother's presence, being left alone there, the mother's return and then departure, the entry of a stranger, and so on. The procedure is designed to provoke a response in the baby which will indicate the baby's attachment to the mother and the sense of security and comfort felt in her presence. Particular attention is paid to the baby's behaviour in the reunion episodes to see if he or she is adequately comforted by the mother.

It was hypothesised that in an effective attachment relationship the child would use the mother as a base to explore, but would be distressed by her absence and would seek closeness on her return. The 'mother absent' episodes are curtailed if the baby is excessively distressed or if the mother wishes to return more quickly.

On the basis of the findings from studies using the Strange Situation procedure, Ainsworth has identified three main attachment types: Type A insecure (anxious/avoidant); Type B secure; Type C insecure (ambivalent).

Babies' behaviour

Type A Insecure (anxious/ avoidant)	During the mother's absence, does not appear distressed; in the reunion episodes, avoids closeness or interaction with the mother; ignores mother on her return or greets her casually, switching between this and avoidance responses such as turning away.

| Type B
Secure | Explores actively in mother's presence; distress in her absence; seeks closeness, interaction or bodily contact in the reunion episodes. |
| Type C
Insecure
(ambivalent) | Anxious before separation from the mother; distressed during separation; ambivalent during the reunion when they both seek and avoid contact with the mother |

Most research on attachment types has been based on the above three categories. However, subsequent research by Main and colleagues suggested that a fourth category might exist.

| Type D
Disorganised and
Disorientated | Main and Solomon (1986) found in their research that a small proportion of babies did not appear to have a coherent strategy for coping with the stresses of the Strange Situation. Their behaviour seemed to be totally disorganised and disoriented; this was characterised by incomplete movements and reactions, sometimes wariness of a stranger, sometimes of mother. |

Research into attachment types

Some interesting findings have emerged from studies where babies were first assessed using the 'strange situation' procedure:

1.   Attachment type related to other aspects of development

Lewis *et al.* (1984) found that 'secure attachment' at 12 months correlated with:

- The quality and sensitivity of mother–child interaction at 6–15 weeks;
- curiosity and problem-solving at age 2;
- social confidence at nursery school at age $3\frac{1}{2}$;
- lack of behaviour problems (boys) at age 6.

Browne (1989) found that 'insecure/avoidant' attachment appeared to be linked to the likelihood of infant maltreatment or abuse. In one study, 70 per cent of maltreated babies were found to insecurely attached to the parents.

Many studies have found that infants categorised as Type B appear to have many advantages over their peers categorised as Type A or Type C. These advantages have revealed themselves in terms of more positive play (Wartner *et al.*, 1994), greater autonomy, interpersonal competence, eagerness to learn during the toddler, pre-school and early school years (Youngblade and Belsky, 1992) and greater responsiveness to unfamiliar adults at school (Turner, 1993). Though there have been some disparities in the literature, it is generally agreed that the quality of attachment is an important aspect of parent–child relationships, one which can predict other social and cognitive aspects of development over the next few years.

2. Stability of security of attachment over time

The significance of research findings depends very much on whether security of attachment is stable over time. There would be little point in drawing conclusions from a measure which might simply reflect the child's emotional state at the time of testing. Therefore, studies have been carried to examine **test–retest reliability** (the same group of infants are assessed twice with a suitable time lag between the tests).

Waters (1978) found an almost exact agreement between babies' 'strange situation' classification at 12 and 28 months. Antonucci and Hewitt (1984) found good reliability between 7 months and 13 months. Main *et al.* (1985) found a strong relationship between security of attachment at 18 months and at 6 years. However, it has been shown that when a child's home circumstances changed, for example, parental divorce, moving house, starting nursery school, security of attachment often changed also, either from secure to insecure or the other way round (Thompson and Lamb, 1983).

In sum, most research found stability over time in security of attachment except in some cases where there was a marked change in the child's home circumstances.

3. Parental responsiveness

In a follow-up study, Ainsworth *et al.* (1986) found that when observed in the home, babies' behaviour was very similar to that observed in the laboratory situation. Furthermore, there appeared to be a link between the attachment types assigned to the babies and the behaviour of their mothers. Babies classified as 'securely attached' cried the least and had mothers who were sensitive and responsive to their needs. Mothers of babies classified as 'anxious/ avoidant' tended to be unresponsive to the babies' social signals and were often relatively cold and rejecting. Mothers of 'ambivalent' babies were inconsistent in their responses to the babies' needs, sometimes responding warmly, at other times ignoring the child's social signals. Ainsworth's early research has been supported by a great deal of more recent research set up to test the hypothesis that sensitive caregiving produces securely attached children. The common factor in the lives of securely attached babies seems to be **contingent responsiveness** from the parents to the child. That is, parents are sensitive and match their responses to the babies' needs.

When very unfavourable family situations have been studied, for instance homes where there are highly stressed, neglectful or abusive parents, serious problems have often been found. For example, parental stress and depression have been found to be linked to the development of insecure attachment in the child (Jarvis and Creasey, 1991). Carlson *et al.* (1989), studying a sample of neglected and badly treated infants, found that about 80 per cent of them fell into the Type D (disorganised and disoriented) category. It seems likely that the highly stressful and inconsistent regime in an abusive home may interfere with the organisation of an effective attachment system. The child's instincts are to seek proximity to the parent; however, because of ill-treatment and rejection, he or she ends up feeling confused about and distrustful of attachment figures.

Despite the above findings, the research carried out has not succeeded in producing a consistent or conclusive pattern which enables us to be sure what features of parental behaviour are most important to the development of secure attachment. There are many other factors that may be important, for example the quality of the relationship between parents, the degree of stress in the home and other possible factors.

4.   Characteristics of the infant

Research findings seem to indicate a strong link between the quality of caregiving and attachment. However, many studies which have claimed such a link have been correlational and one must not overlook the problem of causation which exists in correlational studies (see Chapter 1). Campos *et al.* (1983) point out that differences in maternal behaviour may be due at least in part to the characteristics of the child. A mother may appear to be insensitive because her child is unresponsive, so significant correlations found between maternal responsiveness and security of attachment may not necessarily indicate that causality is from mother to child.

Some researchers have argued that it is **temperamental differences**, widely thought to be inherited, that determine how attachment develops. Belsky and Rovine (1987) found that newborns who showed more temperamental instability (frequent tremors; startle more easily) tended to fall into certain sub-types associated with distress in the Strange Situation. However, Belsky and Rovine propose that both parental responsiveness and infant temperament are important. Children of different temperamental characteristics present different challenges to their caregivers, but also the caregiver's style of responding to the child may determine the kind of attachment relationship which develops between them. In other words, it is a two-way process.

5. *Cross-cultural variations*

In studies carried out in the USA, around 65–70 per cent of babies tend to be classified as Type B (securely attached to their mothers), some 20 per cent as Type A (insecure/avoidant) and around 10 per cent as Type C (insecure/ambivalent). However, some German researchers have found around 40–50 per cent to be Type A (Grossman *et al.*, 1981). In Japan, Miyake *et al.* (1985) classified 35 per cent of babies as Type C. A very substantial contribution to the debate about cross-cultural differences was made by two Dutch researchers, van Ijzendoorn and Kroonenberg (1988). They carried out a meta-analysis of 32 studies which had used the Strange Situation methodology in eight different countries. There were three main findings:

- There were some noticeable **intra-cultural** (within cultures) differences in the way the types were distributed. For example, one of two Japanese studies showed a high proportion of Type Cs but no Type As at all while the other yielded a distribution very similar to that found in Ainsworth's original studies. Overall, van Ijzendoorn and Kroonenberg found intra-cultural differences to be 1.5 times as large as cross-cultural difference

- When the distributions from different cultures were aggregated, the pattern which emerged was very close to Ainsworth's 'standard'.
- While Type Bs were the most common in all cultures, Type As were relatively more frequently found in West European countries, while Type Cs were more common in Israel and Japan.

These findings raise the question of whether 'insecure attachment' is a less satisfactory style of development, as Ainsworth and others believe. Or does it simply reflect *different* styles of interacting? (See Box 2.4.)

BOX 2.4

Cross-cultural differences in attachment types

Takahashi (1990) argues that interpretations of the 'strange situation' types should be very carefully thought through, particularly when they are applied to different cultures. He pointed out that Japanese babies were particularly upset by the 'infant alone' episode because usually, in Japan, babies are *never* left alone at one year old. Therefore, fewer babies were classified as 'securely attached'. Also, it would be difficult for Japanese babies to be assessed as 'insecure/avoidant' since Japanese mothers typically moved immediately towards and picked up their baby.

Sagi and Lewkowicz (1987) suggest that the *meaning* of the Strange Situation may be different for different cultures. The nature of the parent–child relationship varies according to the backgrounds, assumptions and expectations of different cultural groups. For example, German parents perceived some of the behaviour of securely attached babies as hallmarks of a 'spoiled' child. Harwood and Miller (1991) compared Anglo-American and Puerto Rican mothers' reactions to observations of infants who exhibited types A, B or C behaviour. The former perceived independence in babies more favourably while the latter favoured characteristics of obedience and relatedness.

Bretherton (1992) argues that attachment theorists will have to re-think the scope of their work to take account of ecological differences. However, despite misgivings about the usefulness of the Strange Situation in measuring attachment cross-culturally, it could be argued that the differences between cultures add further support to the idea that there is a relationship between caregiving style and the formation of attachments. As different cultures have different styles, it might follow that there would be variations in attachment types.

Criticisms of the attachment construct

Meadows (1986) argues that definitions of terms such as 'attachment behaviour' and 'adequate mothering' need further consideration. Different researchers have sometimes included different criteria in their definitions. For example, Main and Weston (1982) include angry behaviour such as tantrums; other researchers have included 'minutes of crying' or 'number of frowns or smiles'. However, a number of studies indicate that the different behaviours may not be related and may vary from time to time and in different situations (Rutter, 1981)

A number of criticisms of the construct of attachment have centred on the way attachment has been measured and, in particular, the use of the 'strange situation' procedure to determine attachment types:

- The laboratory procedure of introducing a 'stranger' who would approach and make overtures to the baby at set time intervals and without considering the baby's behaviour has been described as unnatural.

  Bronfenbrenner (1979) argues that the Strange Situation provides an ecological setting which might influence the very behaviour being investigated. Rheingold and Eckerman (1973) found that in more natural settings, where a child could approach a stranger in her own time, the child often smiled at and sometimes moved towards the stranger. Nonetheless, despite these findings, it is generally recognised that infants do react differently to people they do not know and are wary of strangers even in familiar surroundings. Also, as we have seen, whether or not it is ecologically valid, the Strange Situation does provide a reliable basis for predictions about other aspects of a child's development.

- Lamb *et al.* (1984) have criticised the fact that the attachment typing arrived at from the Strange Situation procedure was initially based on only 26 American babies. They argue that the classification system was arrived at too quickly using an inadequate sample.

- The assertion that the 'secure attachment' classification is 'normal' must be viewed with caution in the light of studies which have showed variations between cultures (see page 37).

- Smith and Cowie (1991) point out that the Strange Situation procedure measures the relationship between the child and the mother. It cannot be assumed to measure some characteristic of the child. In studies which have used the procedure to assess father–child attachment, it has been found that the attachment type arrived at is often different from that which exists with the mother.

Despite the above concerns and criticisms, the Strange Situation is commonly used internationally and it does seem to allow predictions to be made between the quality of attachment and a whole range of later social and cognitive functions. Lamb *et al.* (1984) argue that the Strange Situation procedure has become the most powerful and useful procedure ever available for the study of socio-emotional development in infancy.

Attachments after infancy

Until the last few years, almost all research into attachment was concerned with very young children. However, it is clear that selective attachment is not something that applies only to infants. If attachment is thought of in terms of the kinds of relationships that reduce anxiety and provide emotional support when we are stressed, it is clear that attachment is in evidence right through all stages of life, including old age (Rutter and Rutter, 1993).

There has been considerable research interest in the factors that may influence stability or change in attachments and also the extent to which early infant–parent attachment may influence a child's later relationships not just with parents but also with siblings, friends, marriage partners or their own children.

The measurement of attachment after infancy

A major problem to face researchers has been how to measure attachment in the years following infancy. As we have seen, it is fairly straightforward in infancy because separation followed by reunion tends to produce very distinctive reactions in the child and because the seeking of closeness is such a widespread indicator of attachment.

Several studies have attempted to measure attachment in older children. For example, Main and Cassidy (1988) successfully used a variation on the Strange Situation with children from 3 to 6 years. For older children and adolescents, a procedure known as the Separation Anxiety Test has been used. In this procedure, the youngsters are asked to respond to photographs showing separation experiences. A procedure known as the Adult Attachment Interview can be used to measure attachment in adults (Main *et al.*, 1985; Pratt and Norris, 1994). The individual is interviewed about his or her early relationships with parents. A technique which has been used to demonstrate the importance of attachment in adulthood is known as the Social Convoy Diagram (Levitt, 1991). This is illustrated in Box 2.5.

Internal working models

The concept of internal working models was originally proposed by Bowlby (1969). It refers to representations in the child's mind of relationships she or he has with parents and other key individuals or attachment figures. These are thought to exist in the form of cognitive structures which are said to contain memories of interactions the child has had with the attachment figure (Bowlby, 1988). These cognitive structures are often referred to as 'schemas' or 'event scripts' which influence the child's interactions with the attachment figure in the light of previous interactions.

Bowlby (1980) argues that though the working model of attachment can change, it is not in a constant state of flux. Once it is developed, it will influence a child's behaviour, affecting memory and attention. Thus the models children build of the relationships they have with parents will regulate how they feel about each parent and how they behave towards them.

Bowlby sees attachment in the school-aged child as being characterised not by the seeking of proximity (closeness) but by more abstract characteristics such as approval and affection. These features, he suggests, become internalised in the child as part of that child's internal working model.

Parent–child pairs of differing attachment types would be expected to have different working models of the relationship. For example, a boy classified as having an insecure/ambivalent relationship with his mother may have an internal working model of her which leads him not to rely on consistent support and comfort when he is upset.

BOX 2.5

Social convoy diagram (adapted from Levitt, 1991)

A technique which demonstrates the importance of attachment in adulthood.

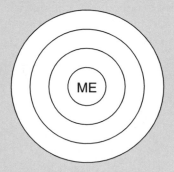

Draw some circles and consider this for yourself.

In the *inner circle*, nearest to yourself, place the names of those people to whom you feel 'so close that it's hard to imagine life without them'.

In the *middle circle*, place those people who are 'not quite as close but still very important'.

In the *outer circle*, place those who don't quite belong in the inner circles but nonetheless are 'close enough and important enough' to have a place in your social network.

Now consider who are the people in your life who provide you with the most support and reassurance – those you would be most likely to confide in, who would look after you if you were ill, who would offer you advice or financial help. It would be very surprising if these were not the people you have placed in the inner circle.

Levitt (1991) carried out a series of studies with people at different stages of the lifespan from young adulthood to old age and from different cultural groups. He found a marked consistency among responses. Most people enter a small number of individuals in the inner circle, usually family – spouse or life partner, parents, children. In-laws are rarely found there, though they often appear in middle or outer circles along with other family and friends.

Levitt (1991) claims that the existence of at least one close relationship seems to be associated fundamentally with personal well-being.

Early attachment and later relationships

Rutter and Rutter (1993) propose that although there is not a lot of solid evidence that early attachment experiences are directly linked to particular attachment relationships in later life, there are some indications that this is so:

> it seems that the experience of selective attachments may in some fashion underlie the development of a range of close relationships in adult life (friendships, sexual love relationships and parent-child relationships) even though the security-providing qualities that characterise attachment in infancy are lacking. (Rutter and Rutter, 1993, p. 125)

He goes on to suggest that individuals' experience of selective attachments seems to improve their capacity to be effective parents. In support, he cites the following research.

(1)   A 36-year-long longitudinal study was carried out by Franz *et al.* (1991). This study showed that the experience of warm and affectionate parenting in early childhood was associated with having a long, happy marriage and close relationships at 41 years of age. However, though these findings suggest continuity in relationships over time, they do not show without doubt that the determining factor was the quality of early attachment.

(2)   Other studies also indicate continuities in relationships. They showed that adults who experienced poor parenting themselves when young tended themselves to have children who were insecurely attached (Parkes *et al.*, 1991). However, there are exceptions. There are many examples of people who are excellent parents and have children who are securely attached, despite their own insecure upbringing. Main *et al.* (1985) found that such mothers, in contrast to those with insecure infants, were able to describe and analyse their own unhappy earlier experiences in a rational way and were able to draw out positive aspects of their own childhood experiences. Mothers who had experienced an unsatisfactory childhood and who themselves had insecure children were unable to discuss their own experiences so rationally. Main suggests that it may be important for people who have experienced an unsatisfactory childhood to develop a balanced perspective and to try to adopt a positive view of themselves which will pay off in later relationships.

Self-assessment questions

1. Outline Bowlby's theory of the nature and functions of attachment. What does Bowlby mean by monotropy?
2. Outline Ainsworth's Strange Situation procedure for measuring the quality of attachment in infancy. Briefly describe the resulting attachment 'types'.
3. In what ways has our understanding of social and emotional development been enhanced by research into 'secure' and 'insecure' attachment? Are these terms culturally valid?
4. Consider some ways of measuring attachment in older children and adults.
5. What is known about the links between the quality of early attachment and later relationships?

SECTION III ATTACHMENT, SEPARATION AND DEPRIVATION

An ongoing concern which began in the late 1940s and early 1950s and still stimulates controversial debate is whether very young pre-school children suffer emotional deprivation if they spend time in day care or childminding situations rather than being brought up in conventional family settings. The debate centres largely on whether mothers of young children should work or should stay at home to look after their children until they are of school age. It has been suggested that very young children should not be deprived of contact with a mother during a particularly sensitive period when the primary attachment relationship is forming. The idea became known as the '**maternal deprivation**' hypothesis and it was first proposed by John Bowlby in a paper to the World Health Organisation in 1951.

Maternal deprivation

Bowlby was concerned about the symptoms observed in institutionalised or hospitalised children. Many exhibited disturbed behaviour, were intellectually retarded and seemed unable to form close relationships with other people. Bowlby believed that a child deprived of the opportunity to form an attachment with a mother or permanent mother figure during the early years of life would develop **social, emotional and/or intellectual problems** in later life.

Among many studies which influenced Bowlby's views were the following:

- His own account of 44 juvenile thieves in a child guidance unit compared with 44 juveniles who were emotionally disturbed, but who had not been accused of a crime. Bowlby observed that the former group contained many individuals who suffered from so-called '**affectionless psychopathy**' (an inability to feel affection for or care about the well-being of others). Moreover, over half of the first group compared with only two of the second had been separated from their mothers for a period of at least a week during the first five years of life. Bowlby concluded that maternal deprivation was the cause of their delinquency and severe emotional disability (Bowlby, 1944).
- Goldfarb's (1943) comparison of two groups of children aged between 10 and 14, fifteen of whom had spent the first three years of life in an institution and fifteen who had spent the same period in foster homes. Compared to the 'fostered' group, the 'institutionalised' group scored lower on tests of intelligence, language and sociability. Goldfarb concluded that the lack of opportunity for the institutionalised children to form an attachment with one person during the first three years of life led to their **intellectual and social retardation**.

Subsequent researchers drew attention to the methodological flaws in these two studies, largely arising from problems of sampling and the lack of appropriate control groups.

According to Bowlby, maternal deprivation could also lead to such conditions as depression, enuresis (bed-wetting) and dwarfism (stunted physical growth).

As we saw in the last section, Bowlby later interpreted many of his earlier observations in the light of ethological theory. He emphasised the **survival function** of the human infant's need to say close to and form an attachment with its mother. He likened this attachment process to **imprinting** in birds (see Box 2.2).

A major aspect of Bowlby's maternal deprivation theory was his proposal that there was a **critical period**, or optimal time, during the first three years of life when this primary attachment should occur.

Bowlby's 'maternal deprivation' theory was also influenced by the work of Harlow and his associates (1958, 1969) into the effects of deprivation in infant monkeys (see Box 2.1). In early studies, Harlow's research showed that infant rhesus monkeys who were separated from their mothers and raised in isolation suffered abnormal social and mating behaviour when they were later placed in the company of other monkeys. As a result of these experiments, Harlow claimed that mothering is crucial for normal development in *all* primates.

Despite many criticisms of his theory, Bowlby's work has had some very worthwhile effects. His work and that of other researchers has led to a much greater awareness of the emotional needs of young children. Also, in a practical sense, it led to many improvements in the care of children in institutions and a move towards fostering and adoption rather than institutional care. It also led to more enlightened care of young children who need to be hospitalised and a recognition of the need for parents to have better access to their children.

A reassessment of maternal deprivation

Bowlby's theory stimulated a large amount of research into the infant–mother relationship and much of it criticised and challenged his more extreme views. In a major review and reassessment of Bowlby's work, Michael Rutter (1972, 1981) supported the view that distortion of early child care could have adverse effects on psychological development. However, he strongly criticised Bowlby's use of the concept of 'maternal deprivation' to cover what is probably a wide range of different problems. Rutter urged researchers to seek more precise descriptions of 'bad' care and 'bad' effects problems and to examine more closely the probable links between them.

Rutter distinguished between the short-term and long-term effects of a child being separated from the parent.

Short-term effects   By short-term effects, Rutter meant the child's immediate response to a depriving experience and to the behaviour shown over the following few months.

He agreed with Bowlby's description of the three stages of distress usually exhibited by a baby who is separated from the parent: protest, despair and detachment (look back at page 19). These three phases are often referred to as the 'syndrome of distress'.

The other syndrome likely to result from 'maternal deprivation', according to Bowlby, is that of developmental retardation, or slowing down of developmental growth, particularly in language and social responsiveness.

After considering the evidence on many factors which are likely to influence a child's response to deprivation (such things as age, sex, temperament, previous mother–child relationship, other separation experiences), Rutter concluded that the syndrome of distress is likely to be due to the disruption of the attachment process, but not necessarily with the mother. Retardation, he believed, can best be explained by the absence of appropriate stimulating experiences

Long-term effects   Long-term was used to refer to effects seen some years later, either following a brief period of separation or after prolonged separation.

After reviewing a wide range of studies (some of them described in the next sub-section) Rutter concluded that:

- Most of the long-term effects of so-called 'maternal deprivation' are likely to be due to the lack of something (**privation**), rather than to any kind of loss (**deprivation**).
- Failure to develop bonds with *anyone*, not just the mother, in early childhood is the main factor in the development of 'affectionless psychopathy'.
- Family discord and the lack of a stable relationship with a parent are associated with later anti-social behaviour and delinquency.
- A lack of stimulation and necessary life experiences are likely to be responsible for intellectual retardation.
- The evidence does not support Bowlby's views concerning the special importance of the bond formed with the mother. The chief bond need not be with a biological parent and it need not be with a female. Rutter stressed the importance of a child's relationships with people other than the mother, in particular the father.

Research findings which have challenged Bowlby's views

Below is a brief outline of some of the research findings which have contradicted or challenged some of Bowlby's views.

Rutter (1972) carried out a study in which he compared a large number of boys aged 9–12 on the Isle of Wight with a similar group in London. All the children in both groups had been separated from their parents for a variety of different reasons at some point in early childhood. Some of the boys went on to become disturbed and delinquent; others did not. Rutter believed that the crucial factor which made the difference was what happened to the boys *after* the separation. Where separation was caused through the illness or death of a parent, the children tended to recover and lead normal lives after the traumatic incident. Where parental separation came about through family discord or divorce, the child often became maladjusted and delinquent. Rutter argued that it is the discord often present in separating or divorcing families and the subsequent difficulties in the family which lead to later behaviour problems rather than the actual separation from a parent.

Freud and Dann (1951) studied six 3-year-old orphans who had spent most of their lives together in a German concentration camp. In the absence of either a mother or father figure, the children appeared to have formed very close and warm attachments with each other. Moreover, although their behaviour was disturbed in some respects, there was no sign of the 'affectionless psychopathy' that had been predicted by Bowlby to occur where children are deprived of mother-love.

Unfortunately, there was no follow-up study of the children's adult lives. Also, it should be borne in mind that this is a case study and therefore lacks the objectivity and precision of stricter methods of study (see page 12).

Clark and Clark (1976) documented much evidence which runs counter to Bowlby's claims that infancy and early childhood years have a special overriding importance in social and emotional development. They proposed instead that the *whole* of development is important, with the infancy period no more so than middle or later childhood.

Tizard and her colleagues (Tizard and Hodges, 1978; Hodges and Tizard, 1989) in a longitudinal study, followed the progress of a group of institutionalised children who were later adopted after the age of four. The group was compared with a similar sample of children who were reared at home. The researchers' aim was to try to discover whether early institutional experience would affect the children's later social and emotional behaviour even if they were adopted.

At the age of 8, it was reported by most of the adoptive parents that the children had formed strong attachments to them. However, many parents reported that the children had some emotional problems. They were often difficult to manage and at school were quarrelsome and unpopular with their peers. These findings were reflected also in the follow-up study when the children were 16.

Tizard concluded:

- Most children had formed attachments with adoptive parents and there was little to support Bowlby's claims of an early critical period for the formation of attachments.
- The first two years of life did appear to be critical in shaping some aspects of later development; the early institutional experiences of the children seemed to have caused some problems of social and emotional adjustment.

Harlow's later research with infant monkeys (see Box 2.2) showed that his early studies may have confused the effects of maternal deprivation with the effects of total isolation. Novak and Harlow (1975) showed that the disturbed behaviour of deprived monkeys was much reduced when they were allowed to interact with other 'therapist' monkeys. This seemed to show that the effects of early deprivation were not irreversible and interactions with peers could be as effective as those with parents in easing the effects of social isolation.

In his review described previously, Rutter concluded that the evidence overwhelmingly supported the importance of deprivation and disadvantage as adverse influences on children's psychological development. The worst effects are experienced by children who have experienced multiple caretaking in early life and have been unable to form strong attachments. However, it appears that humans are far more flexible than Bowlby suggested. While the first few years of life do appear to be important for bond formation and social development, a single, female mothering figure is not essential to healthy development.

Rutter argued that the concept of 'maternal deprivation' should be abandoned. Researchers should try to investigate the *different* kinds of inadequate childcare and look carefully at their separate effects. It is important, also, to look at individual differences in children's responses to stress and deprivation and discover why it is that some children develop normally despite adverse experiences, while others do suffer psychological damage.

Early experience and its later effects

This seems to be a good point at which to summarise some of the insights which have been drawn from research into the effects of early experience on later development.

There is a long history of research which proposes that children's early experiences with their parents determines what they are like in later life. Many of the earlier accounts of child development, particularly those arising from a psychoanalytic tradition, implied also that once the roots of development were established in early infancy, change was difficult or impossible later on. We now know that this is not correct, or at least that the link between early experience and later effects is far more complex than was originally thought. The work of Rutter discussed above and that of other researchers has highlighted a number of methodological and conceptual problems.

Perhaps the most important point is that the long-term outcome attributed to a particular early experience may not be directly due to the experience itself. It may be the outcome of the continuing effects of its short-term consequences. Or it may be the result of a severe and pervasive problem which caused both the disturbing early event and the longer-term effects. An example may make this clearer.

It has long been accepted that children from broken homes are more likely to have later problems such as unsatisfactory social relationships, and delinquency, and to underachieve at school. Many explanations stressed the painful effect on the child of being separated from one parent. It now seems to be a more plausible explanation to attribute children's behaviour problems to family discord, both before and after the divorce, loneliness and changes in discipline. Also, the changed circumstances of the single parent left responsible for the child, for example lowered income or having to go out to work, are likely to have an impact on the child's behaviour (Rutter, 1981).

Distinguishing between different causes of childhood problems is very important, since different preventative measures and different treatments may be important.

Care outside the home: childminding and day care

This section started by raising the ongoing (often heated) debate about whether pre-school children will suffer psychological harm if they are cared for in a day centre or by a childminder whilst their parents are at work. It is clear from the research findings considered above that children do not need to be cared for twenty-four hours a day by a 'single, female mothering figure' as Bowlby suggested. However, related research has considered the quality of alternative care such as childminding and nursery-based day care and the probable effects on young children. Some of this research evidence is outlined below.

Care in a day centre

Most studies of day care have been carried out in the USA. Generally, research suggests that there will be no adverse intellectual or emotional effects on the child, provided the quality of the care is high. Factors such as a stimulating, well-organised environment, committed and caring staff, and a high ratio of staff to children are all important (Belsky and Steinberg, 1978).

However, in the late 1980s, a further controversial debate began. After reviewing a number of recent studies, Belsky and Rovine (1988) showed that infants placed in full-time day care during the first year of life had higher levels of insecure attachment, as measured by the Strange Situation, than those brought up at home or where the mother worked part-time. They concluded that placing infants under one year old in day care for more than 20 hours a week could adversely affect the child's emotional well-being.

These findings do raise concerns. However, there are a number of ways they could be interpreted:

- Firstly, it is possible that babies placed in day care during the first year of life are at real risk.
- An alternative explanation is that it is possible that the higher rate of insecure attachment shown in the infants arises because they have not been in day care for very long. It has been found that the longer babies had been in day care, the less likely were they to show symptoms of insecure attachment. The highest levels were shown by those babies who had been in day care only a short time. Therefore, it is possible that the effect may 'wear off'.
- Clarke-Stewart (1989) has suggested that the 'Strange Situation' procedure may not be appropriate for babies of working mothers, since these babies experience more systematic separations than babies looked after at home. Therefore Belsky and Rovine's conclusions may at least in part be inaccurate

It is clear that much more research must be carried out in order that these issues may be resolved.

Incidentally, researchers are generally agreed that Belsky and Rovine's findings do not apply to infants who are placed in day care *after* the age of one year.

Childminding

There is a mandatory requirement for those who look after other people's children in their own homes (childminders) to be registered with the local authority, who will monitor the conditions in which children are cared for. However, it is generally accepted that there are many unregistered childminders. Studies of childminding include the following.

Mayall and Petrie (1977, 1983) carried out a naturalistic observation study of 39 childminders in the London area. The researchers were highly critical of the bad housing, cramped conditions and unstimulating care that children were exposed to. Many of the children appeared insecure and showed deficits in cognitive and language skills. However, since there was no control group for comparison, it was not clear whether the children's problems arose from the childminding or from other factors arising from the home environment.

Bryant, Harris and Newton (1980) combined methods of survey, interview and naturalistic observation to study childminding in Oxfordshire. Though there were no examples of inadequate conditions and, in general, carers were conscientious and affectionate, few carers considered that their job was to provide stimulation for the children. About 25 per cent of the children appeared to be thriving. However, many of the remaining children were unnaturally quiet, passive and detached and about 25 per cent of the total were either disturbed or in distress or had inadequate cognitive and language skills. However, once again, it is not clear the extent to which these problems arose from the childminding situation or from problems in the home situation.

Jackson and Jackson (1979) found that many unregistered childminders provided poor conditions and little affection or stimulation.

Moss (1987) argues that there is a need to provide childminders with training courses and improved facilities and resources.

A study which compared the behaviour of children who were cared for either by relatives or by childminders or in private day care was carried out by Melhuish (1990). It was found that at the age of 18 months, language ability was highest for children cared for by relatives and lowest for those in nursery care. However, there were no noticeable differences between the three groups in attachment behaviour towards the mother or in cognitive development. Interestingly, the nursery care group showed more prosocial behaviour, such as co-operation and sharing. So while care by relatives would seem to be the preferred situation, care in a nursery setting may have some advantages.

Self-assessment questions

1. What did Bowlby mean by 'maternal deprivation'?
2. Discuss some research which has challenged Bowlby's concept of 'maternal deprivation'. How useful, or otherwise, has this concept been in helping us to understand the effects of early deprivation?
3. Outline some of the conceptual and methodological problems inherent in trying to link early experience to later development.
4. Outline the findings from research which has examined the care of children outside the home.

SECTION IV   CHILDREN'S PLAY

As with many other young mammals, play is a characteristic part of the behaviour of all normal, healthy children. A dominant view in psychology has been that play has important implications for a child's psychological development. This section aims to consider the nature and functions of play and its role in development.

What is play?

A number of problems arise when psychologists attempt to define what they mean by play. One of the main problems is in deciding what to include under the umbrella term of 'play'. Do we confine ourselves to what children do or should we include the activities of adults who enjoy a game of bingo or go down to the pub to play skittles? And if we do confine ourselves to the behaviour of children, what range of activities should be included – painting, playing with bricks, experimenting with sand and water, kicking a football, exploring a new object? Should all these be subsumed under the heading of 'play'?

The range and diversity of all the above activities have presented psychologists with a dilemma in seeking to describe and explain behaviour associated with play, particularly during early childhood. There is much disagreement about the activities that should be categorised as play. There seems to be no simple definition.

Some theorists have looked at the general characteristics and functions of play. For example, Garvey (1977) provides one list of characteristics:

- Play is essentially enjoyable and associated with positive affect (feeling good).
- It is an activity done for its own sake, is rewarding in itself and does not depend on the attainment of goals outside the play situation.
- It is spontaneous and voluntary and is not instigated or controlled by someone else.
- The player needs to be actively involved.
- It is not the same as 'real life' and should not be taken literally.

While intuitively this list of characteristics has appeal, looking at play in terms of an idealised list of features is not as simple as it might appear. There are some features which all play seems to share; we can probably all agree that people play for the sake of enjoyment rather than for externally imposed reasons. However, there are other features which are not necessarily shared by all kinds of play. For example, Sluckin (1981) has suggested that much of what goes on in school playgrounds is anything but free/voluntary/spontaneous since it is strongly influenced by other children (and sometimes adults). Also, there is often evidence of play that does not have 'positive affect' and is characterised by aggression and tears rather than pleasure.

Gardner (1982) believed the purposes of play in the development of the child to be:

greater mastery of the world, more adequate coping with problems and fears, superior understanding of oneself and one's relationship to the world, an initial exploration of the relations between reality and fantasy, an arena in which intuitive, semi-logical forms of thought can be freely tested.

(Gardner, 1982, p. 255)

You will recognise many of these functions of play in the theories and studies which follow.

Social aspects of play

Parten (1932) proposed that socially there is a clear developmental sequence in a child's style of play, particularly in the early years.

- Until the age of 18 months, there is much **solitary play** with objects such as toys.
- The 3-year-old is more likely to engage in **parallel play**, playing alongside other children, sometimes watching and imitating the other child but not truly interacting.
- Around the age of 4, play becomes increasingly **social** and simple interactions take place. Initially these interactions are quite rigid, but they soon involve 'give and take' in the form of turn-taking and co-operation.

Subsequent researchers have confirmed and used Parten's categories quite a lot. However, Cohen (1987) argues that social categorisations of play such as this have limited usefulness since most children mix many different kinds of play. She points out that typically these categories have been derived from observing children in playgroups or nursery schools, whereas much of the play children engage in actually occurs within the family. Therefore, it is likely that such play will involve children of different ages playing together and also children playing with adults, and the patterns of interaction will vary.

Some theories of play

Numerous theories of the nature and purposes of play have been developed, some dating back to the end of the last century. This section will briefly consider a selection of the more recent theories.

Piaget firmly linked the development of play with the development of thought (see Chapter 3) and contends that children's developmental level may be inferred in part from their play. He proposed three broad stages of play activity:

1. **Mastery play** corresponds to the sensori-motor stage of development (birth to two years, approximately). The emphasis is on practice and control of movements, and on exploration of objects through sight and touch. Children's play activity contains many repetitive movements which are indulged in for the

simple pleasure of demonstrating their developing mastery of the skills involved.

2. **Symbolic play** coincides with the pre-operational stage (approximately two to seven). The child employs fantasy and make-believe in play and delights in using one object to symbolise another – so a chair may become a motor car, a sheet a fashionable dress.

3. **Play with rules** characterises the operational stages (from about seven onwards). The child's developing thought processes become more logical and play involves the use of rules and procedures.

Piaget proposed that play is an expression of the process of **assimilation**, where children are attempting to take knowledge of the world around and change it to fit in with their own understanding and experience.

Freud's psychodynamic theory of development (See Chapter 4) viewed play as a means of relieving pent-up emotions. Children may use play to explore and cope with their feelings about life and work out their fears and anxieties (catharsis) in a safe situation. Play can thus be seen both as a defence against problems and as a coping behaviour.

Erikson (1963), a neo-Freudian, contended that:

The child's play is the infantile form of the human ability to deal with experience by creating model situations and to master reality by experiment and planning.

The psychodynamic approach to play is characterised in the use of **play therapy** to treat disturbed children. The basic assumption is that the child's play is a reflection of his or her unconscious mind. During therapy, the child is encouraged to play in a safe, undemanding situation with objects such as dolls, buildings and so on. Through play sessions, the child can act out and come to terms with anxieties.

Vygotsky (1967) saw play as a leading contributor to overall development. He emphasised particularly the rules of play. Confronted with a problem, the child unconsciously devises a make-believe situation which is easier to cope with. Such a 'game' involves the use of a set of rules and procedures which enable the child to take an object from its familiar context and believe that it is something else – so a broom handle can become a horse and the 'rules' of the game allow the child to behave in a manner which is removed from everyday reality.

Vygotsky believed that play creates a '**zone of proximal development**' (see Chapter 3, Section II) where the child can operate at a level which is above that for her normal age; for instance, performing some of the movements of writing for the first time. One way of assessing a child's potential development at a particular time, Vygotsky believed, is to note the distance between the levels of activity reached during play and those of her customary behaviour.

Bruner (1976) stressed the learning potential of play, and viewed play as a means of attaining physical and cognitive skills in young children. Play involves experimentation with smaller actions which may later be combined into a more complex, higher-order skill. Thus, a two-year-old given a set of construction toys, will initially explore and handle the individual pieces. Over a period of time, the child will experiment with possible uses and combinations until eventually he or she will be able to assemble complete constructions with confidence. This kind of play allows a child to understand such things as spatial relations and mechanics in a relaxed, non-threatening setting. Thus, play contributes to problem-solving and an understanding of the use of tools.

Studies of play

Much of the theorising about the importance of play has been done without any real evidence to support claims about its value in development. Nonetheless, over the last 20 years or so, a range of empirical studies have been carried out. It is intended to look at two 'classic' studies in some depth and to look more briefly at a range of others.

1. Play and cognitive development

Sylva *et al.* (1980) carried out a naturalistic observational study of the play of pre-school children in Oxfordshire playgroups and nursery schools. This was part of a large project under the directorship of Jerome Bruner. The researchers were particularly concerned to investigate how play may contribute to cognitive development.

The researchers identified what they called **elaborated play** – rich play which challenges the child and stimulates more complex activity involving the child's fullest capacities. Elaborated play has two important characteristics:

1. It has a clear goal and some means for its achievement
2. It has 'real world feedback, that is, the child is able to assess his or her own progress without referring to anyone else.

The main findings of the study were as follows:

- It was proposed that the richest, most elaborated and extended play occurs in building and construction activities, drawing and art and doing 'school readiness' puzzles. These activities also encourage the child to concentrate for longer periods of time.
- Somewhat behind these activities in importance is play involving pretending, small-scale toys, sand and dough.
- Less elaborated play, such as informal, impromptu games and 'horsing around', appears to serve the functions of social contact and release of tension.
- Young children play longer and better when they operate in pairs rather than alone or in larger groups. The presence of an adult nearby for assurance or brief comment, but not managing the situation, improves the quality of play.

Sylva *et al.*'s study has important implications for the organisation and staffing of nursery schools and playgroups. It emphasises play which offers cognitive challenge. However, by implication, perhaps it underplays the importance of the social challenge found in, for instance, pretend play.

In considering a range of studies that have examined the contribution of play to cognitive development including the Sylva *et al.* one discussed above, Meadows (1986) concluded that there are problems in comparing studies. One such problem arises from differences in how the 'quality' of play was assessed. However, she found that, on the whole, the researchers agreed in two important ways:

- The general level of cognitive complexity of children's play was disappointing. Much of what they did was simple, undemanding and uninventive.
- Where teachers were more than casually involved and the children used a range of materials which made it easy to define a goal and move towards it (for example in art activities), children did show higher levels of play.

2. Exploration

Hutt (1966) carried out a study in which she investigated exploratory behaviour. Exploration has often been confused with play. However, Hutt's experiment made the distinction clear. Exploration is explained as an activity during which children may investigate objects and events in the environment and/or features of their own physical ability.

Children aged from 3 to 5 were presented with a novel and complex object in the form of a red metal box with four brass legs and topped with a lever which, when moved, activated various novel auditory or visual stimuli. Typically, at first, a child concentrated on trying to find out what the novel object could do. This was followed by an attempt to use the object as part of a game. Once the child had become familiar with the object, she or he would investigate it further only if a new features, for example a new sight or sound, was discovered.

Hutt distinguished between the earlier exploratory behaviour and the later play behaviour. Exploration was characterised as fairly serious and focused, essentially asking 'What does this object do?' Play was characterised as being more relaxed and involving a range of activities, essentially asking 'What can I do with this object?'

Though the study was strictly an experiment, it involved some degree of natural observation.

3. What is related to playfulness?

In a follow-up to Hutt's study above, Hutt and Bhavnani (1972) revisited 48 of the children whose exploratory behaviour had been studied. They found that non-exploring in early childhood related to lack of curiosity and adventure in boys, and to problems of personality and social adjustment for girls. Those children who had been earlier categorised as more imaginative explorers were more likely to be judged as independent and curious by their teachers and more likely to score highly on tests of creativity. Hutt proposed a relationship between one form of exploratory play (as investigated in her study) and subsequent personality, creativity and cognitive style. However, this was a correlational study, so we cannot assume that there is a causal link (see page 12) – we must not assume that imaginative play *causes* a child to develop creativity. The imaginative play of some of the children in Hutt's original study might be a by-product of their essential creativity rather than a cause of it.

Connolly and Doyle (1984) found that the amount and complexity of fantasy play in pre-school children was significantly and positively correlated with measures of social competence. Johnson *et al.* (1982) found a positive correlation between the level of constructive play in 4-year-olds and their intelligence scores. This is in accord with the findings of Sylva *et al.*'s study of the value of elaborated play. Again, however, we must be aware of the problem of causality in these correlational studies.

4. Play tutoring

As in other areas of developmental psychology, there has been a trend towards studying children's play in more ecologically valid ways. This means paying more focused attention to the social context in which play happens over a sustained period of time.

A group of studies in the USA have highlighted the benefits of **play tutoring** with deprived pre-school children. Play tutoring is a technique pioneered by Smilansky (1968) and summarised by Christie (1986). It involves adults engaging children in play, usually with verbal guidance and suggestions and sometimes acting as role models in fantasy play. Several studies found that play tutoring encouraged cognitive, language and social development in children. However, a study by Smith, Dalgleish and Herzmark (1981) compared play tutoring to **skills tutoring**, where adults interacted with children in structured activities such as jigsaws and sorting shapes. Groups of 4-year-old children in a nursery school experienced equal amounts of either play tutoring or skills tutoring. Both groups showed improvements on measures of social, cognitive and language skills and neither group was superior to the other. The researchers concluded that the crucial factor that caused the improvements was adult involvement, particularly verbal stimulation, and this may have accounted for the findings of earlier studies of play tutoring.

What is the value of play?

So what can be concluded about the value of play and its significance in childhood development? The truth is that there is little conclusive evidence that play is essential to healthy development. In some cultures, children seem to play very little, yet they develop normally. The pervading feeling among researchers seems to be that while play may have benefits, they are unlikely to be of crucial importance. Other activities may fulfil the same functions. However, Meadows (1986) argued that play cannot be written off as useless. It is a source of enjoyment and pleasure which probably contributes to a child's emotional well-being.

It is a potential source of feelings of competence and achievement, and so a contributor to the child's self-esteem and feelings of self-efficacy. It is part of the child's social worlds of peers and of adults. (Meadows, 1986, p. 30)

Self-assessment questions

1. What do you understand by 'play'? Outline some difficulties experienced by psychologists in their efforts to define 'play'.
2. List some differences you might observe between the play of three-year-old children and that of eight-year-old children.
3. Discuss theory and evidence which suggest that play contributes to cognitive development.
4. What is 'exploratory play'? Briefly outline the findings of a relevant study.
5. What do you conclude about the value of play and its significance in childhood development?

Further reading

Bowlby, J. (1988) *A Secure Base: Clinical Applications of Attachment Theory* (London: Tavistock/Routledge).
Durkin, K. (1995) *Developmental Social Psychology: From Infancy to Old Age* (Cambridge, Mass.: Blackwell).
Garvey, C. (1991) *Play* (2nd edn) (London: Fontana/Open Books).
Rutter, M. (1981) *Maternal Deprivation Reassessed* (2nd edn) (Harmondsworth: Penguin).
Schaffer, R. (1977) *Mothering* (Glasgow: Fontana/Open Books).

"I WAS LIKE YOU — THOUGHT
I KNEW IT ALL — THEN THEY
STARTED ON THINGS CALLED
WORDS ! "

Cognitive Development 3

At the end of this chapter you should be able to:

1. describe and evaluate Piaget's theory of cognitive development;
2. discuss the psychometric approach to cognitive functioning;
3. have an appreciation of other approaches to cognitive development, including those of Vygotsky, Bruner and information-processing theorists within cognitive science;
4. consider the educational implications of theories of cognitive development;
5. critically evaluate research and theories into language acquisition.

INTRODUCTION

The term 'cognitive', which is derived from the Latin *cognosco* (to know), refers to all those psychological activities involved in the acquisition, processing, organisation and use of knowledge – in other words, all those abilities associated with thinking and knowing. The cognitive processes of perception and memory have been the most widely studied.

Cognitive abilities include also a child's measured intelligence, levels of thinking and even, to some extent, creativity and the way interpersonal relationships are conducted. Since language is the medium through which thinking usually takes place, and since much intelligent and creative activity is expressed through language, this, too, is usually regarded as a cognitive activity.

Two key questions dominate the study of cognitive development:

1. What changes in cognitive functioning occur as the child grows older?
2. What factors may be responsible for these changes?

The best known and most influential approach to these questions is that of the Swiss biologist-turned-psychologist, Jean Piaget. Piaget's theory focuses mainly on logical thinking, reasoning and problem-solving, and is less directly concerned with processes such as perception and memory. Piaget's theory will be considered in some detail and the section will also include a brief review of three other theoretical approaches drawn from the work of Vygotsky (1978), Bruner (1966, 1986) and theorists within the information-processing approach of cognitive science. The chapter will also examine factors associated with the development of intelligence test performance – the psychometric approach to cognitive functioning.

Issues in the study of cognitive development

Before considering theories of cognitive development, it is important to note two major issues, or controversies, which relate to the study of child development, and which are particularly pertinent when considering the study of cognitive development.

1. *Maturation versus learning*

The first issue arises from the fact that we are still unable to unravel the interaction between **maturation** – the genetically controlled biological and behavioural changes that take place during life – and **learning** – the changes that come about through the experiences the individual has with the environment. This issue relates to the discussion on the interaction of biological and social factors in development in Chapter 1 and it would be helpful if you would look back at this.

2. *Competence and performance*

The second important issue has concerned many researchers whose work has involved the study of young children. A problem sometimes arises in distinguishing between what children actually know and can do – that is, their **competence** – and the extent to which children make use of their ability to deal with tasks and problems – that is, their **performance**. Children may possess abilities that they do not use in some situations.

The problem of competence and performance can be illustrated in a study in which pre-school children were asked to sort objects belonging to different categories (vehicles, trees, people, furniture). They were asked to put objects belonging to the same category either into separate plastic bags or on to different pieces of paper. The children were found to be more successful in sorting objects when asked to place them in bags than when asked to place them on pieces of paper. Hence, a child who failed to put the objects representing trees on to one piece of paper – a failure in performance – probably did possess the competence of understanding the concept we call trees, but did not demonstrate it (Markman *et al.*, 1981).

The reasons why children's performance may sometimes not adequately reflect their competence are complex and it is only during the last twenty years or so that investigators have considered them. The context and relevance of the situation in which the child is operating, her interpretation of the language used by the researcher and her assumptions about the intentions of the researcher are all factors which may affect the child's performance. (See the discussion of the work of Bryant and Donaldson later in this chapter.)

SECTION I   PIAGET'S THEORY OF COGNITIVE DEVELOPMENT

Most psychologists would agree that Jean Piaget (1936/1952) was the most influential developmental psychologist of the twentieth century. Largely as a result of his work, cognition has been a major focus in child development research since the late 1950s when his work was translated from French into English.

For over half a century Piaget made detailed observations of children's activities, talked to children, listened to them talking to each other, and devised and presented many 'tests' of children's thinking. His methods of study, which included the **clinical interview** and **naturalistic observation** (see Chapter 1), were in sharp contrast to the rigorous and strictly controlled methods used by the behaviourists. In his studies, Piaget did not manipulate variables in the manner of formal experiments. His early research programme attempted instead to describe the kinds of thinking characteristic of children up to adolescence. Further, Piaget's interest was not in the uniqueness of individual children, but rather in the similarities between children of roughly equivalent ages.

Piaget's findings led him to propose a theory of how children form the concepts involved in thinking – that is, a theory which suggests that children develop more sophisticated ways of thinking mainly as a consequence of maturation.

A concept is the idea an individual has about a particular class of objects (including animate objects) or events, grouped together on the basis of the things they have in common. It is through concepts that we are able to think about and make sense of the world. Thus a small child will have a concept of 'daddy', 'dog' or 'table', of 'softness' and 'hardness', of 'small things' and 'large things', of 'more than' and 'less than'. When children encounter new objects and experiences, they try to make sense of them by fitting them into their existing concepts. Consider the two-year-old girl who has formed the concept of 'bird' as an object that flies in the sky. One day she sees her first aeroplane and tries to link it to her concept of 'bird'. But the noise, the size and the shape do not fit her existing concept. If she questions her parents, they will provide a new word and explain the differences between birds and aeroplanes, therefore allowing the child to create a new concept.

Piaget believed that the way in which we are able to form and deal with concepts changes as we move through childhood into adolescence. A child's thinking is not simply a less well informed version of an adult's, but differs from it in a number of important ways which are discussed below.

Schemata and operations (variant cognitive structures)

Piaget saw the structure of the intellect in terms of **schemata** and **operations**.

A **schema** is the internal representation of some specific physical or mental action. The newborn child, he believes, is endowed with a number of innate schemata which correspond to reflex responses, for example the looking schema, the grasping schema, the sucking schema, and so on. As the child develops, these innate schemata integrate with each other and become more elaborate, and entirely new schemata are formed as the child responds to the environment.

Fundamental to intelligence are schemata consisting of knowledge about objects/events and knowledge of how to do things. In any intellectual or physical act, there is always a schema of some kind present, a kind of cognitive plan which the individual uses to deal with a particular problem.

An **operation** is a higher-order mental structure which is not present at birth, and is usually not acquired until middle childhood.

An operation involves the child in knowing more complex rules about how the environment works. It has the characteristic of being **reversible**. This means that an operation can be regarded as a mental activity which can be reversed – done backwards, so to speak. The rules of arithmetic involve operations which are reversible. For example, a child of five will readily understand the process of addition ($2 + 3 = 5$) but will not appreciate that this process is reversible by subtraction ($5 - 3 = 2$). The older child who is capable of operational thinking will recognise that addition is reversible by subtraction and division is reversible by multiplication.

Look at Figure 3.2 on page 71 and read the account of task 1 set for children by Piaget. When asked the final question, 'Does the "sausage" have the same amount of plasticine as the "cake"?', the answer given by a child of 4 or 5 usually is very different from the answer given by a child of 7 or 8. The older child will usually reply without hesitation 'of course they are the same'. The younger child typically says that the 'sausage' now contains more plasticine than the 'cake'. The younger child's thinking seems to be dominated by the appearance of objects. Moreover, she or he is not capable of performing the mental operation of reversibility, or mentally reversing the moulding of the 'sausage'.

Children's cognitive structures change as they grow older. Hence, Piaget terms 'schemata' and 'operations' **variant cognitive structures**.

Adaptation to the environment (invariant functions)

Piaget based his theory firmly within a biological framework, and **adaptation** is a key concept. In order to survive, every individual must adapt to the demands of the environment.

Intellectual development is seen as the adaptation of cognitive structures (schemata and operations) to meet the demands of the environment. Such adaptation takes place through the processes of **assimilation** and **accommodation**. Assimilation refers to the process whereby a new object or idea is understood in terms of concepts or actions (schemata) the child already possesses. Accommodation is a complementary process which enables all individuals to modify concepts and actions to fit new situations, objects or information.

Consider again the example described earlier of the child who first encounters an aeroplane. Her initial interpretation of it as a bird is an example of assimilation – she assimilates the aeroplane into her schema of 'bird'. On acquiring new information about the characteristics of an aeroplane, she accommodates to the new situation and consequently develops a new schema.

The twin processes of assimilation and accommodation continue throughout life as we adapt our behaviour and ideas to changing circumstances. Assimilation is the process that enables an individual to deal with new situations and new problems by using existing schemata. Accommodation, on the other hand, is the process which involves the changing of existing schemata or the development of new schemata. It is because of the unchanging nature of these processes that Piaget referred to assimilation and accommodation as **invariant functions**.

Before a child has acquired new knowledge, he or she is in a state of what Piaget called **equilibrium** (or cognitive harmony). When this state of equilibrium is disturbed – that is when something new or demanding is encountered – the processes of assimilation and accommodation function to restore it. Piaget proposes a process of **equilibration** which acts to ensure that accommodation is consolidated via assimilation, and that a balance is maintained between the two. In this way, mental structures change and cognitive ability gradually progresses.

Piaget's developmental stages

Piaget has identified a number of distinct stages of intellectual development. He proposed that the child moves through each of these stages in turn, in the sequence and at approximately the ages shown below. The speed at which he or she moves through each stage, although influenced by the child's particular experiences, is essentially controlled by biologically determined maturational processes. The process cannot be hastened – a child must be maturationally ready before progressing to the next stage. At each stage new, more sophisticated levels of thinking are added to the child's cognitive repertoire.

Stage 1 Sensori-motor (approximately birth to two years)

In this stage the child experiences the world mainly through **immediate perceptions** and through **physical activity**, without thought as adults know it. For example, not until about eight months does a child have any concept of the **permanence of objects**. Until then, out of sight is out of mind, and the child will not attempt to look for a previously visible object which is placed out of sight as she or he watches. The child's thinking is dominated by the 'here and now'. With the acquisition of the object concept and when other means of knowing, such as memory and language, are available to her, the sensori-motor stage is at an end. The child can now anticipate the future and think about the past.

Stage 2 *Pre-operational (approximately two to seven)*

This is the stage that has been most extensively studied by Piaget. It marks a long period of transition which culminates in the emergence of operational thinking. With the development of language the child is now capable of symbolic thought, though Piaget argues, the child's intellectual capabilities are still largely dominated by his perceptions, rather than by a conceptual grasp of situations and events.

Piaget describes a number of limitations to a child's thinking which exist at this stage of development. These limitations are described below.

1. **Egocentrism** refers to the child's inability to see the world from anything but his own point of view. The child is not capable of understanding that there can be viewpoints other than his own. Thus, if a small boy is asked to say what someone sitting on the other side of a room is able to see, he will describe things from his own perspective only; a little girl may tell you that she has a sister, but will strenuously deny that her sister has a sister!

   Figure 3.1 illustrates Piaget's famous 'three mountains task' which was designed to illustrate the egocentrism of young children.

2. **Centration** involves attending to (centring on) only one feature of a situation and ignoring others, no matter how relevant. The child's inability to de-centre is apparent in Piaget's famous **conservation** tasks, some of which are described in Figure 3.2.

   In task 1 the younger pre-operational child will exhibit an inability to conserve – that is, will be unable to grasp the fact that the amount of plasticine remains the same even though the appearance of one may change. Similarly, in task 2, even though the child has agreed that the two 'fat' beakers contain the same amount of liquid, when the contents of one are poured into a tall, thin beaker, the child will now usually contend that we have

FIGURE 3.1

Piaget's 'mountains task' (Piaget and Inhelder, 1956)

Piaget's 'mountains task' showing three mountains viewed (a) from the front and (b) from the top.

(a)

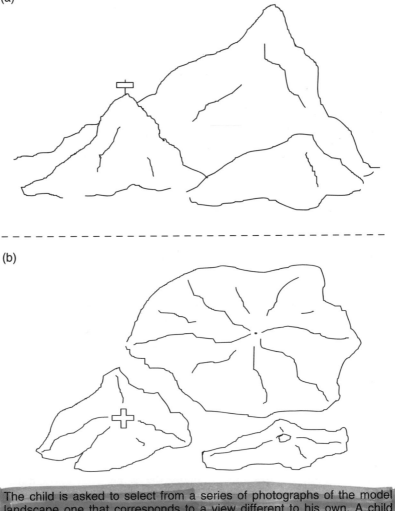

(b)

The child is asked to select from a series of photographs of the model landscape one that corresponds to a view different to his own. A child under eight does not seem to be able to imagine what other views would be like.

FIGURE 3.2

Typical Piagetian conservation tasks

Task 1   **Conservation of substance**

1. The child is shown two identical balls of plasticine and is asked 'Are these two "cakes" the same?'

2. The experimenter rolls out one ball of plasticine into a 'sausage' shape. The child is asked 'Does the sausage have the same amount of plasticine as the "cake"?'

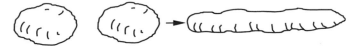

Task 2   **Conservation of volume**

 (a)   (b)

1. The child is shown a short, 'fat' beaker (a) containing milk and is asked to pour milk from a jug into a second identical beaker (b) until it has the same amount of milk as the first beaker. The child agrees that the amount of milk in each beaker is identical.

2. The child is then shown a tall 'thin' beaker and is asked to pour the contents of one of the original beakers into it. He is then asked 'Is there the same in (c) as there is in (a)?'

Task 3   **Conservation of number**

1. The child is shown counters placed in two identical rows (A and B). The child agrees that the two rows have the same number of counters.

2. The experimenter 'bunches up' the counters in row B. The child is asked 'Do the rows still contain the same number of counters?'

more liquid than before, simply because the level has risen higher. This illustrates an inability to conserve volume. In task 3, the pre-operational child will claim that the two rows in part 2 of the experiment do not now contain the same number of counters.

All these conservation experiments are the same in that they first involve a phase in which the child is presented with two entities and is asked to agree that they are 'the same'. Then the appearance of one entity is transformed while the child watches. The child is then asked to judge whether the two things are still the same. Piaget carried out similar tasks with area, length, weight, and so on.

3. **Irreversibility** – the conservation experiments also show the inability of pre-operational children to work backwards mentally to their starting point. Look back to page 67 and re-read the discussion of the importance of reversibility to the development of operational thinking.

Stage 3   Concrete operations (approximately seven to eleven years)

The main features of this stage are

1. the acquisition of reversible thinking, and
2. the ability to de-centre.

Hence, the child confronted with conservation tasks is capable of understanding the concept of invariance, partly because she or he realises that the transformation of shape, volume, spatial distributions, etc. is capable of being reversed, and partly because his or her thinking is no longer dominated by only one feature of a situation.

Piaget maintains that conservation takes place in a definite order, with the conservation of number coming first at approximately 6–7 years and conservation of volume being achieved last at about 11 or 12 years of age. The child also becomes less egocentric, and is now capable of seeing objects and events from the viewpoint of another.

Another important feature of this stage is the child's increasing ability to handle such concepts as **classification** – the ability to group objects together logically in terms of their common characteristics – and **seriation** – the ability to arrange items in rank order in terms, for example, of their colour or size.

The stage of concrete operations is so-called because the child needs to manipulate and experiment with real objects, in in order to solve problems in a logical way. For example, the child at this stage will have difficulty dealing with the verbal problem 'Joan is taller than Susan; Joan is smaller than Mary; who is the smallest?' in his head, but would have no difficulty if given three dolls to represent Joan, Susan and Mary.

Stage 4   Formal operations (approximately eleven years onwards)

This stage marks the emergence of the ability to reason in the abstract without having to rely on concrete objects or events. The child's thinking increasingly resembles that of the adult. He is able to solve a problem in his head by systematically testing out several propositions, by isolating such propositions and at the same time considering their interrelatedness.

Figure 3.3 illustrates Piaget's 'pendulum task', which was used to investigate formal operational thinking.

FIGURE 3.3

Piaget's 'pendulum task' designed to investigate formal operational thinking

The child is given several weights and a length of string suspended from a hook, and is told that he or she can vary the length of the string, change the weight and vary the strength of 'push'. The task is to find out which of these different factors affects the time taken to complete one swing of the pendulum.

The pre-operational child typically thinks the strength of 'push' is the only important factor.

The concrete operational child will attempt to investigate the different factors – different weights, shorter or longer string, etc., but does so randomly rather than systematically.

The formal operational child systematically tests each factor. He or she sets up a hypothesis that one or the other factor is important and tests it out until all possibilities have been investigated.

Evaluation of Piaget's theory

1. *Methodological considerations*

- Piaget's reliance on the clinical interview method has been criticised. It has been suggested that because there were no set questions and no standard method of presentation, there may have been a tendency to 'lead' children into views that were not strictly their own. Piaget himself was aware of these problems and much of his later work employed more strictly controlled methods.
- Bryant (1974) argued that the design of many Piagetian tasks made it very difficult for children to give correct answers. Piaget, he felt, may have underestimated the language and memory skills of young children. By a slight rewording of a Piagetian question or the use of a more realistic example, Bryant showed that children under five were capable of more sophisticated thought than Piaget claimed.

2. *Cognitive abilities in infancy*

A great deal of modern research into infant cognition shows that Piaget underestimated some of the cognitive abilities of babies. The following studies are among those which have challenged some of his assumptions:

- Piaget's belief that a child has no concept of the permanence of objects until the age of 8 or 9 months was challenged by Bower (1981). In a series of experiments with babies, Bower showed that infants as young as 4–6 weeks have some ability to appreciate the existence of objects that disappear from view. When the babies were presented with a moving object which disappeared behind a screen and then reappeared at the other side, many of them moved their eyes to follow the anticipated movement of the object. However, later experiments appeared to suggest that the same object moved to a number of different positions is perceived by babies under 5 months as a series of *different* objects. Bower concluded that up to about 5 months of age, a child does not understand that place and movement are linked.
- Piaget proposed that during the sensori-motor period, a baby's thinking is dominated by the 'here and now' and shows no

evidence of the internal representation of objects and events. However, studies of memory in very young babies by Rovee-Collier (1993) shows that they may be capable of some kinds of internal representation long before Piaget suggested. Rovee-Collier demonstrated that babies as young as 3 months could remember for as long as a week kicking actions they made to move a mobile placed over their cots.

3. Egocentrism

Piaget's 'mountains task' was designed to assess whether a child can take the point of view of another person. Using this model, Piaget claimed that children under about eight years do not perform successfully. Margaret Donaldson (1978) described a series of experiments, carried out by her colleagues, which shows that young children between three and a half and five years old are quite capable of appreciating the viewpoint of another person. Figure 3.4 contains a description of the 'naughty boy and policeman task' carried out by Hughes (1975).

Why should the experiment described by Donaldson produce findings which were so different from those of Piaget when he used the 'mountains task'? Firstly, in Donaldson's experiment, a great deal of care was taken to ensure that the children fully understood the task, and in particular, the meaning of 'to hide'. Secondly, Donaldson claimed that the 'policeman' task 'made sense' to the child and that its realism and interest-value captured the child's imagination.

> the task requires the child to act in ways which are in line with certain very basic human purposes (escape and pursuit). It makes human sense . . . in this context, he shows none of the difficulty in 'decentring' which Piaget ascribes to him . . . the 'mountains task' is abstract in a psychologically very important sense, in the sense that it is abstracted from all basic human purposes and feelings and endeavours. (Donaldson, 1978)

4. Conservation

Many psychologists have contested Piaget's claim that children in the pre-operational stage are unable to conserve. It has been pointed out that it is by no means certain that young children use and interpret words in the same way as adults do and failure in

FIGURE 3.4

The 'boy and policeman' task

A model shown to pre-school children in an experiment designed to investigate egocentrism (Donaldson, 1978)

CHILD

1. Two 'walls' are set up to form a cross.

2. A 'policeman' doll is placed on the model so that he can see the areas marked A and C, but cannot see B and D because they are obstructed by the wall.

3. The child is given a 'boy' doll and asked to place it on the model where the policeman cannot see it.

4. The task is repeated several times using two policeman dolls which are placed in varying positions on the model. On each occasion the child is asked to place the boy where the policeman cannot see him.

5. Ninety per cent of the children tested placed the 'boy' doll correctly so that neither 'policeman' could see it.

Source: Donaldson (1978).

conservation tasks may, in some cases, be accounted for in terms of the difficulties children experience with word meanings, for example 'less than' and 'more than' and so on.

As in the 'policeman' task, context too may be an important factor in conservation experiments. In a replication of one of Piaget's number tasks, McGarrigle (reported in Donaldson, 1978) found, as did Piaget, that few children under six appeared to understand conservation of number (refer back to task 3 in Figure 3.2). However, the task was repeated, but this time a 'naughty' teddy bear was introduced, who proceeded to rearrange one row of counters while 'messing about'. When asked on this occasion if both rows contained the same number, a large proportion (63 per cent) of the children gave the correct answer, indicating their ability to conserve number.

Why should 'naughty teddy' have made such a difference? Donaldson argued that in the earlier experiment, the child may have thought that because the experimenter (an important adult) had rearranged the counters, it seemed reasonable to assume that something must have changed. This experiment and the policeman task are illustrations of the problematical nature of the relationship between a child's competence and his performance, discussed earlier. However, a study by Eames *et al.* (1990) failed to replicate the 'naughty teddy' findings. The researchers suggested that experimenter effects in the McGarrigle study might have been responsible for the discrepancy.

5. Formal operational thinking

Some research has shown that the kind of abstract thinking described by Piaget as occurring at the formal operational stage is not attained by all teenagers or adults. A study by Lewis (1981) showed that only 50–60 per cent of 17-year-olds used formal operational logic in problem-solving tasks. Keating (1980) suggests that only about 50–60 per cent of those aged 17–20 in Western countries *ever* use formal operational thinking, and if they do so, it is not consistently employed.

6. The concept of stages

Piaget proposed that the development of the intellect occurs in 'clear-cut', qualitatively different stages, each of which builds upon and replaces the level of adaptation reached in the previous stage.

Some later investigators claimed that their findings supported this view of stage-like changes in cognitive behaviour (Neimark, 1975). Other investigators have been more critical and argued that discontinuous, step-like changes in cognitive development are unlikely and that development proceeds in a continuous manner (Keating, 1980).

Bee (1995) argues that the evidence does not support Piaget's notion of development occurring through a number of coherent, general stages. Rather, she feels, it is a much more gradual process where skills which existed at an earlier age in a more rudimentary form are gradually improved.

Despite the criticisms of Piaget's theory, it is worth noting that the vast majority of critical studies contain a tribute to the man whose great intellectual scope provided such a monumental contribution to our understanding of child development.

Cross-cultural studies of Piagetian ideas

Several cross-cultural studies have supported Piaget's view that the stages of cognitive development are the same for children in many different countries and cultures. For example, conservation tasks were set for groups of 7- to 11-year-old children from the Meru of Tanzania (Nyiti, 1976), from the Themne of Sierra Leone (Kamara and Easley, 1977) and the Kamba of Kenya (Kiminyo, 1977). In all these cultures, the average age at which the children were able to solve the conservation tasks was very similar to that for children from Europe and North America. As Piaget's theory would predict, some 11- to 12-year-olds who had not attended school had more difficulty solving conservation of volume tasks than children of the same age who had attended school.

Findings from a study by Jahoda (1983) were consistent with the idea proposed by Donaldson that the context and relevance of the tasks set have an important bearing on a child's cognitive ability. Jahoda found that 9-year-old children in Harare, Zimbabwe, showed evidence of abstract thinking when playing a shopping game with a mock shop. In particular, they demonstrated a greater understanding of concepts such as profit and loss than did British children of the same age. The Harare children were highly involved in their parents' small businesses and Jahoda argued that because of this, they had grasped principles of trading at an early age. The shopping game was therefore more relevant and interesting to them.

Implications of Piaget's theory for education

Although Piaget's theory was not directly concerned with what goes on in the classroom, his work has had a major impact on the way children are taught, particularly at the primary school level. Some of the educational implications of his theory are outlined below.

1. The concept of 'readiness' Because of Piaget, parents and teachers are aware that a child's intellect is *qualitatively* different from that of an adult. Therefore, it is important that teachers should be sensitive to the child's level of development and his ability to understand and deal with concepts of varying kinds. For example, it would not make sense to expect a child of 6 to be able to grasp a problem which involved conservation of volume. Asking a child to cope with tasks or solve problems before he is ready to deal with the concepts involved will result in confusion and distress and may prevent the child from ever fully appreciating some concepts.

2. Active involvement in a stimulating environment Piaget emphasised the importance of active participation and interaction with the environment. It is now generally recognised that *active* involvement in learning leads to greater understanding and retention. Therefore, teachers should provide an appropriate environment in the form of rich and varied materials and activities which will stimulate the child's natural curiosity and help him to make the transition to a new stage of development. Opportunities to learn by discovery will encourage children to explore the environment and to learn through their own activities.

3. Questioning children Questioning children also encourages them to be active in their own learning. Where an incorrect answer is given, the teacher should look for clues which may provide insight into the child's thought processes.

4. Use of concrete materials Children below the formal operational level should be introduced to new concepts through concrete objects, building up gradually, where appropriate, to more abstract reasoning.

5. Assimilation and accommodation In order for children to accommodate new ideas and experiences, the teacher should allow them first to assimilate them. New concepts should therefore be linked to what children know and have experienced already. (See also Donaldson's work, page 75, and Jahoda's study, page 78, on the importance of context and relevance to a child's thought processes.)

Self-assessment questions

1. Discuss two controversial issues which relate to the study of cognitive development.
2. Briefly describe Piaget's methods of investigating children's thought processes.
3. Define the terms 'schema' and 'operation' as used by Piaget. Why are these known as 'variant cognitive structures'?
4. Briefly explain the processes of assimilation, accommodation and equilibration.
5. List the key features of children's thought processes at each of Piaget's developmental stages. What factor did Piaget believe principally governs the speed at which children progress through these stages?
6. Evaluate Piaget's theory in the light of more recent research.
7. Discuss some of the educational implications of Piaget's theory.

SECTION II   COGNITIVE DEVELOPMENT IN A SOCIAL CONTEXT

As we have seen, Piaget's view of cognitive development assumed that there are psychological structures in people's minds which affect their thought processes and which become increasingly more sophisticated with age. Cognitive development is thought of as individuals constructing their own internal mental model of external reality, relatively independently of other people. However, many developmental psychologists have also investigated *social* influences on a child's developing thought processes. This approach takes the view that children develop more sophisticated ways of thinking because adults are available as teachers and models to guide them through increasingly more demanding situations. The work of Vygotsky (1967, 1978) and Bruner (1966, 1986) is highly influential in the study of cognitive development in a social context. Both will be discussed below.

The influence of Vygotsky

The work of Vygotsky (1896–1934), a Russian psychologist, was unknown in the West until it began to be translated in the 1960s. Even in Russia, much of his work was denigrated or censored by the oppressive Stalinist regime following the Russian revolution.

Like Piaget, Vygotsky saw the child as a curious, problem-solving being who plays an active part in her own development. Where he differed from Piaget was in his view of the importance of the role of other, more knowledgeable people in the child's development. Vygotsky argued that the child acquires the mechanisms of thinking and learning as a result of the social interactions between the child and the adults around her. The child's knowledge and skills develop because of this co-operative process involving 'experts' and a 'novice'. The more expert person is seen as providing a framework or 'scaffolding' within which a child works towards greater understanding. In the early stages of learning something new, the adult provides plenty of props and verbal prompts. An example might be a situation where a very young child is learning to handle a construction toy for the first time. Initially, the parent gives the child much help, and model what is required. As the task becomes more familiar and easier to handle, the parent leaves more and more for the child to do until eventually he or she can cope with the whole task alone. Butterworth's (1987) studies into infant–parent interaction see scaffolding processes at work as the mother engages the child in ritual language games and rhymes and encourages turn-taking. The concept of scaffolding will be considered again later in this section.

The importance of language and culture

As so much of social interaction, both in the home and in school, involves language, Vygotsky saw language development and cognitive development as closely interrelated. It is through language, he believed, that an individual organises his or her perceptions and thought processes. Thus, he placed more emphasis than did Piaget on the importance of language development, though he stressed that this should be seen in the context of the individual's culture and the help and support available in that culture.

Vygotsky stressed the importance of three major elements in the process towards fully developed cognitive ability:

- Firstly, the child responds to the world through action. This often does not require the use of language.
- Secondly, the child is able to reflect upon her own thought processes through language and may use strategies such as talking herself through a problem.

- Thirdly, understanding is reached through co-operation with others in a wide variety of **social settings**. These will involve interactions with parents, peers, teachers and other people significant in the life of the child. They will also involve the child in learning through elements of her own culture – through art and language, explanations and comparisons, songs and play.

Vygotsky stresses the importance of cultural experiences and the social interactions that occur within the child's culture. It is within this cultural framework that the child constructs her understanding of the world.

The zone of proximal development (ZPD)

An idea central to Vygotsky's theory is the 'zone of proximal development' (ZPD). This is the area between the child's actual developmental level and the potential developmental level which could be achieved with the help of adults or more experienced peers. For example, a child may attempt to emulate and master activities such as writing performed by older siblings and this may act as a stimulus to the child's own development.

Unlike Piaget, Vygotsky did not believe that it was necessary for a child to be 'ready' before he was able to learn something new. He argued that adults could and should provide a child with activities above his developmental level, far enough above to provide challenge, but not so far that it would demoralise or confuse. In other words, in helping children to learn, adults should provide experiences that fall within the ZPD, so that they might achieve something they would not do so alone.

Bruner's theory

The American psychologist, Jerome Bruner (1966, 1986), has been heavily influenced by the work of Vygotsky and has extended and applied his ideas in education

Bruner suggested that children develop three main ways of internally representing the environment to themselves on their way to acquiring the mature thought processes of the adult. These three **modes of representation** are the **enactive**, the **iconic** and the **symbolic**.

In the **enactive mode**, thinking is based entirely on physical actions and uses neither imagery nor words. For a baby playing with a toy, the movement involved becomes her internal representation of the toy. Enactive representation operates throughout life and is apparent in many physical activities, for example, throwing a ball, swimming, cycling, which we learn by doing and which we do not represent internally through language or images.

When a child becomes capable of representing the environment through mental images, **iconic representation** is possible. These mental images may be visual (sight), auditory (hearing), olfactory (smell) or tactile (touch). They provide a means whereby children may experience and build up a picture of the environment, even though they may be unable to describe it in words.

Finally, the transition from the iconic to the **symbolic mode** occurs and the child is able to represent the environment through language and later through other symbolic systems such as number and music. Symbolic representation leads to thought of a much more flexible and abstract kind, allowing the individual not only to represent reality but to manipulate and transform it.

A classic experiment by Bruner and Kenney (1966) exemplified the limitations of iconic thinking. Children from five to seven were shown an arrangement of glass tumblers which were placed on a board in order according to height and diameter (see Figure 3.5).

FIGURE 3.5

Bruner and Kenney's (1966) experiment

When the glasses were removed, all the children were capable of replacing them in the correct positions. Then the glasses were removed and one glass was replaced on the board, but in a different position. The children were asked to replace the rest of the glasses so as to retain the original pattern. The older children, who were capable of symbolic thought, were able to complete the task satisfactorily, whereas the younger, iconic representers, were not. Bruner and Kenney suggested that the younger children were unable to restructure and transform their original image of the array to enable them to cope with the new situation.

Comparisons with Piaget

Bruner's modes of representation have obvious similarities with Piaget's stages of development. However, a major difference arises from Bruner's insistence that although we acquire these modes sequentially during childhood, the adult retains and uses all three throughout life. We do not 'pass through' the earlier modes, and although adult thinking employs mainly the symbolic mode, we employ enactive and iconic thinking also when the need arises.

Like Vygotsky, Bruner placed greater emphasis than did Piaget on the part played by experience. He stresses that cognitive growth is significantly influenced by such variables as culture, family and education. In particular he stressed the value to the developing thought processes of a child of instruction by expert adults.

In contrast with Piaget, Bruner stresses the importance of language to the child's developing thought processes. Children who still depend upon iconic thought are dominated by the images they perceive; their ability to restructure and reflect upon these images is limited. Parents and teachers should encourage children to describe problems and events by talking and writing about their experiences in order to encourage symbolic rather than iconic representation.

Educational implications of Vygotsky's and Bruner's theories

There are a number of practical implications of Vygotsky's theory which have been taken up by modern researchers and applied to educational settings. These are discussed below:

(1) Vygotsky's view suggests that meaning is socially constructed and arises from the interactions between a child and more

experienced peers and adults. This departs quite strongly from the child-centred model of education which arose from Piaget's theory and from traditional, more didactic methods of teaching. Teachers influenced by Vygotskian theory would not view children solely as individuals who develop mental competence through their own actions, even though this may be an important experience. Rather they would offer abundant opportunities for children to develop concepts and skills through interaction with others, particularly more expert others.

(2)   The notion of scaffolding is particularly important in educational settings. Failure by teachers to provide appropriate supporting frameworks for children's learning or to build upon the knowledge and experience that children bring to the classroom may well result in a failure to achieve their full potential. Box 3.1 illustrates how scaffolding may enhance learning.

(3)   The importance of language is central to both Vygotsky's and Bruner's theories In the school setting, children should be provided with opportunities not just to listen, watch and do, but to engage in discussion and conversation both with teachers and with peers. By encouraging children to use language to express their thoughts, teachers can help them to move beyond their immediate perceptions towards greater understanding.

(4)   Close links between parents and teachers can enhance a child's opportunity to learn and make it more relevant and interesting. Wells (1985) suggests that some of a child's most important learning experiences occur at home where parent and child interact and have shared goals.

(5)   Piaget emphasised the teacher as a facilitator who provides the right environment and materials for children to 'discover' their own learning. Both Vygotsky and Bruner believe that the intervention of the teacher is crucial to a child's learning. However, this intervention should be tailored to the child's level of development and ZPD. Help and encouragement should be freely available. However, where a child is succeeding in a task, relatively little help need be given and she should be allowed to learn how to work independently. And even where a child is not succeeding, she may have sufficient knowledge for the teacher to direct her to another activity which is within the ZPD. In this way, the demands placed upon children will not be so simple as to become boring, nor so complex that they become demoralised and give up (Wood, 1988).

BOX 3.1

Scaffolding in educational contexts

Bruner and his colleagues carried out a number of research studies to examine the role of scaffolding in learning. In one, carried out by Wood, Bruner and Ross (1976), the researchers suggested that there are a number of factors which characterise effective scaffolding when a tutor attempts to develop a child's learning:

- **Recruitment** The tutor's initial goal is to capture children's interest and motivate them to attempt the task.
- **Reduction of degrees of freedom** The tutor must simplify the task and break it down into manageable steps in order for the child to achieve success.
- **Direction maintenance** In the early stages of the task, the tutor should encourage the child and motivate her to succeed. Later on, the child should find the task motivating in its own right.
- **Marking critical features** The tutor should emphasise relevant aspects of the task, in order that the child may judge how far her end-product differs from a correct solution.
- **Demonstration** The tutor should demonstrate a correct solution, or where the child has already produced a part solution, should offer explanations of any discrepancy. This should lead to the child imitating and then improving her effort.

The above is based on data from an observational study carried out by the researchers with 3-, 4- and 5-year-old children. A tutor taught each individual child to build a three-dimensional structure, a task the children would have been unable to do on their own. It was agreed in advance that the tutor would allow the children to complete as much as possible by themselves and would offer verbal help before demonstrating the task. The tutor's behaviour at each stage of the task was dependent upon the child's success or failure. This study illustrates well the process of scaffolding. The tutor guided the children through a task, at each stage allowing the child's level of achievement to determine the next level of tutoring. She worked within the ZPD (zone of proximal development), the area between what the child could do on her own and what she could achieve with help.

(6) Vygotsky's theory emphasises the importance of adults being aware of a child's ZPD and moulding their scaffolding behaviour to suit the child's existing knowledge and developmental level. However, this could be difficult in a school situation, where teachers are frequently responsible for the learning of 30-plus pupils. So how might it be possible for teachers to handle this situation?

There is a growing body of research which suggests that **peer tutoring** may be one answer. Foot *et al.* (1990) have used Vygotsky's model in explaining how peer tutoring operates. One child (the tutor) is more expert than the other (the tutee) on the task in hand. Each child is aware that the aim is for the 'expert' to improve the knowledge or skills of the 'novice'. However, the expert is only slightly ahead of the novice and is therefore better able to understand the difficulties involved and to scaffold the novice effectively within the latter's ZPD. Thus the tutoring is effective when it is only slightly beyond the tutee's capabilities and falls within the ZPD.

(7) A body of research findings is growing on ways in which children in a classroom situation can examine and negotiate meanings through processes such as conversation, active participation and carrying out tasks of particular relevance to themselves (e.g. Cowie and Ruddock, 1988, 1991; Salmon and Claire, 1984). Bennett and Dunne (1989) found that **co-operative group work** was effective in encouraging children to anticipate and respond appropriately to the behaviour of other children. The researchers found that those children who had engaged in co-operative group work – activities within small groups where children were required to co-operate with each other and to discuss the activity – were less competitive, less concerned with status and more likely to display logical thinking than were children who had worked alone. However, the value of co-operative group work depends very much on the way the learning is structured. Some researchers have argued that not all co-operative group situations enhances a child's cognitive development. Slavin (1987) has stressed the value of motivation and inter-group competitiveness. Brown and Palenscar (1989) have emphasised that much depends on the child's initial ability and social status. They argue that the benefits of co-operative learning will be felt most by children who have only an incomplete understanding of the situation and who are faced with a situation which they can take seriously, but which conflicts with their own views.

Conclusions

Meadows (1995) concludes that

> The best candidate for social experience affecting cognitive development that a theory offers is Vygotsky's idea of 'scaffold-

ing' . . . There is some evidence that parenting that is notably lacking in scaffolding and child-contingent discussion is associated with later difficulties in concentration and the development and elaboration of activities. (p. 30)

However, she points out that, as yet, we know very little about how common scaffolding is in adults' dealings with children, whether there is an optimum amount of scaffolding that is effective, whether cultural differences that influence language development apply also to cognitive development, and whether there are alternative ways of achieving the same result (some cultures do not appear to engage in scaffolding, as it is recognised in Anglo-American settings). Also, it is not known how scaffolding affects children: among other things, it may provide models of cognitive skills or of self-scaffolding (the process through which more mature learners may guide themselves through difficult tasks). She argues that further research is necessary in order to clarify these and other issues

Self-assessment questions

1. What are the most important differences between Vygotsky's theory of cognitive development and that of Piaget?
2. What does Vygotsky mean by the 'zone of proximal development'?
3. Outline some of the main features of the concept of 'scaffolding' in relation to Vygotsky's theory.
4. Briefly discuss the three major ways in which, according to Bruner, individuals represent the environment to themselves.
5. Discuss some of the educational implications of Vygotsky's and Bruner's theories.

SECTION III THE MEASUREMENT OF INTELLIGENCE

Traditionally this approach to studying cognitive functioning, or intelligence, has focused on individual differences in performance on specially devised tests. Often referred to as the psychometric approach, it has a major weakness in that it focuses on the measurement of intelligence but does not examine its development.

What is intelligence?

The idea of 'intelligence' or 'ability' is a far-reaching and powerful concept in everyday life. It is used freely to describe differences between people and to explain why individuals behave as they do. Terms such as 'bright', 'quick-thinking', 'dull' and 'slow' are frequently used to label people as being of a certain type. Despite the confidence with which these terms are used, finding a precise definition of intelligence that all psychologists can agree upon is very difficult. Some early definitions implied that intelligence is an entity – something one has a lot or a little of. More recent definitions have stressed the idea of intelligent behaviour which is aimed at successful adaptation to the environment. But what is intelligent behaviour? One child may have an exceptional talent for music while another is particularly good at solving mathematical problems; yet another child may excel at creative writing. Which child is the more intelligent?

Sternberg (1984) argues that any definition of intelligence must recognise the cultural context in which the definition is being applied. What is classed as intelligent behaviour in one culture may not be so highly regarded in another. This idea will be considered later.

In Western societies, the definition of intelligence is often closely linked to the notion of **intelligence quotient (IQ)**. This is the score derived from an intelligence test and it will be discussed later. IQ tests have traditionally emphasised powers of reasoning and verbal and mathematical abilities. Since intelligence is often equated with the ability to do intelligence tests, some psychologists have suggested that intelligence is 'what the tests measure', a rather circular definition.

Intelligence tests: a historical sketch

The earliest examples of intelligence tests were provided at the end of the last century by **Sir Francis Galton** in England and **J. McK. Cattell** in America. These early tests which were based on the measurement of simple sensory processes such as the speed of reaction times and judging the difference between two weights did not prove useful as measures of intelligence.

Simon–Binet　The first tests to resemble modern intelligence tests were devised by the French psychologist **Alfred Binet** and his co-researcher, **Theodore Simon**. In 1905, Binet was requested by the French government to devise tests which would identify children who needed special educational help. Using the judgements of school teachers on what constituted 'average' performance on a range of tasks involving reasoning and judgement, Binet first undertook to identify the 'mental level' of the 'normal' child in various different age groups. From this work, a number of age-related scales were devised based on the concept of **mental age**. Thus, a seven-year-old child who satisfactorily completed all those items normally completed by the average eight-year-old was said to have a mental age of eight; the ten-year-old who was able to complete only those tasks expected of eight-year-olds would also be assigned a mental age of eight.

The result of this work was the Simon–Binet (1905) test, which is generally regarded as the first intelligence test.

Intelligence quotient   Later researchers contended that in order for a more complete assessment to be made of the ability levels of children of different age groups who exhibit the same mental age, some account should be taken of the child's chronological, or actual age. In 1912, **Stern** introduced the idea of an **intelligence quotient** (IQ) which could be calculated as follows:

$$IQ = \frac{\text{Mental Age (MA)}}{\text{Chronological Age (CA)}} \times 100$$

It can be seen that when MA and CA are the same, using this calculation, IQ is 100, that is, average. This way of calculating IQ is not used any longer. Today, a child's test performance is compared directly to norms (average scores) drawn from a large group of children of the same age. However, an IQ of 100 is still used as the average score.

Stanford–Binet   In 1916, the Simon–Binet test was revised by **Lewis Terman** of Stanford University. The Stanford–Binet test as it became known was originally designed for children but was later extended to measure IQ in adults. The Stanford–Binet Intelligence Scale was revised many times, the most recent revision being in 1986. Before the 1986 revision, the IQ score was derived from an amalgam of all the items and would not reflect differences between a child's performance in for example numerical ability compared to verbal or spatial ability.

Wechsler   The most widely used test of adult intelligence, the Wechsler Adult Intelligence Scale, was devised in 1939 and this was followed later by the Wechsler Intelligence Scale for Children

(WISC). Both these tests have subsequently been revised. Because it was felt that the Stanford–Binet scales relied too heavily on language ability, the Wechsler scales provide measures not just on a verbal scale but also a non-verbal performance scale, which requires the manipulation or arrangement of blocks, pictures and other displays.

British Ability Scales The Stanford–Binet and Wechsler test were designed mainly for use with American populations. An important milestone so far as Britain is concerned is the British Ability Scales designed for 2- to 17-year-olds (Elliott *et al.*, 1983). This test, in addition to using traditional items concerned with reasoning, short-term memory and so on, measures aspects of development and moral reasoning.

Infant tests In 1969 the Bayley Scales of Infant Development (revised in 1993) were constructed. Since a child under 2 years old has limited or non-existent spoken language, these were designed primarily to measure sensory and motor skills such as reaching for a dangling ring (designed for a typical 3-month-old), putting cubes in a cup on request (9 months) or building a tower from 3 cubes (17 months). Tests of this kind have been useful for identifying infants and toddlers who may not be developing normally. However, in general, the scores derived from these tests do not correlate highly with later scores drawn from tests such as the Stanford–Binet or WISC. It seems, therefore, that these tests are not tapping the same kinds of abilities as those measured by the common childhood or adult intelligence tests (Colombo, 1993).

The relationship between intelligence and IQ

Though IQ scores purport to be a measure of intelligence, the relationship between 'intelligence' and 'IQ' cannot be considered in the same way as, for example, that between 'weight' and 'pounds and ounces'. Whilst we accept a numerical value expressed in pounds and ounces as an objective and exact indication of the weight of something, because of the complexity and uncertainty surrounding definitions of intelligence, the same cannot be said for an IQ score in relation to intelligence. Continuing the analogy between weight and intelligence, claiming that someone who weighs 60 lb is half as heavy as someone who weighs 120 lb is legitimate; arguing that someone with an IQ of 70 is only half as intelligent as someone with an IQ of 140 would be nonsensical.

Predictive ability of IQ scores

Crucial questions about IQ tests are whether they are stable and whether they predict anything helpful in relation to a child's later development. Before dealing with these questions directly, it is necessary to examine the concepts of **reliability** and **validity**.

Reliability   In order for it to be considered reliable, a test given to the same individual on two or more occasions should yield the same or nearly the same score; in other words, it should be consistent. This can be assessed using the **test–retest** method. The test is given to the same group of individuals on two different occasions, with a suitable time-lag to prevent them from remembering the test items (or two different versions of the same test may be used). The technique of correlation (see Chapter 1) is applied to the two sets of scores to examine the degree of similarity between them. The resulting correlation coefficient, known as a **reliability coefficient**, should be in the region of 0.90 (that for the Wechsler Intelligence Scale is 0.91). A perfect match between two sets of scores would yield a correlation coefficient of 1.00.

Validity   It is necessary also to demonstrate that the test is measuring what it claims to measure, that is, intelligent behaviour. This is its validity. One way of doing this is to examine the test's **predictive validity**. For example, children's scores on an IQ tests can be correlated with some *future* measure of intelligence, such as school achievement or a different IQ test. The stronger the correlation, the more likely it is that the two measures are tapping the same abilities.

There are other kinds of reliability and validity which are established when a psychometric test is being developed. For an account of these, see Malim and Birch (1997).

Stability of test scores   As has already been pointed out, scores on infant IQ tests such as the Bayley do not correlate highly with later IQs. A typical correlation coefficient between scores on the Bayley at one year old and scores on the Binet at four years old is only about 0.2 to 0.3. From the age of about three onwards, reliability in IQ test performance increases. Typically, the correlations between IQ scores in middle childhood are in the region of 0.80 (Honzik, 1986). The older the child the more stable the IQ score becomes.

What do IQ scores predict?   When psychologists have compared children's IQ scores with tests of their school performance, the correlation consistently found is around 0.60 (Carver, 1990). This is a strong but by no means perfect correlation (remember that a perfect correlation would be 1.00). It tells us that for the majority of children, the higher their IQ score, the more likely they are to achieve well in school. However, there will be some children with high IQ scores who do not excel at school while some with lower IQ scores do. This is an important point to remember.

Problems with the use of IQ tests

Advocates of psychometric tests have drawn attention to the great value of IQ testing as a reliable and standard means of comparing individuals to others. The results of tests, it is claimed, can be a valuable source of information in a wide range of situations, from diagnosing children's learning difficulties to helping individuals to make educational and career choices. However, there have been a number of criticisms associated with their use:

1. Achievement or aptitude

It is claimed that IQ tests do not measure knowledge and skills acquired through learning but are measures of actual or potential 'brightness' and intellectual capacity. Indeed, some theorists, for example Burt (1958) see this capacity as largely innate and inherited. As such, IQ tests are referred to as **aptitude tests** and are viewed as qualitatively different from the sorts of tests used in schools (such as those of reading, mathematics and so on) and referred to as **achievement** (or attainment) **tests**. However, many researchers (Ginsburg, 1972; Stott, 1978) argue that questions in IQ tests are learned (though not necessarily in the formal sense) in the same way that answers to achievement tests are. Like achievement tests they should be seen as measures of *present* performance, rather than as measures of capacity or future performance. As with other measures of present performance, levels of success are likely to be affected by numerous factors both within and external to the test-taker.

2. Culture and IQ tests

One of the most controversial issues in IQ testing is the question of whether tests are biased in favour of white, middle-class people. If so, their use with groups whose social or cultural experience is very different would seem to be unfair. This is a particularly important issue with verbal tests that require competence in a particular language. A child whose first language was not English could not be expected to score as highly on verbal items as a child from a solely English-speaking home. And even where English is the first language, the vocabulary used may differ significantly between middle-class and working-class homes. One of the most widely used tests thought to be relatively culture-free is **Raven's Progressive Matrices** which uses non-verbal items in the form of shapes and symbols. However, cultural factors, it has been claimed, can also influence performance on non-verbal items depending upon the particular experiences of test-takers and how familiar they are with the materials and content of the tests (Irvine, 1966; Simon, 1971). Vernon (1969) reflects the view of many psychologists when he argues that there can be no such thing as a truly culture-fair test.

The importance of social and cultural influences on IQ testing is illustrated by Warburton (1951) who described some of the difficulties encountered in devising ability tests for Gurkha recruits. Brought up in a less competitive society than our own, they were not motivated to succeed in what appeared to be irrelevant, abstract tasks and they were unaccustomed to working within a set time limit. Consequently, their achievement, even on 'performance' tests was thought not to be a reflection of true ability. The messages from this study are still relevant today.

3. Labelling and the self-fulfilling prophecy

One area in which the concept of intelligence has been and still is influential is that of education. The most significant example of the use of IQ tests to select pupils to receive different kinds of schooling can be seen in the 11-plus examinations, which still exist but are much less common than in the 1950s and 1960s. And within the education system, teachers sometimes make use of intelligence tests to make decisions about the allocation of pupils to particular classes or to groups within classes. Such a tendency to select, to categorise and to label is thought by many psychologists to be potentially harmful (Gould, 1981). Studies have illustrated the possible effects of a **self-fulfilling prophecy**, where people who are treated in a particular way because of some label that is applied tend to develop behaviour and characteristics generally associated with the label. Thus, if teacher, parents and child form certain expectations about school performance based on an IQ score, this might lead the child to do as well or as badly as everyone expects. An intriguing example of the self-fulfilling prophecy can be seen in Rosenthal and Jacobson's (1968) study. At the beginning of a school year, a group of teachers were told that 20 children joining their classes had high IQ scores and were expected to do well in the coming year. In fact, the children were of average IQ. In line with teachers' expectations, all the children performed very well and scored highly in school tests a year later. This is held as a classic study of the possible effects of teacher expectation, though it should be noted that some psychologists have criticised the design of the study and the ambiguity of the results (Shackleton and Fletcher, 1984). Others have condemned the study on ethical grounds.

Alternative views of intelligence

Over the past decade or so, a number of psychologists have attempted to go beyond the traditional psychometric approach to intelligence with its heavy emphasis on verbal and reasoning skills. Gardner (1983) and Sternberg (1985, 1988) have attempted to understand intelligence in terms of a complex interaction of various cognitive and other systems. Each theory will be briefly discussed below.

Gardner's theory of multiple intelligences

Gardner (1983) has put forward a theory based partly upon the results of tests and partly on research from neuropsychology. The theory has three fundamental principles:

1. There exists seven distinct intelligences as follows:

    - linguistic (language skills such as reading, writing, speaking and listening)
    - logical-mathematical (numerical skills)
    - spatial (understanding relationships in space as in driving or playing chess)
    - musical (skills such as singing or playing an instrument)
    - bodily kinaesthetic (using the body as in dance or athletics)
    - interpersonal (understanding and relating to others)
    - intrapersonal (understanding oneself)

2. The intelligences are independent of each other. They operate as modular systems without a 'central control' to co-ordinate them. In other words, a person's abilities as assessed under one intelligence should in theory be uncorrelated with the person's abilities as assessed under another intelligence.
3. Though they are separate and independent of each other, the intelligences interact and work together whenever the need arises; for example solving a mathematical word problem would require linguistic and logical-mathematical intelligence to work together.

Gardner believes that each intelligence resides in a separate portion of the brain and that a particular intelligence could be isolated by studying brain-damaged patients. Damage in one area of the brain could impair one intelligence leaving the others intact. The phenomenon of severely retarded individuals who have one exceptional skill such as playing a musical instrument or manipulating numbers provides evidence for the independent existence of one particular intelligence.

The first three intelligences proposed by Gardner are very much in line with those measured in conventional IQ tests. However, Gardner's inclusion of the other abilities as part of intelligence represents a new and interesting approach as does his attempt to explore the roles of physiological and cognitive processes in intelligence.

Among criticisms made of Gardner's theory is that the kinds of intelligences he proposes are not easily measurable. However, Gardner replies that the intelligences he proposes may be measurable by conventional IQ tests but can be assessed through the activities engaged in by children at school, such as composition or athletic activities (Gardner and Feldman, 1985).

Sternberg (1990) suggests that whilst Gardner's theory is at present too vague to be substantiated in detail, it represents an important contribution to understanding the human mind and intelligence.

Sternberg's triarchic theory of intelligence

Sternberg's triarchic (governed by three systems) theory of intelligence (Sternberg, 1985, 1988) seeks to explain the relationship between

1. intelligence and the internal world of the individual, that is the mental mechanisms that underlie intelligent behaviour (the **componential sub-theory**);
2. intelligence and the external world of the individual, that is the use of these mental mechanisms in everyday life in order to adapt to the environment in an intelligent way (the **contextual sub-theory**); and
3. intelligence and experience or the role played by life experience in linking the individual's internal and external worlds (the **experiential sub-theory**).

1. The componential sub-theory

Sternberg proposes that intelligent functioning, for instance trying to solve a mathematical problem, involves three basic information-processing mechanisms or components. These are:

- **Metacomponents**, which include higher-order processes involved in identifying the nature of the problem, developing a strategy for its solution and evaluating the success of the solution;
- **Performance components**, which include lower-order processes involved in actually solving the problem according to the plans laid down by the metacomponents;
- **Knowledge-acquisition components**, which include processes involved in learning new material, such as sifting out relevant from irrelevant information.

Other components have been considered by Sternberg. These include **retention components** – processes involved in retrieval of information form memory – and **transfer components** – processes involved in generalising (transferring information from one situation to another).

The components function together in a highly interactive way and are not easy to study in isolation from each other. Metacomponents activate performance and knowledge components, which in turn provide feedback to the metacomponents.

Understanding the nature of the components, Sternberg argues, is not sufficient to allow an understanding of the nature of intelligence, as there is more to intelligence than a number of information-processing components. Nor is it sufficient to assess an individual's intelligence solely through IQ tests. The other two aspects of the triarchic theory go some way to explaining the other elements of intelligence which contribute to individual differences in intelligent behaviour – outside of testing situations as well as within them.

2.   The experiential sub-theory

The information-processing components discussed above are always applied to tasks and situations where the person has some level of previous experience. The essence of the experiential aspect of the triarchic theory is that an individual's intelligence can only be understood if account is taken not just of the components but of his/her level of experience.

Intelligence is measured most effectively where the tasks being undertaken are either relatively **novel** (not totally outside the individual's understanding, but close to the limits) or in the process of becoming **automised** (performed automatically).

- **Novelty.** Different sources of evidence suggest that assessing the ability to deal with relative novelty is a good way of measuring intelligence. In studies with children, Davidson and Sternberg (1984) found that those who were intellectually gifted had the ability to deal with novelty in a problem-solving situation without being given helpful cues, whereas less gifted children benefited from help. Sternberg contends that the various components of intelligence that are involved in dealing with novelty in particular situations provide apt measures of intellectual ability.
- **Automisation.** Equally, Sternberg believes that the ability to automise information, as in skilled reading, is a key aspect of intelligence. Poor comprehenders are often those who have not automised the elementary processes of reading and therefore have not the resources to allocate to more complex comprehension processes. Thus, the ability to automise allows more resources to be devoted to novelty. Similarly, if one is able to deal effectively with novelty, more resources are available for automisation.

3.   The contextual sub-theory

According to this aspect of the theory, intelligence is not a random mental activity that happens to involve certain information-processing components. Rather, it is purposely directed towards one or more of three behavioural goals – adaptation to an environment, shaping of an environment, and selection of an environment.

- **Adaptation**. The components of information-processing and the importance of dealing with novelty and automisation of information-processing are seen by Sternberg as universal in that they operate in the same way for individuals in one culture as they do for those in all other cultures. However, the way these components show themselves in the experience and behaviour of individuals will vary from culture to culture. What is intelligent in one culture may be seen as unintelligent in another.
- **Shaping**. This involves adapting the environment to one's own preferred style of operating rather than the other way round. Sternberg sees this as a key feature of intelligent thought and behaviour: 'In science, the greatest scientists are those who set the paradigms (shaping) rather than those who merely follow them (adaptation)' (Sternberg, 1990, p. 281).
- **Selection**. This involves renouncing one environment in favour of another. It sometimes occurs when both adaptation and shaping fail. For example, if one has failed to adapt to the demands of a particular job or to shape the nature of those demands to make them fit in with one's needs, the intelligent thing to do may be to select a new environment by changing one's job.

It can be seen that a major feature of Sternberg's theory is his emphasis upon the need to go further than studying intelligent behaviour as represented by typical problems in IQ tests. Bee (1989) argues that standard IQ tests have failed to assess many of the kinds of abilities featured in Sternberg's contextual and experiential sub-theories and which are so relevant to intelligent functioning in the 'real world'. However, Sternberg himself is developing a test based on his triarchic theory of intelligence. In addition to providing scores for componential skills, it will also assess coping with novelty skills, automisation skills and practical intellectual skills.

Origins of differences in IQ: the heredity/environment issue

The question of the origins of differences in IQ has inevitably centred around disputes about **nature versus nurture**. During the last century, Francis Galton (1869) studied the relative effects of heredity (nature) and environment (nurture) on the development of intelligence. Subsequently, this issue developed into probably the most controversial and divisive debate to be encountered in psychology.

The question that concerned psychologists was, which is the more important influence on the development of differences in intelligence: heredity (that is, genetic inheritance) or environment (usually defined as all the experiences an individual is exposed to from the time of conception)? Psychologists now know that this is far too simplistic a question. Differences in intelligence are the result of an interaction between heredity and environment. No psychological characteristic can be entirely one or the other. Some aspects of development, for example temperament, may initially be inherited, but they can be influenced by such things as the parents' style of child-rearing. Nonetheless, there is still a good deal of disagreement about the *relative* importance of each. Let us examine some of the available evidence.

Family and twin studies

An important source of evidence relating to the inheritance of intelligence came from studies which correlated IQ scores between people of varying degrees of genetic relationship, for example parents paired with children, siblings (including twins) paired with each other, cousins paired with each other. Figure 3.6 shows the correlation coefficients arrived at from three individual studies (Newman *et al.*, 1937; Shields, 1962; Burt, 1966) and from a survey which examined 111 studies on familial resemblances in measured intelligence (Bouchard and McGue, 1981).

Of particular interest is the data relating to **twin studies**. But first some facts about twins. Twins of two different kinds; monozygotic (**MZ**) or 'identical' twins and dizygotic (**DZ**) or 'fraternal' twins. DZ twins have developed from two separately fertilised ova and are no more alike genetically than any two children of the same parents. MZ twins have developed from a single fertilised ovum and are thought to start life genetically identical. Differences in behaviour between identical twins must, it is thought, be attributed almost entirely to the effects of the environment.

FIGURE 3.6

Family studies of intelligence showing IQ correlation coefficients

	Name of study			
	Newman et al. (1937)	Shields (1962)	Burt (1966)	Bouchard and McGue (1981)*
Relationship				
Monozygotic twins				
Reared together	0.91	0.76	0.94	0.86
Reared apart	0.67	0.77	0.77	0.72
Dizygotic twins				
Reared together	0.64	0.51	0.55	0.60
Siblings				
Reared together				0.47
Reared apart				0.24
Single parent-offspring				
Reared together				0.42
Reared apart				0.22
Cousins				0.15

*Median correlation.

Examining the data in Figure 3.6 a number of points can be made:

1. Overall the data clearly shows that the closer the family relationship, the higher is the average correlation-coefficient between IQ scores and therefore the more similar are the IQ scores. It also shows of course that correlation coefficients rise as the *environments* become more similar.
2. The highest correlation coefficients relate to MZ twins, indicating that they have more similar IQs than any other pairs. Hereditarians would attribute this to the greater degree of genetic similarity between MZ twins. However, it is probable that they were also *treated* more similarly than DZ twins.
3. Even MZ twins *reared apart* have more similar IQs than DZ twins *reared together*. Hereditarians claim this as powerful support for genetic influences on intelligence.

Evaluation of twin studies As noted above, hereditarians claimed that the evidence from twin studies overwhelmingly supported the role of genetic inheritance in intelligence. However, environmentalists have made a number of criticisms of twin studies:

1. Different studies used different intelligence tests; it is therefore difficult to make a valid comparison between them.
2. Many of the MZ twins reared apart were in fact brought up in very similar homes and in some cases were raised by members of the same family. This suggests that their environments may have been quite similar (Kamin, 1977). An example in one study (Newman *et al.*, 1937) where an MZ pair were brought up in very different environments revealed an IQ difference between the twins of 24 points.
3. Some of the early studies are likely to have suffered from sampling inaccuracies because at that time there was no reliable method of identifying true MZ twins.
4. Herman (1984) pointed out that families who produce twins may not be typical of the general population. Therefore, generalisations from twin studies should not be made.
5. The data produced by Burt is open to question since the results of at least some of his twin studies are thought to have been faked (Burt's data are not included in the Bouchard and McGue review).

Adoption studies

A large number of studies have compared the IQs of adopted children with that of both their adoptive parents and their natural parents. The assumption is that if heredity is the more important influence the correlation between children's IQ scores and those of their natural parents will be higher than the correlation with their adoptive parents.

Two early adoption studies (Burks, 1928; Leahy, 1935) found very low correlations of 0.13 and 0.18, respectively, between the IQs of children and their adoptive parents. The correlation for children and natural parents living together is about 0.50. It seems from these figures that environment is important, though less so than heredity.

Hereditarians claimed that foster/adoption studies offer powerful support for a high heritability component to IQ. However, environmentalists argued that there are major flaws in the early studies cited by hereditarians. For example, Kamin (1977) drew attention to the process of **selective placement** practised by adoption agencies. He made two main points:

1. Selective placement involves placing children in homes which resemble as closely as possible the home environment of their natural parents. Thus the children of 'bright' mothers may be placed in homes with high-IQ adoptive parents, whereas the children of 'less bright' mothers may be placed in homes where the adoptive parents' IQs resemble that of the natural parents. Therefore, selective placement could account for the similarity between the IQ of adopted children and their natural parents even if they have not lived together.
2. The correlation between the IQ of children and adoptive parents is likely to be artificially lowered because of the nature of adoptive parents as a group relative to parents in general. Because of the conditions laid down by adoption agencies, adoptive parents are likely to be emotionally stable, financially secure, not alcoholic, etc. Also, there is likely to be less variance in their IQs than that of the children they adopt. This could artificially reduce the correlations between the IQs of the two groups.

Later studies attempted to avoid some of the problems in the early adoption studies and concentrated on parents who had brought up both adopted and natural children (Scarr and Weinberg, 1977; Horn *et al.*, 1979). In both studies, the correlation of mother–natural child IQs was very similar to the correlation of mother–adoptive child IQs (0.22 and 0.20, respectively, in the Scarr study). This provides no support for the high heritability of intelligence since the second relationship did not involve similar genes.

A study which supported the environmentalist case in highlighting the effects of a 'good' environment on IQ was carried out by Schiff *et al.* (1978) in France. They studied 32 children born to parents of low socio-economic status who were adopted before they were 6 months by parents of high socio-economic status. A comparison was made between the children's IQs and those of their biological siblings who had been reared by their natural mothers. The average IQ of the adopted group was 111 while that of the 'naturally reared' group was 95.

Environmental influences

After much research, there appears to be a general consensus on the environmental conditions that enhance the development of an individual's intellectual potential: these conditions include good pre-natal and post-natal nutrition and health care; intellectual stimulation; a stable emotional climate in the home; parental encouragement and support. There follows an outline of some of the studies which have contributed to this view:

1. A classic longitudinal study carried out by Skeels (1966) studied a group of children brought up in an unstimulating orphanage environment. At 19 months, their mean IQ score was 64. Some of the children were removed from the orphanage and given individual attention. At age six, the latter group showed a mean IQ of 96, compared with 60–70 in the institutionalised group.
2. Studying 12-year-old children, Fraser (1959) found a strong, positive correlation between high IQ and factors such as the level of parental encouragement, general family atmosphere and the amount of book-reading in the home.
3. Wiseman (1964) found a strong correlation between the standard of child care and IQ.
4. Bayley (1970) contended that IQ differences between children of low and high socio-economic status become progressively greater between birth and entrance to school, suggesting that the quality of the environment amplifies any genetic differences present at birth.

Environmental enrichment

Because children from underprivileged homes tend to be at a disadvantage intellectually, a number of programmes were mounted which aimed to provide greater intellectual stimulation for these children. The first and best known of these programmes is **Project Headstart**.

Headstart   In 1965, funds were allocated in the USA to provide enriched learning experiences for pre-school children from deprived homes. A variety of approaches was used. In some, teachers visited children and their parents at home to provide intellectually stimulating activities of the kind that children from 'better-off' homes tend to receive from their parents. In other programmes, the children attended classes where they took part in special learning activities.

Early follow-up studies showed that the project had not been as successful as had been hoped, in that no lasting IQ gains were found in children who had participated compared with those who had not. However, later follow-up studies highlighted some lasting benefits. Compared with a control group of children who had not received pre-school enrichment, participants in Headstart at age 15 were a full grade ahead, scored higher on tests of reading, arithmetic and language use and exhibited less antisocial behaviour (Zigler and Berman, 1983; Lee *et al.*, 1988). Significantly, programmes that actively involved parents in stimulating their child's intellectual development have tended to produce the greatest benefits (Darlington, 1986).

Even larger and more lasting benefits are found when an enrichment programme is started in infancy. Ramey (1992; 1993) reported a study which followed the progress of a large sample of infants (6–12 weeks) who had been randomly allocated to one of two groups. One group received specially enriched day care up to their entrance to kindergarten, and the other (a control group) received medical care and nutritional supplements but no enriched day care. At all ages, the average IQ scores of the children in the 'enriched' group were higher than those of the control group: 44 per cent of the control group children had IQ scores classified as borderline or retarded (scores below 85) compared with only 12.8 per cent of the 'enriched' group. Additionally, the 'enriched' group achieved significantly higher scores on reading and mathematics tests at age 12. These findings show that the intellectual power of disadvantaged children can be significantly increased if they are given stimulating experiences early in life.

The race and IQ controversy

Box 3.2 outlines the main arguments in a debate which began in 1969 over whether or not genetically determined differences in intelligence exist between different racial groups.

BOX 3.2
Race and IQ

A lively and often bitter debate developed over the years. The question arose as to whether or not genetically determined differences in intelligence existed between different racial groups. It is an undisputed fact that using standard IQ tests, black Americans score on average approximately 15 points below the average of the white population (Shuey, 1966); the controversy arose from how this information was interpreted.

The debate began in 1969 with the publication of an article by Arthur Jensen in the USA in which he claimed that genetic factors were strongly implicated in the average Negro–white intelligence differences found. He based this view on an 80 per cent heritability estimate, which was calculated from studies of the white population. (Heritability relates to the proportion of a trait's (for example, intelligence) variance within a particular population, which can be attributed to genetic differences.) He added that the evidence did not support the possibility of strong environmental influences. In view of the implications of this view for social policy and in particular the allocation of resources for such enrichment projects as Headstart, a heated exchange began between hereditarians and environmentalists. There follows a summary of some of the more important points made:

1. Jensen's use of an 80 per cent heritability estimate is based on *within-group* differences, i.e. differences within the white population. It does not follow that conclusions can be drawn about *between-group* differences, i.e. differences between black and white populations (Mackenzie, 1984).
2. Tobias (1974) pointed out Jensen's failure to take account of the possible cumulative effects of generations of environmental deprivation suffered by American blacks in the form of poverty, malnutrition, prejudice and lack of educational opportunity. It is well known that the effects of poverty and malnutrition can persist for at least two generations after improvements in conditions have taken place.
3. Kamin (1977) argued that the complex interaction between genetic factors and environmental influences is not well understood. No study has yet been able to estimate the extent to which different environment can affect intellectual development.
4. Fontana (1988) argued that a starting point for the debate must be the difficulties in defining and measuring intelligence. Concepts of intelligence and the methods for measuring it in western white societies are **culture bound**, that is, they may not be valid for other cultures.
5. Race, like intelligence, has no agreed definition though most commonly it refers to a group sharing a common gene pool. However, known differences in gene structure are greater *within* a racial population than *between* such populations (Bodmer, 1972).

6. Where black or mixed-race children are adopted before they are one year old and reared by well-educated, high-income white families, they score an average of 15 IQ points higher than under-privileged black children reared in their biological families (Scarr and Weinberg, 1977).
7. Fontana (1988) suggests that 'there are no conclusive grounds for supposing genetic differences in intelligence exist between races. Such measurable differences as do exist would seem to be far too strongly contaminated by environmental variables to allow us to explain their origins with any confidence' (p. 102).

Nature/nurture: an interactionist approach

As we have seen, the nature/nurture debate in intelligence was concerned with the role of genes and environment in determining measured intelligence. Much of the research discussed has served to highlight the complexity, and some would argue the futility, of trying to unravel the relative contributions of each.

In a classic paper in 1958, Anastasi argued that the only fruitful course for psychologists is to ask how the two *interact* rather than which has the greater influence. Both genes and environment influence behaviour. Different environments acting on the same genetic structure would produce different behaviours. Conversely, individuals who were genetically different but sharing the same environment would also exhibit different behaviours. It is therefore more logical to accept that heredity and environment interact and to consider the question of how changes in one may affect the influence of the other. (See Chapter 1.)

Norm of reaction. Anastasi and others have used the concept of 'norm of reaction' in relation to the question of how heredity and environment may interact. Genetic structure is seen as imposing a top and bottom limit on an individual's potential behaviour. Where within this range the individual's behaviour (in this case IQ) will fall is determined by the kind of environment experienced. Thus, individuals who are exposed to a rich stimulating and emotionally supportive environment would be expected to develop to their full intellectual potential. Scarr-Salapatek (1971) maintained that indi-viduals have a reaction range of 20–25 points. Thus an IQ score can vary within this range depending upon the kind of environment encountered.

A classic theory proposed by Hebb (1949) illustrates the concept of 'norm of reaction'. Hebb distinguished two kinds of intelligence which he called **Intelligence A** and **Intelligence B**. Intelligence A is seen as the individual's genetic potential or the basic given qualities of the central nervous system; Intelligence B relates to the amount of Intelligence A that is realised as a result of experience, learning and other environmental factors. However, there is no way of observing Intelligence A or B, much less comparing them between individuals. In 1969, Vernon added the term **Intelligence C** as being that portion of Intelligence B which is measurable by IQ tests.

Because of the difficulty of assessing genetic potential and the interaction with various environments, the usefulness of 'norm of reaction' is at present limited. Moreover, recent developments in genetics suggest that genetic structure is more flexible than had been thought. Rigid upper and lower limits may not exist. Nonetheless, until more conclusive evidence is available, it serves to remind educationists and social policy-makers of the complex interaction between heredity and environment and the need to ensure that all individuals receive the best possible environmental conditions. It may also encourage researchers to develop more searching studies of the social and educational practices which might reduce IQ differences between groups.

Note that a more detailed account of the nature/nurture debate in psychology can be found in Wadeley *et al.* (1997). A more complete discussion of theories of intelligence and of different kinds of IQ tests can be found in Birch and Hayward (1994).

Self-assessment questions

1. How would you define 'intelligence'?
2. Briefly describe some widely used IQ tests. How is an IQ score currently arrived at?
3. What are thought to be the main benefits of IQ testing? Discuss some of the controversies arising from the use of IQ tests.
4. Critically evaluate some evidence which offers support for the role of 'nature' in the heredity/environment debate.
5. Referring to evidence, discuss some environmental factors which are likely to enhance the development of the intellect.
5. Briefly discuss the main issues arising from the controversy surrounding race and IQ.
6. Outline the interactionist approach to the nature/nurture debate in intelligence.

SECTION IV INFORMATION-PROCESSING APPROACHES TO COGNITIVE DEVELOPMENT

This is a relatively new approach to the study of cognitive development which has gathered momentum over the last two decades, particularly in the United States. Information-processing theorists, while in some cases influenced by Piaget, do not subscribe to a single, unifying theory in their work. Their aim is to understand how an individual interprets, stores, retrieves and evaluates information. Typically, this approach has included the following:

- A detailed study of processes such as perception, memory, the use of strategies, reaction times, the efficiency with which attention can be allocated and so on.
- An attempt to understand what aspects of information-processing change with age and which are relatively stable. For example, it is known that children's ability to handle several items of information at one time increases with age and that their performance will suffer if this capacity is overloaded.

Information-processing theorists tend to view the human mind as being similar to a computer. The physiology of the brain, with the nerves and connective tissues, are seen as the 'hardware' of cognition, with the processes occurring during cognition being viewed as the 'software' or 'programs'. Typically, information-processing theorists present people with problem-solving tasks and then investigate the strategies used to solve them. Often, computer simulation techniques are used (computer simulation refers to attempts to replicate human thinking by using computers).

Within the information-processing approach to children's thinking, there currently exist two main strands:

- *Study of developmental structures and processes* This approach, without necessarily inferring that distinct stages of development exist, assumes that children's thought processes develop in a clearly sequential way.
- *Study of individual differences* Researchers in this field are interested in identifying the kinds of basic information-processing capacities or strategies that might underlie differences between people in relation to their cognitive functioning.

Aspects of these two approaches are discussed below:

Developmental aspects of information processing

The work of Case (1978, 1985) exemplifies this approach. Some of his propositions can be summarised as follows:

- **Sequential development** Cognitive development occurs in an orderly sequence, during which the child's information-processing capacities become increasingly more proficient.
- **Working memory** The crucial concept in explaining development was thought to be the amount of '**working memory**' or '**M space**' (roughly equivalent to short-term memory) the child possesses at a particular time. Case argued that tasks that the child encounters can be described in terms of the amount of M space they require. As children develop, the amount of working memory increases and this is responsible for their increasing ability to handle cognitive tasks, such as problem-solving and remembering things.

Meadows (1995) argues that although it is feasible that the size of the memory stores increases as children grow older, it does not follow that this is responsible for the increasing proficiency that occurs in memory and information-processing skills as the child develops. More important, she suggests, are the changes that occur as a result of the child's increasing experience of handling cognitive tasks. Dealing with knowledge, studying and exploring in school lead to the child becoming more 'expert' at remembering things and solving problems.

Other research has examined a wide range of information-processing phenomena. Some of this research is outlined below.

1. Efficiency in information-processing

Clearly information-processing becomes more efficient as a child grows older. The best evidence for this is that they become *faster* at solving-problems and performing other cognitive tasks. Kail and Park (1992) found increases with age in children's performance in a wide range of activities such as simple perceptual motor tasks (for example, tapping), reaction times to a stimulus (for example, pressing a button when a light is flashed) and simple addition. Results with children in Korea were very similar to those for children in the United States which adds some cross-cultural validity to this proposition. Hale *et al.* (1993) argue that efficiency in information-processing is brought about by physical changes in the brain which allows increasing speed of both responses and mental activity.

2. *Use of rules*

Some researchers have found that in addition to an increase in speed of information-processing, children increasingly acquire a basic set of rules when solving problems. As the child grows older and gains more experience, these rules are applied to a wider and wider range of problems. Siegler (1981) studied children solving a range of different problems (see an example in Figure 3.7) and concluded that almost all but the very youngest children behaved as if they were following one of four rules:

- *Rule 1* where children paid attention to only one aspect of the problem set (usually the number of weights) and seemed incapable of handling other dimensions.
- *Rule 2* Here children still paid attention only to the number of weights unless there was an equal number on each side. In this case they also took account of the distance of the weights from the central point.
- *Rule 3* where children attempted to take account of more than one aspect of the problem but did not do so systematically and often ended up making a guess at the solution.
- *Rule 4* Here, the child was able systematically to test out different possibilities and arrived at the correct solution (comparing distance times weight for each side).

FIGURE 3.7
Siegler's (1981) balance scale

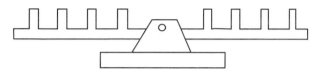

This is similar to the balance scale used by Siegler in his experiments.

The scale has a series of pegs on either side of the centre piece, as indicated above. Weights can be placed on the pegs.

Children are asked to predict which way the balance will fall depending on the number and location of the weights.

Siegler proposed that children developed the rules in an orderly sequence, starting with Rule 1. It is clear that the sequence has many similarities with Piaget's description of children's development of problem-solving abilities (see Section I). However, Siegler proposed that whether a child uses a particular rule depends not so much on age, but on the child's experience of solving particular kinds of problems and the extent to which the child has been able to practice aspects of the task concerned. This is in keeping with the findings from the cross-cultural study by Jahoda (1983) discussed in Section I, which highlighted the importance of experience to cognitive development.

3. Meta-cognition

Meta-cognition refers to a children's knowledge and understanding of cognitive processes, particularly their own cognitive skills – knowing about knowing, if you like. Here are some examples:

- A child who says 'I won't be able to solve this problem because I don't remember how to convert from fractions to decimals' is demonstrating her awareness of the limits of her own cognition in relation to a particular task.
- When children can describe the best ways of studying or explain why they find one particular kind of mental arithmetic task more difficult to do than another they are showing awareness of their own cognitive processes. Such awareness of one's own cognitive processes, or meta-cognition, is part of a larger category of cognitive skills that information-processing theorists call **executive processes**. These include (i) contemplating different strategies, (ii) planning how to solve a problem.

Meta-cognition and the idea of a **central executive system** have played a dominant part in the information-processing approaches already described (for example, those of Siegler, 1981, and Case, 1985) and theorists see cognition as becoming increasingly proficient and controlled as a child develops and receives more and more education.

Study of individual differences in information-processing

Whilst some researchers have been studying developmental changes or sequences, others have concerned themselves with individual differences. In general, their strategy has been to compare performance on standard IQ tests with some measure of information-processing skill. Some of these measures and tentative findings are as follows:

- *Speed of information processing* A number of researchers have found that individuals with faster reaction times or speed of performance on an assortment of tasks also have higher IQ scores on standard tests (Vernon, 1987). Further, some studies have linked speed of processing both to IQ and to the functioning of the central nervous system. For example, it is now possible to measure speed of conduction of neural (nerve cell) impulses such as those in the nerves of the arm. Vernon and Mori (1992) found that there was a relationship between this measure and measures of IQ.
- *Comparisons of normal-IQ and retarded children* DeLoache and Brown (1987) compared searching strategies used by 2-year-old children who were developing normally with those of children of the same age who appeared to show delayed development. In a task where the children were set to search for a toy hidden in the room, the search strategies and skill of the two groups did not differ. However, when the experimenter discreetly removed the toy from its location before the children started to search there was a difference. The normally-developing children searched in various other locations, whereas the delayed-development children continued to search in the place where they had first seen the toy hidden. It appeared that they were not able to change their strategies. This and other studies suggest that flexibility in the use of information-processing strategies may be another key factor underlying individual differences in cognitive ability.

Evaluation of the information-processing approach

As we have seen earlier in this chapter, before the information-processing approach was developed, there were two main approaches to studying cognitive development. The first – the psychometric or IQ approach – was concerned solely with measuring cognitive ability. The other approach, exemplified by the theories of Piaget's and his followers, focused on the development of cognitive structures and processes.

The information-processing approach has complemented and provided some important links between the other two approaches, as indicated below:

- It now seems likely that while there are some basic inborn strategies which develop with age (such as noting differences and similarities) some of the changes in cognitive ability that Piaget attributed to changes in structure are heavily influenced by experience. For example, the more often a child plays with coloured shapes, the more proficient she will become at classifying objects. Therefore individual differences in cognitive ability can be thought of as arising from inborn differences in the efficiency of basic cognitive processes coupled with differences in experience.
- There are some practical applications of the information-processing approach. For example, studies of recognition memory in infancy provide a means for the early identification of retarded children or those that may be at risk of later problems. This could lead to the identification of particular kinds of training that would be helpful to children with learning difficulties.

The information-processing approach, then, shows much promise and is an important addition to other approaches to the understanding of cognitive development. However, this approach is not yet sufficiently well-developed to explain all the differences that are observed among children on Piagetian tasks. Additionally, there are not yet any tests of information-processing ability that could justifiably replace the use of IQ tests in educational and clinical settings.

Self-assessment questions

1. How does the information-processing approach to cognitive development differ from that of Piaget?
2. Outline some of the research which has examined developmental aspects of information-processing.
3. Briefly indicate some findings from research which has been concerned with individual differences in information-processing.
4. Outline the main strengths and weaknesses of the information-processing approach to cognitive development.

SECTION IV LANGUAGE ACQUISITION

The basic units of a language are words and each word is made up of sounds, known as **phonemes**, which correspond roughly to the letters of the alphabet. Phonemes combine together to form **morphemes** which are the smallest units of language to have a grammatical purpose. For example, the word 'pin' is made of four phonemes – p-i-n-s – and two morphemes – 'pin', which is a word, and 's', which serves the purpose of converting the word to the plural.

In the remarkably short time-span of about three years, young children progress from speaking their first word at approximately 12 months, to producing fluent, grammatically correct speech. Without any deliberate training, children are able to acquire a working knowledge of grammar, or **syntax** (combining morphemes so that they obey systematic rules) by the time that they are about four and a half. At the same time, their understanding of the meaning of words and sentences (**semantics**) and their appreciation of how language is used in different social contexts (**pragmatics**) develops rapidly.

Psychologists are interested in a number of questions about language acquisition. These include the following:

- What accounts for the rapid progress in mastering such a complex and intricate system as language? To what extent does language acquisition depend upon biological factors and to what extent upon learning?
- How far is it important to examine the child's developing competence in various social contexts?
- What role is played by adults in providing the kind of environment within which the child's language development will flourish?

These and other questions will be explored in what follows.

Sequence of language acquisition

There are three main phases of early language acquisition:

Babbling The first sounds made are cries, which reflect the child's physical state of well-being, followed soon by gurgles, coos and chuckles, which are not strictly speaking language, but are thought to represent what Vygotsky called the 'pre-intellectual' stage. At about six or seven months, the child begins to babble, producing syllable-like sounds, for example, 'gaga', 'dada'. All babies, including those who are deaf, in all cultures produce these same speech-like sounds. This suggests that maturation, rather than learning, is responsible. A major, longitudinal study of children's language by Wells (1985) confirmed that there appears to be 'a universal sequence of development, at least in general outline'. (p. 224). Towards the end of the first year, the sounds made begin to resemble the particular language that is spoken around the child. Parents seem to spend a lot of time interpreting the meaning intended in a baby's actions and vocalisations (Snow, 1977). Indeed, they often go beyond the actual meaning for example:

Baby: Dadadada.
Mother: Yes, that's Daddy. He has gone to work.

This is an example of 'scaffolding' (see Section II).

One-word utterances   At about 12 months, a child produces the first understandable words, for example, 'mama', 'dog', 'no'. Children's active vocabulary by the age of 18 months is, on average, about 30 words, though they will understand and react correctly to many more that they cannot yet utter.

Early sentences   At about the age of two years, children begin to put two words together to form simple sentences, for example, 'Mummy go', 'Teddy fall'. These words are not randomly linked, but appear to be 'telegraphic' versions of adult sentences, in which essential nouns, verbs and occasional adjectives are uttered (see Roger Brown's work below). From the start, it seems, the child is capable of following simple rules of grammar. At this stage, children seem to be adept at interpreting other people's responses. For example, if the word 'milk' is not understood, they may change it to 'give' or 'want it' (Wilcox and Webster, 1980).

Shortly after about the age of two years, a child can consistently produce three- and four-word utterances. This is followed by a rapid increase in the use of grammatical rules and a child is able to alter the word arrangement in a sentence to change the meaning, for example, 'Lucy is singing' becomes 'Is Lucy singing?' By the age of three, children begin to use more complex sentences and their language is generally understood by adults, even outside the family. By about the age of four and a half, the child's language is very similar to that of an adult.

Some studies of language acquisition

Trevarthen (1974) studied babies from birth to six months with the aid of recording devices. He noted a particular kind of behaviour in babies as young as six weeks which he termed 'pre-speech'. He suggested that this was a primitive attempt at speech by moving the lips and tongue, sometimes vocally, at other times soundlessly. He noted also that as early as two months, babies make soft, low vowel sounds in response to others. This responsive vocalisation may be the beginning of 'taking turns' as children and adults do in conversation later on.

In a pioneering, longitudinal study lasting 10 years, Brown and Bellugi (1964) used naturalistic observation techniques to study the development of language in three children under two and a half, Adam, Eve and Sarah. The children were visited in their homes and tape recordings made of conversations between child and mother. The tape recordings were later transcribed and analysed by Brown and his colleagues. The following are among the insights obtained from Brown's work:

- Early sentences produced by young children up to about two and a half are short and incomplete grammatically. However, the words retained are 'telegraphic' in that they preserve the meaning of the message, while the smaller 'functor' words, which are not essential to the meaning, are left out, for example, 'baby highchair', meaning 'Baby is in the highchair'. Correct word-order is invariably retained.
- Children up to the age of four or five have difficulty in correctly expressing a negative (I will *not* walk), past tenses (I shout*ed*), irregular plurals (mice).
- Early sentences are much the same whatever language children speak. Whether they are English, Russian or Chinese, the same variety of meanings are expressed, for example, statements about location ('spoon table'), possession ('my doll'), actions ('Mummy dance').

Brown's then-innovatory approach to the study of language acquisition produced a vast amount of data which has provided material for many further studies. However, the study had some limitations. Because of the nature and size of the sample, it was difficult to generalise findings to all children. Also, child speech was analysed from a typed transcript of the recordings. It was noted by

Robinson (1981) that features of the language used, such as intonation, pitch and stress, were not included and the caretaker's utterances and the context in which the utterances were made were often left out.

Gelman and Shatz (1977) found that adults talking to children usually speak differently to children from the way they do to adults. Typically, they use shorter sentences, speak in a high-pitched voice and emphasise key words and phrases. The length and complexity of the sentences used are also adjusted to suit the child's level of comprehension. This simplified form of speech used by adults when talking to children is known as the **Baby Talk Register (BTR)**. It used to be known as 'motherese' but this term is now considered to be sexist. It is thought that the way parents adjust their language to suit a child's level plays an important part in the acquisition of language. Gelman and Shatz also tape-recorded 4-year-olds presenting a new toy to adults and to younger children. The 4-year-olds used shorter, less complex sentences when they were speaking to the 2-year-olds, showing that even at this early age they had acquired the skill of adjusting their use of language to suit their listener's linguistic level.

Cazden (1965) found that a group of children whose utterances were **commented** upon on a regular basis over a period of three months showed more progress in language development than a similar group whose utterances were **expanded upon** and imitation of correct language encouraged. The following is an example:

Child's utterance	Expansion by adult	Comment by adult
Me play.	You are playing.	What are you playing with?

These findings were confirmed by Nelson *et al.* (1973) who compared children whose utterances were **recast** (commented upon in the same context) with those whose utterances were **expanded upon**. Children whose utterances were recast used more complex grammatical forms of language than did children whose language was just expanded.

Theories of language acquisition

Traditionally, two broad theoretical approaches have been taken in an attempt to explain language development. These are **learning**

theory and **nativist theory**. Each of these will be considered in turn. In addition, approaches will be discussed which have emphasised the importance of **social interaction** on the development of language

Learning theory

Learning theorists view reinforcement and imitation as the principal mechanisms governing a child's acquisition of language. Skinner (1957) distinguished three ways in which speech may be encouraged:

1. The child uses **echoic** responses, i.e. imitates sounds made by others, who immediately show approval. In line with the principles of operant conditioning (see Chapter 4), this reinforcement increases the likelihood of the word being repeated on future occasions in the presence of the object.
2. The child produces a **mand**, i.e. a random sound, which then has a meaning attached by others; e.g. on hearing 'dada' the parent uses it to form a word and encourages the child to repeat it.
3. A **tact** response is made, where the child utters a word, usually imitated, in the presence of the object, and is rewarded by approval.

Gradually, through the processes of imitation, trial and error and reinforcement, children develop and refine their language until it matches that of the parents.

Limitations of the learning theory approach   Learning theory cannot explain:

- the remarkable rate of language acquisition. An impossible number of utterances would need to be imitated/reinforced if these were the only mechanisms responsible;
- the many different responses that may be made to the same verbal stimuli;
- the creative and novel utterances made by children. 'Mouses', 'I seed', 'He goed' – all common childhood utterances – are unlikely to have been acquired though imitation and reinforcement. Herriot (1970) argued that these 'virtuous errors' arise because the child is actively trying to apply 'correct' grammatical rules, and has not had sufficient experience to remember the irregular morphemes.

The learning theory explanation relies heavily on the role of the caretaker in acting as a model for the child's speech and providing reinforcement. However, Brown and others observed that parents rarely correct a child's grammar or reinforce grammatically correct statements. Rather, they tend to be interested in the truth or correctness of the utterances. McNeill (1966) showed that when parents do attempt to correct a child's speech the results are often disappointing, as the following dialogue demonstrates:

Child:	Nobody don't like me
Mother:	No, say 'nobody likes me'
Child:	Nobody don't like me

After eight repetitions:

Child: Oh, nobody don't likes me.

Dodd (1972) studied babies' utterances during the babbling stage and found there was no imitation of sounds made by an attentive adult, though the amount of babbling increased.

Imitation and reinforcement clearly play a part in language acquisition since children end up speaking the language they hear around them, but learning theory does not appear to provide the whole explanation, as the studies by Gelman and Shatz (1977) and those by Cazden (1965) and Nelson *et al.* (1973) show. These studies appear to show that the involvement of adults and older children who use an appropriate form of BTR and who recast a child's utterances in an accessible form provide an environment in which language will develop effectively.

Nativist theory

Chomsky (1968) strongly opposed Skinner's learning theory explanation of language acquisition and stressed the likelihood of some biologically based predisposition to acquire language. He maintained that humans possess an inborn brain mechanism which he terms a '**language acquisition device**'. The language acquisition device contains certain information about the structure of language which is progressively used as the child matures.

At some level, all languages share common elements. Chomsky calls these common features 'linguistic universals'. One sort of 'universal' relates to the existence of nouns, adjectives and verbs, which are common to all languages. These 'universals' exist at the 'deep' structural level in languages. Throughout the language acquisition device the child has an innate awareness of these universals. The differences that exist between the various languages, Chomsky suggests, exist at the 'surface' structure.

Put at its simplest level, the surface structure represents the actual words and phrases which make up a sentence, while the deep structure corresponds more or less to the meaning of the sentence. The understanding of how to transform this deep structure into the surface structure is what Chomsky terms **transformational grammar**. When children are exposed to language, they are able to 'scan' what is heard, extract the underlying grammatical rules and apply them in new situations and in varying forms (transformations).

Here are two examples which make this clearer

1. Take these two sentences:

   John was chased by a bull
   A bull chased John

   The surface structure of these two sentences is very different. Every word has a different position, the form of the verb has changed and the subject is different in each case. Yet the deep meaning of the two sentences is the same.

2. Now look at these sentences:

   Some children are easy to please
   Some children are anxious to please

   One word only has changed, but the deep meaning is quite different. In the first sentence, the children are the object who are easily pleased; in the second, they are the active subject, wanting to please.

Arguments in favour of Chomsky's theory include:

• The existence of 'linguistic universals' must point to an innate capacity of language in humans. Chomsky argues that this predisposition is not shared by other species. However, studies aimed at investigating whether non-human primates can acquire language have cast some doubt on this assertion since they suggest that chimpanzees appear to be able to use human language, albeit in a limited form (see Gardner and Gardner, 1969; Premack and Premack, 1972).

- The fact that children acquire language so competently in such a short time span is quite remarkable, particularly in view of the fragmented and often distorted samples of speech they are exposed to in the home. Such a feat could not be accomplished without the existence of an inborn capacity for language. However, it should be remembered that a child does not acquire language in isolation from the social context in which it occurs. It is likely that speech heard by the child is interpreted in conjunction with its social context.

- All human beings possess common physiological features related to language, such as finely turned vocal chords, and language areas in the cortex of the brain. Furthermore, virtually all children, regardless of their intellectual ability, acquire language at approximately the same age and in the same sequence (Lenneberg, 1967).

- The findings of studies by Brown and Bellugi (1964), Herriot (1970) and McNeill (1966) previously referred to, suggest that children appear to have an inborn capacity to use 'rules' of language. This is illustrated in their language through their production of 'errors' (for example, 'I wented'). This would be consistent with the existence of a LAD. However, some psychologists have suggested that the use of rules by children in their early speech is the result not so much of an inborn LAD, but of the child's **prelinguistic knowledge**. By this is meant that, before children are capable of using language, they are able to communicate and understand the communications of others through gestures, facial expressions and actions.

Criticisms of Chomsky's theory include the following:

- It has been suggested that Chomsky's theory over-emphasises the structure of sentences, while neglecting their meaning. For example, the theory cannot explain single or two-word utterances since they contain no grammatical structure. Bloom (1970), researching childhood utterances, maintained that the meaning of the utterance must be taken into account. One of the children she studied produced the utterance 'Mummy sock' in two different contexts, one where her mother was putting a sock on the child's foot, the other while picking up her mother's sock. The intended meanings are very different.

- Language acquisition is not just about knowing the structures or the rules, but also about learning the *social* functions of language. You cannot divorce language from the context in which it is used. Bruner (1983) saw language as 'a by-product (and a vehicle) of culture transmission'.
- The theory tends to ignore the fact that parents modify and simplify their language to help their understanding. (Look back at the references to the BTR on page 118.) Chomsky is suggesting that the environment is inadequate for language learning.
- The theory appears to suggest that children's linguistic achievements proceed quite separately from their intellectual development, that learning to talk about something is separate from forming a concept of it.

Language and social interaction

The learning theory approach to language acquisition suggests that language is acquired through the influence of the environment. This is thought to occur in the form of parents' modelling and reinforcing appropriate language. Nativist theory implies that the environment is of less importance. What is crucial is the child's innate tendency to acquire language. A third approach highlights the importance of the social interaction which occurs between children and the people around them. Essentially, this view suggests that children begin to master the social context and then later add language to their repertoire.

Some of the research already discussed supports this social interaction hypothesis – for example, studies by Gelman and Shatz (1977) into the influence of the BTR, and by Nelson *et al.* (1973) into the effectiveness of adults recasting a child's sentences.

Another line of research has focused on the development of **joint attention** and mutual understanding of gestures. Joint attention relates to the communication that occurs through the shared understanding of gestures between a child and adult when they are focusing together on an object. Butterworth (1987) has described how as early as 6 months, babies will follow the mother's gaze to look at something, and by about 9 months will start pointing to direct the mother's attention to an object. Often the mother names the object or comments on it. This form of non-verbal communication between a child and adult together with the experiences of 'turn taking' and the mother's verbal comments seem to be an important forerunner to the development of language and the skills of communication. Bruner (1983) has called these early interactive processes and later 'scaffolding' (see Section II) the Language Acquisition Support System.

Self-assessment questions

1. Outline the main phases of language acquisition in children.
2. What insights did the studies of Brown and his colleagues provide about language acquisition? What were the shortcomings of this research?
3. Explain what is meant by the Baby Talk Register.
4. Briefly outline both the learning theory and the nativist approach to language acquisition. Comment on the shortcomings of each.
5. Outline the findings of research which shows that early social interaction plays an important part in the acquisition of language.

Further reading

Bee, H. (1995) *The Developing Child* (7th edn) (NY: HarperCollins) chs 7 and 8.
De Villiers, P. A. and De Villiers, J. (1979) *Early Language* (London: Fontana).
Donaldson, M. (1978) *Children's Minds* (Glasgow: Fontana/Collins).
Meadows, S. (1995) 'Cognitive Development', in P. E. Bryant and A. M. Colman (eds), *Developmental Psychology* (Harlow: Longman).

"IT'S REALLY REINFORCING, SEEING HIM WITH HIS SUCCESSFUL THEORY!"

Approaches to Social Development

At the end of this chapter you should be able to:

1. describe and evaluate psychodynamic, learning theory and cognitive approaches to development;
2. compare and contrast these three approaches.

Three major theoretical approaches have contributed to our knowledge of the development of social and moral behaviour:

1. The psychodynamic approach, which arises from Freud's theory of personality development and has been upheld by neo-Freudians such as Erikson;
2. The learning theory approach, which is based on the work of the early behaviourists such as Watson, Pavlov and Thorndike and more recently the work of Skinner, the 'father of behaviourism' and that of Bandura and others into social learning theory;
3. The cognitive-developmental approach which was initially derived from Piaget's theory of cognitive development but more recently has encompassed work by other theorists. The study of social cognition, ways in which children think about relationships, can also be included within the cognitive approach.

Each approach will be considered in turn.

SECTION 1   THE PSYCHODYNAMIC APPROACH

Freud (1856–1939)

Freud's psychoanalytic view of child development has had a profound effect on psychological thinking since its introduction in the early part of this century.

Originally trained as a doctor, Freud's interest in neurology led him to specialise in nervous disorders. He noted that many neurotic disorders exhibited by his patients appeared to stem from former traumatic experiences, rather than from physical complaints. Freud developed his now famous psychoanalytic treatment of emotional and personality disorders. Psychoanalysis involves the use of three major techniques:

- **'Free association'** where patients are encouraged to relax and express the free flow of thoughts entering their minds;
- **Analysis of dreams**;
- Interpretation of '**slips of speech**' and other 'accidental' events.

Each of these techniques, Freud believed would penetrate the **unconscious mind** of the patient and reveal thoughts, feelings and motivations of which the patients was not consciously aware.

It was from **case studies** of his patients that Freud developed his famous theory of the human mind and personality, a theory which continued to grow and develop throughout his life. The term **psychoanalysis** can refer to both the treatment and the theory.

Central to psychoanalytic theory are Freud's belief in

- the existence of an unconscious mind, built up during childhood, harbouring repressed memories which motivate and influence conscious thoughts and behaviour. Freud's view of the unconscious mind was largely negative in that he believed the contents were repressed because they were painful or threatening.
- the existence of **instincts** which motivate and regulate human behaviour even in childhood: for example, **Eros** (a general life instinct made up of life-preserving and sexual drives) and **Thanatos** (a death instinct which involves aggressive and destructive drives). The source of these instincts is psychic energy and the most dominant, the **libido**, is sexual in nature. Freud regarded the libido as a force which compels humans to behave in ways which are likely to reproduce the species. He proposed that the amount of psychic energy for a particular individual is fixed and that energy could be linked to objects, people, thoughts and actions. He called this process **cathexis**.
- the importance of **defence mechanisms** such as **repression** (removing painful experiences from conscious memory), **regression** (reverting back to earlier ways of behaving in order to

escape from stressful events); **projection** (expressing one's own disturbing feelings or attitudes as though they arose from another person); **sublimation** (expressing basic drives, for example, aggressive tendencies, in a substitute activity such as art).

An important concept introduced by Freud is that of **identification**, a psychological mechanism which aims to explain the increasing similarity between the behaviour of children and older generations. Identification is the mechanism through which an individual adopts the attitudes, beliefs and behaviour of another person.

Structure of the personality

Freud held that the personality consisted of three major structures, the **id**, the **ego** and the **superego.** Each part of the personality has its own function, and in the healthy, mature personality the three parts produce balanced, well-integrated behaviour. Note that these parts of the personality should in no way be thought of as tangible, biological entities.

- **Id** The id is biologically determined and is the most primitive part of the personality. It represents all the instinctual drives: sexual, aggressive and those concerned with the satisfaction of bodily needs. It operates on the 'pleasure principle', that is to say, it seeks to obtain pleasure and avoid pain The id is irrational and impulsive and is unaffected by social restrictions. In the newborn baby, all mental processes are id processes.
- **Ego** As the infant develops and attempts to adapt to the demands of the outside world, the ego emerges. It operates on the 'reality principle', that is to say, gratification of needs are postponed until the appropriate time and place. For example, the young child learns that hunger will only be satisfied when someone is available to prepare food. This does not imply that the ego is concerned with what is 'right' or 'good', only that it takes account of the constraints and restrictions of the outside world. The ego is often said to be the 'executive' or 'manager' of the personality, in that it attempts to strike a balance between the realities of the outside world and the irrational, self-seeking drives of the id.

- **Superego**   Around the age of four to six, the third part of the personality, the superego, emerges. Roughly equivalent to the conscience, the superego represents the individual's own internal framework of what is 'right' and 'wrong' as represented by the moral sanctions and inhibitions which exist in the surrounding culture Any violation of its often unrealistically high standards results in the individual experiencing guilt and anxiety. (The superego will be discussed in more detail in Chapter 5.)

Freud believed that the three parts of the personality are in continual conflict, with the id trying to attain gratification of impulses and the superego setting, often unreasonably high, moral standards. The ego is obliged to maintain an appropriate balance between these two opposing forces and the external demands of social reality.

Development of the personality

Freud proposed that in the course of development children pass through a series of stages. During each stage satisfaction is gained as the libido (or sexual energy) is directed towards a different part of the body. He referred to 'sexual instincts', though in attributing this term to children he used the term 'sexual' in a rather special way to mean something like 'physical pleasurable'. Each stage entails a set of problems to be overcome in relation to later development. Failure to negotiate satisfactorily a particular stage results in fixation, or halting of development at that stage. Fixation causes the individual to retain some of the characteristics of that stage in later life and in severe cases results in neuroses in adult life.

Below is a brief description of Freud's psychosexual stages:

Oral stage (birth to 1 year)

The id is dominant. Libidinal energy is centred on the mouth and the child gains satisfaction from sucking and biting. Freud proposed that:

1. The oral stage can be subdivided into the passive, receptive, sucking subphase of the earlier months and the later active, aggressive, biting subphase.

2. Fixation may be caused either by the over-indulgence or by the frustration of a child's oral needs. A child whose oral needs are not satisfied or are over-indulged will exhibit the characteristics of this stage in later life. Fixation may express itself in addictions such as smoking, gluttony or alcoholism; nailbiting; the excessive use of sarcasm.

Anal stage (second year of life)

This stage focuses on pleasurable sensations experienced in the mucous membranes of the rectum. The child gains satisfaction from expelling and withholding faeces and is now in a position to exercise some control over these bodily functions. He or she can either please the parents by being 'clean' or can thwart them by making a mess. Thus the pleasurable sensations associated with 'letting go' or 'holding on' become associated with behaviour that has social implications. A significant event in the child's life is the parents' efforts to impose toilet training. Fixation at the anal stage, perhaps resulting from parent/child conflict over toilet training, may give rise to a personality who is exceedingly preoccupied with cleanliness and orderliness (expelling) or who is mean, obstinate and obsessive in adulthood (withholding).

Phallic stage (3 to 6)

Now libidinal energy centres on the genitals and feelings become overtly sexual. Describing first the sequence of events for the male child, Freud defined important issues arising from the **Oedipus complex**. The boy's fantasies include wishes for sexual intimacy with his mother. He envies his father's intimate relationship with his mother and fears punishment in the form of castration for his forbidden wishes. The Oedipus complex is resolved when the child identifies with his father in order to appease him and to become like him in as many ways as possible.

Freud's account of the progress of female children through the Phallic stage is less clear-cut and he proposed various explanation for the girl's eventual identification with her mother. Possibly the most widely reported, the **Electra complex**, is that the girl, believing herself to be already castrated, since she does not possess a penis, suffers **penis envy**. This leads her to seek a strong love attachment to her father, the possessor of a penis, and finally to identify with her mother in order to become like her.

The satisfactory resolution of the Oedipus/Electra complex results in the child identifying with the same-sexed parent. Two important consequences stem from this identification:

1. The child adopts the gender-role which will be assumed through life.
2. The child adopts the parents' moral standards, attitudes and prohibitions, together with the moral norms of the society they reflect. Thus, the superego is born and the values and beliefs of a culture are passed on from one generation to the next.

If, through insensitive handling by adults, the child does not satisfactorily overcome the Oedipus/Electra complex, problems lie ahead. Psychoanalysts believe that fixation at the phallic stage lies behind most adult neuroses.

Latency period (6 to puberty)

This is a period of relative calm following the turmoil of the phallic stage. During this time, the libido is submerged and does not centre upon any bodily area. It is a time of ego-development, particularly in relation to social and intellectual skills.

Genital stage (puberty)

Hormonal changes now stimulate the re-emergence of the libido. There is renewed interest in sexual pleasure and all previous sexual drives associated with particular regions of the body come together in an integrated set of adult sexual attitudes and feelings.

Studies of Freud's theories

Freud's work has generated an immense amount of research both into aspects of the theory of psychoanalysis and into the effectiveness of psychoanalysis as a therapy. Detailed reviews of experimental investigations have been carried out by Kline (1981) and Fisher and Greenberg (1977). Below is a selection of empirical studies which have attempted to test aspects of the theory.

The oral personality

As noted earlier, fixation may be caused either by the over-indulgence or by the frustration of a child's oral needs.

Fisher and Greenberg (1977) see the oral personality as being preoccupied with issues of giving and taking, concerns about independence and dependence, extremes of optimism and pessimism, unusual ambivalence, impatience and the continued use of the oral channel for gratification.

A number of studies have examined whether these traits do tend to exist together in a single cluster or whether two clusters exist reflecting the oral passive (sucking) and oral aggressive (biting) subphases. Kline and Storey (1977) reviewed these investigations and found the strongest support for the oral personality in Goldman-Eisler's (1948) studies where traits such as pessimism, passivity, aloofness, oral verbal aggression and autonomy were found to cluster together as were their opposites. However, Goldman-Eisler provided evidence only of face validity for the scales used. Lazare *et al.* (1966) provided similar results using Goldman-Eisler's items in a questionnaire. In their own study, Kline and Storey (1977) found that characteristics associated with the first 'optimistic' subphase of the oral stage (including dependency, fluency, sociability and relaxation) tended to cluster together as did characteristics (including independence, verbal aggression, envy, coldness and hostility, malice, ambition and impatience) of the second 'pessimistic subphase.

A second series of investigations examined the relationship between feeding practices and later behaviour. For example, Yarrow (1973) found a significant correlation between the time spent feeding and later thumb-sucking, those children with the shortest feeding times being the most persistent thumb-suckers. Though some support is claimed for the effects of fixation in the oral stage, an alternative explanation might be that children whose greater need for sucking, for whatever reason, led them to feed more quickly and later to satisfy the need through thumb-sucking.

The anal personality

As we have seen, Freud proposed that anal fixation is linked to the child's conflicts with the parents during potty training. The struggle which results either from over-harsh potty training or from exceptionally intense pleasure associated with the anal period can later reveal itself in the character traits of orderliness, rigidity, obstinacy and a dislike of waste. The kind of personality in which these traits are combined is known as the anal or obsessive-compulsive personality. Three major reviews of research evidence (Kline, 1972; Fisher and Greenberg, 1977; Pollak, 1979) concluded that these traits do tend to cluster together in the anally-oriented personality. However, Hill (1976) identified major methodological weaknesses in six of the studies considered by Kline to be sound ones. Howarth (1982) recognised that there does appear to be a personality type characterised by the orderly, pedantic, self-controlled and controlling individual who runs the bureaucracy of most nations who might be described as an anally-oriented personality. Fonagy (1981) points out that no evidence exist which suggests that this type of personality received toilet training that was different from that of less obsessive–compulsive types.

Defence mechanisms

Many researchers have attempted to demonstrate the effects of repression ('motivated forgetting') in the laboratory, often by causing an individual to experience anxiety in relation to a particular kind of material or activity and then looking to see if the rate of forgetting increased. Holmes (1974) in a review of such studies found no conclusive evidence of repression. However, Wilkinson and Carghill (1955) claimed that stories with an Oedipal theme were remembered less well than those that were neutral. Levinger and Clark (1961) showed that when asked to remember association words they had produced in response to a number of emotional and neutral stimulus words, participants recalled significantly less of the emotional associations. Kline (1972) claimed that these findings provide clear evidence of repression operating in memory. However, using Levinger and Clark's stimulus words, Parkin *et al.* (1982) found that if participants delayed recall for one week, emotional associations were *better* recalled than were neutral ones. They concluded that these findings support the known relationship between arousal levels and memory and offer no support for Freud's theory of repression. However, an objection to this study and others like it is that the stimuli used may be too trivial and artificial to activate the deep emotional responses described by Freud.

Evaluation of Freudian theory

Eysenck and Wilson (1973) have raised objections to psychoanalytic theory on a number of counts:

- Freud's use of a limited sample composed mainly of adults who were suffering some psychological disturbance prevents generalisation of this theory to all human beings.
- His use of the clinical case study method was criticised. Accounts of his sessions with patients were not written up until some time later and may have been inaccurate and selective.
- Freud used no quantitative data or statistical analysis in support of his theories.
- Most of the processes described by Freud, for example instinctual drives and defence mechanisms, cannot be directly observed and inferences drawn about human behaviour are often open to alternative explanations. This makes the generation of precise and testable hypotheses difficult. Not only can the theory not be supported, it cannot be refuted – a serious violation of the scientific method according to Popper (1959).
- Freudian theory is unable to predict an individual's development. It can be used only to explain something after an event.

Criticisms have been made of Freud's over-emphasis on the role of biological factors in personality development. His insistence that the goal of all behaviour is to satisfy biological needs was not shared by other psychodynamic theorists such as Jung, Adler and Erikson. Whilst recognising the importance of biological factors, these theorists subscribed also to the *social* nature of human beings.

Kline (1984) whilst agreeing that some aspects of the theory, for example instinctual drives, cannot easily be tested and should be abandoned, other aspects can generate testable hypotheses which conform to the demands of the scientific method. Those hypotheses which can be tested should be restated in a refutable form and then subjected to an objective, empirical examination. Kline believes that psychoanalytic theory offers a coherent account of human behaviour in all its complexity and he pleads for bold and original thinking in future attempts to investigate Freudian concepts.

The final comment should perhaps draw attention to the profound effect that Freud's theory has had on psychological thinking and on disciplines such as history, art and English literature:

it seems madness to jettison a set of ideas as stimulating as Freud's because they do not conform to a conventionalised methodology at present in favour in psychology. What is required is scientific psychology that combines theoretical rigour with the rich comprehensiveness of psychoanalysis. (Kline, 1984, p. 157)

Self-assessment questions

1. Explain the following terms as used by Freud: Id, Ego, Superego, Libido, Cathexis, Defence mechanism.
2. Briefly describe the psychosexual stages of development, noting the consequences for adult life of fixation in these stages, as proposed by Freud.
3. Discuss the major objections to Freudian theory.
4. Evaluate some studies which have attempted to provide evidence in support of Freud's psychodynamic theory of development.
5. What difficulties might be encountered by researchers who attempt to test Freudian ideas?

SECTION II   THE LEARNING THEORY APPROACH

Learning theorists are a group of psychologists who believe that socialisation is influenced mainly by external, environmental factors, rather than by factors within the individual. They do not deny that maturation plays a part in development, but rather suggest that the process is of limited value in explaining changes in behaviour. Their beliefs are rooted in the work of associationists, Ivan Pavlov and Edward Thorndike, and the early behaviourists, John Watson and Clark Hull, all of whom studied learning in the form of conditioning.

According to psychologists who subscribe to the learning theory view of development, human beings are quite similar at birth and have the potential to develop into similar adults. However, throughout their development, each individual has varying experiences and receives different treatment from others. Over time, these diverse experiences accumulate and result in unique individuals, each with their own typical patterns of behaviour. For example, one person lives in a loving, caring environment, so she develops into a happy, optimistic personality; another lives in a deprived environment where he is mistreated, and he grows up withdrawn and unsociable. According to learning theorists, the same individual might have been totally different had her/his life experiences taken a different course.

Three theories of learning are used to account for how a child may develop such a complex pattern of behaviours, concepts and habits. Two of these theories are based upon conditioning processes, where new associations are formed between objects and events in the environment and the individual's responses. The third theory, social learning theory, proposes that changes in behaviour are brought about by an individual observing and imitating the behaviour of others. Each of the three theories will be considered in turn.

Classical conditioning

Reflex behaviour is involuntary; it arises automatically in response to an appropriate stimulus; examples are salivating at the smell of food, feeling fear when faced with something frightening. The theory of classical conditioning aims to account for the way in which reflex behaviour may become associated with a new stimulus that does not naturally activate that behaviour. Put simply, an individual may lean to respond in a particular way to a given stimulus because of its association with something else.

Pavlov (1927), a physiologist, was studying the salivary reflex in dogs when he observed that the dogs salivated not only at the sight and smell of food, a 'natural' response, but also at the sight of food container alone. Through a series of experiments, he demonstrated that dogs could be conditioned to salivate to other 'unnatural' stimuli, such as a buzzer being sounded, provided the stimulus was repeatedly presented at, or slightly before, the presentation of food. Such a pairing caused an association to be formed between the buzzer and the food and subsequently between the buzzer and the salivation response. A **conditional reflex** had been formed.

Figure 4.1 illustrates the process of classical conditioning and the terminology associated with it.

Pavlov further demonstrated that the following processes could occur after conditioning:

- If the conditional stimulus continues to be present but without the food, the salivating response would cease or become **extinguished**.

FIGURE 4.1

The process of classical conditioning

The Process of Classical Conditioning

Procedure	Response
Before Conditioning	
Food (UCS) ⟶	Salivation (UCR)
Buzzer (CS) ⟶	No response or irrelevant response
During Conditioning	
Food plus buzzer (UCS) (CS) ⟶	Salivation (UCR)
Repeated pairing of the UCS and CS	
After Conditioning	
Buzzer (CS) ⟶	Salivation (CR)

Key:
UCS   Unconditional stimulus
CS   Conditional stimulus
UCR   Unconditional response
CR   Conditional response

Source: Malim, Birch and Hayward (1996).

- After extinction, the conditioned response, salivation may reappear when the relevant stimulus is present, though it is much weaker. This reappearance is known as a **spontaneous recovery**.
- The dog would **generalise** its response by salivating to sounds similar to the buzzer.
- The opposite process to generalisation is **discrimination**: if two different tones were sounded but food was presented with only one of them, the dog would learn to discriminate between them and salivate only to the tone associated with food.

Classical conditioning in infants

Pavlov's procedures and terminology were soon applied to experimentation with young children. Watson and Rayner (1920) demonstrated that fear could be developed through classical conditioning and could be eliminated in the same way. Watson proposed that the emotion of fear (UCR) in infants is a natural response to a loud noise (UCS). He produced a fear of rats (and indeed of all white furry things) (CR) in a nine-month-old baby by repeatedly associating the appearance of a rat (CS) with the sound of a loud gong (UCS). This is the, now notorious, 'Little Albert' study which has been heavily criticised for its unethical procedures (see Box 1.3, Chapter 1).

Learning theorists propose that classical conditioning may be responsible for the development of many phobias (irrational fears). For example, the child who undergoes a frightening experience associated with the presence of a dog may develop a long-lasting fear of dogs. Marquis (1931) demonstrated the process of classical conditioning in ten newborn babies by sounding a buzzer shortly before or at the same time as they received their bottle. After this treatment had continued for eight days, it was noted that the infants made sucking movements and generally increased their activity when the buzzer was presented without the food. Marquis concluded that 'systematic training of the human infant . . . can be started at birth'.

Studies of classical conditioning have demonstrated the existence of a powerful process capable of influencing reflex behaviour in both animals and human beings. This is of special interest in relation to humans because of the role classical conditioning plays in the development of emotional responses. For example, at a very early age, things or people that are present when a child feels happy and content become a conditioned stimulus for these same contented feelings in later life. Similarly, those associated with unpleasant or stressful feelings may become conditioned stimuli for feelings of anger and anxiety later on.

Operant conditioning

Unlike classical conditioning, operant, or instrumental conditioning is concerned with voluntary rather than reflex behaviour. The theory is based on Thorndike's (1913) **Law of Effect** which states that behaviour resulting in pleasant consequences is likely to be repeated in the same circumstances, whereas that which has no such pleasant consequences dies away.

Thorndike investigated this type of learning with cats using a 'puzzle box' – a cage with a door that could only be opened from inside by pulling a loop of string. Typically a cat was placed in the box and tried hard to escape. In the course of its efforts, by chance it pulled the string and escaped through the open door. Several more trials were carried out and eventually the cat pulled the string immediately it was placed in the box. Thorndike measured the time taken by the cat to escape as an indicator of learning. His data showed that learning the correct 'escape' behaviour happened gradually – a situation he named **trial and error learning**. The reward (freedom) he contended was responsible for 'stamping in' the appropriate response. Operant conditioning is similar in principle to Thorndike's trial-and-error learning.

In his book *Behaviour of Organisms* (1938), Skinner described a series of laboratory experiments he conducted with rats. He constructed a small box containing a lever, a food dispenser and (sometimes) a panel to display lighted stimuli. A rat placed in the box spontaneously explores its surroundings and eventually, by accident, presses the lever. This activates the food dispenser and a pellet of food is presented to the rat. Subsequently, each time the animal's behaviour approximates to what is required, food is presented until eventually the 'reward' known as **reinforcement** is produced only when the animal presses the lever. This procedure is known as **behaviour shaping**; the desired behaviour is shaped by rewarding a series of responses that are **successive approximations** – that is, they approximate more and more closely to the desirable behaviour. The desirable behaviour, in this case, lever pressing, was named an operant. The reward, which increases the likelihood of the behaviour (or operant) being repeated, is the **reinforcer**. The process whereby the food is presented in response to the lever-pressing behaviour is known as **positive reinforcement.**

Skinner and others have repeatedly demonstrated that the techniques of operant conditioning can be used to produce quite complex behaviour in animals. By carefully shaping the component behaviours, he trained pigeons to act as pilots in rockets and to play table tennis.

As with classical conditioning, generalisation, discrimination and extinction can be demonstrated:

- An animal may **generalise** its response to situations which are similar but not identical to the one in which it was originally conditioned. Therefore, if a rat is conditioned to respond when a one-inch plastic square is presented, it will also press the lever in response to a circle of a similar size.
- A rat may be conditioned to **discriminate** between the circle and the square if it is reinforced only when it presses the bar in response to one of them, but not the other.
- If reinforcement is discontinued, **extinction** of the operant response will occur. For reasons which are not clear, this takes longer than with classical conditioning.

Schedules of reinforcement Skinner also demonstrated that the kind of patterns, or schedules, of reinforcement given would differentially affect the kind of learning which occurred. The two main schedules are

- **Continuous reinforcement** – when a reward is given to every instance of the desired behaviour.
- **Partial reinforcement** – where an animal is reinforced only some of the time.

The four partial reinforcement schedules that are not commonly used are:

1. **Fixed interval**: the animal is reinforced after regular time intervals, say every 50 seconds, provided at least one lever-pressing response is made during the time.
2. **Variable interval**: reinforcement is given *on average* every, say, 50 seconds, though not precisely at the same time intervals.
3. **Fixed ratio**: the animal is reinforced after a regular number of lever-pressing responses, say after every four responses.
4. **Variable ratio**: reinforcement is given *on average* every, say, four responses, though not exactly after each fourth response.

Each schedule has a different effect on learning. In general, continuous reinforcement produces the quickest learning, while partial reinforcement produces learning which lasts longer in the absence of reinforcement.

The consequences of behaviour Skinner believed that behaviour is shaped by its consequences. We have already noted that one such consequence is positive reinforcement, something which is pleasant. Other consequences might be **negative reinforcement** and **punishment**.

Negative reinforcement refers to the removal or avoidance of something unpleasant. For example, an electric shock is switched off when the rat presses the lever. This is known as **escape learning**. Skinner showed also that if a light is flashed just before an electric shock is given, the rat would learn to press the lever in response to the light, thus avoiding the shock – an example of **avoidance learning**. Like positive reinforcement, negative reinforcement results in the desired behaviour being **strengthened**.

Secondary reinforcement   Some stimuli, known as **secondary reinforcers,** become reinforcing because they are associated with primary reinforcers such as food or water. Thus, Skinner found that a rat would press the lever in response to the clicking noise heard when a food pellet was delivered, even on occasions when no food was in fact produced.

The conventional view of operant conditioning was that reinforcement is only effective it is given quickly following a response such as bar-pressing – a principle known as **contiguity**. The principle of secondary reinforcement has proved useful in overcoming the adverse effects of delayed reward. For example, secondary reinforcers such as clicking noises are useful for training animals, as in a circus when it would be difficult to give a reward immediately after the animal's response.

Punishment refers to the delivery of an undesirable stimulus following a response – for example, when an electric shock is given in response to the lever-pressing behaviour. Skinner believed that just as reinforcement (positive and negative) can be used to strengthen a response, making it more likely to be repeated, so punishment *weakens* the response and makes it less likely to recur. However, he argued that punishment is not a suitable technique for controlling behaviour, since it simply suppresses unwanted behaviour without strengthening desirable behaviour. Studies with rats carried out by Estes (1970) showed that punishment appeared only to diminish lever-pressing behaviour for a short time, but did not weaken it in the long term.

Whether or not punishment is effective with children is a vexed question. Studies have shown that in the short term it appears to suppress undesirable behaviour. It can, however, have unintended emotional effects such as anger and frustration and, in some circumstances, it may actually become reinforcing, as in the case of the child whose tantrums are designed to gain attention. In these circumstances, it may increase, rather than reduce, the unwanted behaviour.

Operant conditioning with humans

As with classical conditioning, research has shown that infant behaviour may be shaped through the techniques of operant conditioning. For example, in a study of language acquisition, Rheingold *et al.* (1959) and Bloom (1979) showed that the number of sounds made by three-month-old babies could be increased if an adult reinforced the infant's utterances with verbal responses.

Operant methods have also been systematically used in order to change undesirable behaviour in humans. This is known as the technique of behaviour modification, which is discussed in greater detail in Birch and Hayward (1994). The use of reinforcement to improve the classroom behaviour of disruptive children, to teach basic hygiene routines to the mentally handicapped, and to encourage autistic children to communicate has received a large measure of success. In all cases, the techniques used operate on the basis of ignoring undesirable behaviour, resulting in its extinction, and reinforcing desirable behaviour which should then be repeated.

Within the home environment, parents use many of the techniques of operant conditioning, albeit unconsciously. Consider how a young child is potty trained or learns table manners. Reinforcement in the form of praise and hugs is freely given as the child proceeds. And as Skinner indicated, partial, rather than continuous reinforcement is usually more effective, particularly with an older child. The child who is praised for being helpful around the home is more likely to repeat the behaviour if the praise is given only some of the time.

Social learning theory

Theorists who have attempted to use the insights derived from classical and operant conditioning to account for the development of complex human social behaviours have experienced some difficulties. Critics have questioned the validity of extrapolating the findings of animal experiments to human behaviour and have also raised doubts as to the likelihood of all complex human behaviour being derived from reinforcement of the spontaneous responses of the young child. The concept of observational learning (or imitation) had been proposed to explain language acquisition during early childhood and seemed appropriate also to the acquisition of social behaviour. The scope of learning theory was therefore enlarged to include the process of observational learning (or modelling) to explain how children may learn new behaviour by imitating another person.

Observational learning

Observational learning has been extensively studied by Bandura and his colleagues (Bandura and MacDonald, 1963; Bandura, 1977). A long series of experiments was carried out, mainly using nursery-school children as subjects.

In his most famous studies Bandura exposed groups of children to either a real-life situation or to a film in which a model knocked down and beat a rubber 'Bobo' doll. The children were then given the opportunity to reproduce the behaviour observed and their responses were compared with those of a control group who had not seen the model. Findings indicated that the children behaved more aggressively than did the control group, and also reproduced many of the specific acts of the model.

In a later study Bandura (1965) showed that children may learn the behaviour of a model without necessarily reproducing that behaviour. Three groups of children were shown a film of a model behaving aggressively; one group saw the model punished for the behaviour, one saw the model rewarded, and the third group observed neither reward nor punishment. Subsequent observation of the children's behaviour revealed different levels of imitation. The 'model punished' group reproduced less aggressive behaviour than did the other two groups. Bandura concluded that vicarious punishment (experiencing the model's punishment as though it were administered to oneself) had influenced the children's learning of the aggressive behaviour. However, when the children were then offered rewards for imitating the model's behaviour, all three groups produced equally aggressive behaviour. It is therefore necessary to distinguish between **acquisition** of behaviour, and the **performance** of that behaviour.

In their time, Bandura's experiments were not questioned from an ethical standpoint. However, in our more enlightened times, perhaps we should question the ethics of placing children in a room and forcing them to witness ten minutes of adult violence. Today, this might be called abuse. Also, the experimental hypothesis actually *predicted* a negative effect on the children.

Bandura and others went on to investigate what characteristics of a model were most likely to encourage imitation in children. Studies have shown that children are more likely to perform behaviour imitated from models who are:

- similar in some respects to themselves;
- exhibit power and control over some desirable commodity;
- are seen to be rewarded for their actions;
- are warm and nurturant.

The importance of cognitive factors

Unlike traditional learning theorists, social learning theorists emphasise the important cognitive, or mediating, variables, which intervene between a stimulus and response. Bandura proposed that the ability to observe and then reproduce behaviour involves at least four mediating skills:

- **paying attention** to appropriate and distinctive features of the behaviour whilst ignoring irrelevant and distracting aspects of the model;
- retaining the critical features of the performance in **memory**;
- accurate **duplication** of the model's behaviour;
- being **motivated** to reproduce the behaviour observed and justifying it in terms of internal, external or vicarious rewards

These processes, Bandura contended, are evident in all kinds of modelling, from the imitation of single acts to the reproduction of complex social behaviour. Imitation is seen as a powerful mechanism of social learning for children. For example, a small boy may pretend to shave like his father, and in Bandura's view, gender role identity (see Chapter 5) arises from a child repeatedly observing appropriate models.

Identification

Identification is a concept derived originally from psychoanalysis and introduced by Freud. It is said to be the process through which a child adopts the feelings, attitudes and behaviour of other people, initially the parents. It is similar to imitation in that it involves the child copying the behaviour of others, but where imitation involves copying very specific acts, identification is more concerned with copying general styles of behaviour and becoming like other important people in our lives. Most psychologists view identification as a fundamental process in the socialisation of the child. For example, a very young child may identify with his father and act in ways he believes his father would act. Later, he may identify with a whole social group and act according to the group identity involved.

Evaluation of the learning theory view of development

- The learning theorists aim to account for all behaviour changes in human beings, including those which occur during development. So far as classical and operant conditioning processes are concerned, numerous studies have shown beyond doubt that the behaviour of young children can be conditioned by both methods. However, critics question whether these studies, most of which have been concerned with controlled, laboratory-based situations, have really addressed the question of how conditioning affects development.

- The question is asked, also, whether behaviour that must be continuously reinforced resembles that which develops naturally and continues to be exhibited without regular reinforcement. The literature on conditioning lacks clear notions of when and why certain kinds of conditioning are possible and what responses are suitable for conditioning at different points in development.

- Studies of learning by observation, with their emphasis on modelling in children of different ages and in a variety of situations, appear to provide a more coherent view of the role of learning in development. However, this approach too often suffers from the limitations inherent in attempting to telescope the whole socialisation process into a single, usually laboratory-based, situation.

- Whatever the role of learning in development, it is clear that other factors also play a part. Learning theorists do not address themselves to the role of biological factors in the development process.

- Learning theorists view the child as continually changing as a result of conditioning and imitation of models. This view implies that the child is passive being who is capable only of responding to external influences. Other theorists, of whom the most notable is Piaget, emphasise children's active role in their own development.

- Perhaps the main limitation of the learning theory approach to human development is its failure to explain spontaneous changes in behaviour that cannot easily be accounted for by either conditioning or modelling, for example the emergence of a novel or creative idea or the unexpected solving of a problem.

Self-assessment questions

1. What do you understand by the 'learning theory' approach to development? Briefly outline three types of learning which are believed to be involved in the developmental process.
2. How might learning theorists explain the development of a phobia, or irrational fear?
3. What is meant by behaviour shaping? Describe an instance of the use of behaviour-shaping techniques to condition animal behaviour. How might these principles apply to the development of behaviour in humans?
4. Referring to appropriate studies, briefly outline Bandura's social learning theory approach.
5. What do you understand by identification? What is its role in the socialisation process?
6. Evaluate the learning theory approach to human development.

SECTION III   THE COGNITIVE-DEVELOPMENTAL APPROACH

Psychoanalytic theories centre almost exclusively on children's emotional development and the impact on development of their relationships with a few key people. The learning theory approach emphasises the central role that reinforcement plays in children's development and also the importance of imitating appropriate models. Cognitive-developmental theory emphasises the importance to social and emotional behaviour of the child's developing thought processes and the exploration of objects. Traditionally, this approach centred upon Piaget's theory (see Chapter 3 for a description and evaluation). However, other theories of cognitive development have also been considered in Chapter 3 and all may be said to have contributed to the cognitive-developmental approach.

Over the past 25 years or so, it has been recognised that children's personal and social development is strongly influenced by the way in which they think and reason about themselves and other people. A relatively new term has entered the psychological literature, that of **social cognition**.

Social cognition

The first thing to note is that the term 'social cognition' means different things to different researchers. Durkin (1995) distinguishes between **individual social cognition**, the most widely used approach to social cognition, and **cognition as a product of social interaction**. These two approaches will be briefly considered below:

Individual social cognition

This approach focuses on people's perceptions, thinking and reasoning about other human beings and about social relationships. Developmental psychologists have addressed a number of questions in this area of social cognition. These include the following:

- How do children understand and conceptualise the social world – the people around them, relationships between themselves and others?
- What changes take place in such reasoning and concepts as children develop?
- What is the relationship between cognition and social behaviour?

The following areas are among those that have been studied:

- Children's perceptions of themselves and the development of the self-concept (see Section III of Chapter 5).
- Conceptions of relationships between themselves and other people, for example, authority relations and friendships.
- Development of moral reasoning (see Section I of Chapter 5).
- Gender role development (see Section II of Chapter 5).
- Many areas are drawn from social psychology. For example person perception and attribution theory.

Initially, a good deal of research on individual social cognition was strongly influenced by Piaget's work. Therefore, many of the underlying principles were based upon his theory. For example:

- **Stages of development**   Children's social thinking and reasoning develop through a sequence of stages. All children pass through these stages in the same order and at approximately the same age. Each new stage incorporates and builds upon the characteristics of preceding stages.
- **Developing thought processes**   Various features of children's thought processes at different stages of development have an effect on how they perceive and understand social situations. As a child develops, thought processes change:

  - from simple to complex, that is, from their tendency to focus on only one feature of a situation or problem to their ability to take account of many considerations at one time;
  - from concrete thinking (where reasoning must be linked to something concrete) to abstract thinking (the ability to think and reason in one's head);
  - from rigid to more flexible thinking

  These ways of thinking affect a child's understanding of social situations and relationships.
- **Taking someone else's perspective**   Piaget considered that children below the age of about six or seven are **egocentric**. He believed, therefore, that they are unable to view a problem or a situation from the point of view of another person. As noted in Chapter 3, more recent studies indicate that very young children may not be as egocentric as Piaget believed. Nonetheless, it is clear that the ability to take someone else's perspective (sometimes called role-taking ability) becomes more skilful and sophisticated as a child develops. This ability influences the way the child perceives and reacts to social situations.

While experimental methods have been used to study individual social cognition, these have often appeared unduly constraining and unrealistic in the context of children's social understanding and behaviour. More often, variations on Piaget's clinical interview method have been used. Typically, a child is told a story about an imaginary social or moral situation. The interviewer then attempts to elicit the child's understanding of the motives and behaviour of characters in the story. Examples of this approach can be seen in Kohlberg's (1969) work on moral reasoning and Selman's (1976) work on perspective-taking and friendships in children.

Cognition as a product of social interaction

This has been a less widely used approach to the study of social cognition. It is concerned with the ways in which interactions with other people – adults or children – influence, enhance and guide the development of cognitive abilities. It takes the view that social cognition is a *social* process: that is, something which occurs as people interact with each other. This is in contrast to the individual approach to social cognition, which tends to emphasise that development occurs as a result of activities *within* the individual.

Paradoxically, this second approach to social cognition has also been influenced by Piaget. Piaget's belief in the relevance of social interaction to cognitive development has tended to be overlooked. In the 1970s, neo-Piagetian researchers working in Geneva re-established this aspect of his theory and drew on concepts from social psychology to reinterpret it. However, a discussion of this research is beyond the scope of this book.

Another important influence on the 'social' approach to social cognition comes from Vygotskyan theory and this was considered in some detail in Section II of Chapter 3. As we saw in that account, Vygotsky argued that the child acquires the mechanisms of thinking and learning as a result of social interactions with adults and peers. To explain how these interactions may guide and enhance a child's cognitive development, he proposed the concepts of the **zone of proximal development** – the area between a child's actual developmental level and the potential level achievable – and of **scaffolding** – a supporting framework provided by adults and sometimes peers (see Section II of Chapter 3).

Many of the early parent–child social interactions, such as **contingent responding** and **social referencing** discussed in Chapter 2, Section I, might also be considered under the heading of social cognition.

Evaluation of the cognitive-developmental approach

The cognitive-developmental perspective is fast becoming the most important influence on the study of development. It links behaviour to the kind of cognition or thinking ability expected at the age or level of development a child is at. As we have seen, Piaget's theory of cognitive development was the starting point, though the approach is not necessarily tied directly to Piaget's ideas. For example, the work of Kohlberg has been influential in the field of moral development and gender role development. A general criticism has been that most research carried out from a cognitive developmental perspective has viewed development from the standpoint of individual social cognition, emphasising the individual's perceptions and reasoning about other people and the environment, while neglecting the influence of the surrounding culture. The environment is taken as fixed and the child is thought to develop an understanding of the world because of emerging cognitive processes, which are the same for everyone. However, more and more cognitive-developmental research is starting to be carried out into how aspects of development are influenced by the social interactions and relationships a child experiences. Some of this research will be referred to in the remaining section of this chapter.

Self-assessment questions

1. Briefly explain your understanding of the cognitive-developmental approach to social behaviour.
2. What do you understand by 'social cognition'?
3. Briefly distinguish between two different developmental approaches to social cognition.

Which approach to development?

Three major developmental approaches have been discussed. There are a number of fundamental differences between them. For example:

- *Active-v-passive nature of the child* Psychodynamic and learning theorists view the child as largely passive, at the mercy of inner drives (in the former case) and the influence of the environment (in the latter case). Traditional cognitive-developmental theorists stress the active, problem-solving nature of the child. Some theorists, such as Vygotsky and Bruner, emphasise the importance of social interactions between the child and other people.

- *Direction of development*   The basic assumption of both the psychodynamic and cognitive approaches is that development is directional. This implies that children advance and improve as they move from infancy to maturity. The mature behaviour of the adult is seen as the ideal goal of development. In contrast, learning theorists make no assumptions about the direction of development or the value of the changes that occur.
- *Biological influences*   Both Piaget and Freud see development as being influenced by biological changes. In contrast, learning theorists emphasise environmental influences and the role of conditioning and observational learning.

The three approaches arise from theories which focus on different facets of behaviour and make different assumptions about the nature of development. Each has its strengths and weaknesses and each makes an important contribution to our understanding of development.

Further reading

Bee, H. (1995) *The Developing Child* (7th edn) (New York: HarperCollins).
Glassman, W. E. (1995) *Approaches to Psychology* (Buckingham, Philadelphia: Open University Press).
McGurk, H. (1975) *Growing and Changing* (London: Methuen).
Walker, S. (1984) *Learning Theory and Behaviour Modification* (London: Methuen).

" THIS IS GOING TO LOOK GOOD ON MY C.V. FOR THE CONSTRUCTION ENGINEERING JOB ! "

Social 5
Behaviour

At the end of this chapter you should be able to:

1. discuss psychodynamic, learning theory and cognitive-developmental approaches to moral development;
2. evaluate these approaches to moral development in the light of empirical evidence;
3. discuss research into (a) the effects of parental style, (b) peer group influences, and (c) wider social influences on moral development;
4. describe and assess the findings from research into gender role development;
5. evaluate alternative explanations of the origins of gender role behaviour;
6. discuss findings from studies of children's developing understanding of the self and of the minds of other people (theory of mind);
7. evaluate research into the development of self-esteem in children and consider some practical implications of research findings.

SECTION I   MORAL DEVELOPMENT

The study of moral development has been a topic of research in psychology for over 60 years. An investigation of how a child develops moral values involves looking at the processes through which the child adopts and internalises the rules and standards of behaviour that are expected in the society that he or she grows up in. **Internalisation** may be defined as the process through which standards and values become a part of one's own motive system and guide behaviour, even in the absence of pressure from others.

The major theories that have arisen from the study of moral developmental fall into three main categories:

1. the psychodynamic approach arising from Freud's theory:
2. the social learning view which draws on the work of Skinner and Bandura; and
3. the cognitive-developmental approach characterised by the theories of Piaget, Kohlberg and Eisenberg.

Each of these approaches focuses on a particular aspect of the child's experiences and largely ignores other important considerations. For example, psychodynamic theory emphasises the emotional aspects of moral development, whereas cognitive-developmental theories stress the links between children's levels of moral reasoning and their stage of cognitive development. Learning theorists emphasise the role of reinforcement, punishment and observational learning.

Each of these three theories will be discussed, together with a brief account of Gilligan's theory of moral orientations and research into child-rearing styles and peer-group influence.

Psychodynamic approach

The first complete theory of moral internalisation was Freud's. The central thrust of the theory, which is concerned with the development of the superego or moral arm of the personality, is as follows.

During the **phallic stage** of psychosexual development (see the account of Freud's theory in Chapter 3), the boy encounters the **Oedipus complex**. Overwhelmed by feelings of love for his mother and fear of retaliation from his father, the boy identifies with his father. This involves the child taking over all his father's beliefs, values and attitudes, and through his father, the moral standards and values of the culture he is growing up in. Thus the **superego** is born.

A similar process exists for a girl as she encounters the Electra complex. Freud, however, though aware that the theory was less well-defined for girls than for boys, believed that females develop a weaker superego and consequently are less moral than men. This has, not unexpectedly, angered modern-day feminists.

The superego

The superego, which is unconscious, consists of two distinct parts: the **ego-ideal** and the **conscience**. The ego-ideal is concerned with what is right and proper. It represents the child's image of the sort of virtuous behaviour the parents would approve of. The conscience, on the other hand, watches over what is bad. It intercepts and censors immoral impulses from the id and prevents them from entering the consciousness of the ego.

The superego, then, represents the child's internalisation of rules and prohibitions, initially imposed by the parents, but later adopted by the child in the form of self-discipline independent of parental approval or displeasure. Thus children become capable of controlling their own behaviour and preventing themselves from indulging in the sorts of behaviour forbidden by their parents. Transgression of moral rules is likely to be followed by feelings of guilt and anxiety.

Psychodynamic theory predicts that the individual with a strong superego is likely to experience greater feelings of guilt in a situation involving a moral dilemma than does the individual with a weaker superego, and is therefore less likely to transgress the rules. This theory is widely accepted by psychoanalytic theorists, with minor variations, although its main support comes from scattered observations of adult patients (Hoffman, 1984). However, Hoffman questions whether a largely unconscious, internalised control system can account for all the complexities of moral behaviour. Other researchers have suggested that although the superego persists during childhood it is disrupted in adolescence by hormonal changes, social demands and new information about the world that may contradict it (Erikson, 1970).

Social learning approach

Social learning theorists typically avoid terms such as 'moral internalisation' and concern themselves solely with observable behaviour. However, in attempting to explain moral behaviour, they do describe a similar phenomenon: the individual's ability to behave in a moral way, or refrain from violating moral rules in conditions of temptation, even when no other person is present.

Social learning theory states that initially a child's behaviour is controlled by rewards and punishments from the parents. Because of a history of experiences where a child is punished for transgressing the rules, painful anxiety will subsequently be experienced whenever the rules are broken, or in situations involving temptation to behave amorally, even if no other person is present. This explanation has much in common with the concept of the superego.

Bandura's work on observational learning also contributes to the social learning view of moral development. It is assumed that one way children learn moral behaviour is by observing and emulating models who behave in a moral way. Observation of models who are punished for amoral behaviour is said to cause the child to experience vicarious punishment, resulting in the child avoiding that behaviour.

A great deal of research has been inspired by social learning theory, but much of it has serious drawbacks. Perhaps the biggest shortcoming arises from the frequent use of controlled experiments in which a single adult–child interaction is used to indicate the presence or absence of moral behaviour in the child. Such a situation cannot adequately reflect the complexities of the 'real life' socialisation process.

A study by Bandura and MacDonald (1963) which claims support for the social learning view will be discussed later in this chapter.

Cognitive-developmental approach

Piaget (1932/1977) emphasised the cognitive aspect of moral development, believing that a child's moral thinking is linked to her or his stage of cognitive development. Using his own type of clinical methodology, Piaget investigated children's attitudes to **rules** in the game of marbles and their responses to **right and wrong** and **judgement**, as depicted in a series of short stories. A well-known example of the latter is the story where children are asked to judge who is naughtier, a boy who accidentally breaks several cups or a boy who breaks one cup while trying to steal jam from the cupboard.

After analysing the responses of numerous children of varying stages of cognitive levels, Piaget concluded that there are two broad stages of moral thinking:

1. The stage of **heteronomous morality** or **moral realism**: in this stage, the child complies strictly with rules, which are viewed as sacred and unalterable. Right and wrong are seen in 'black and white' terms and a particular act is judged on the size of its **consequences**, rather than the intentions of the actor. Thus, the child who broke several cups is 'naughtier' than the child who broke only one cup, irrespective of the intentions involved.

2. The shift to the second stage, referred to as **autonomous morality,** or **moral relativism**, occurs around the age of seven or eight. Rules are viewed as established and maintained through nego- tiation and agreement within the social group. Judgements of right and wrong are based on **intentions** as well as consequences. Hence the child who broke a cup in the course of stealing is seen as committing the more serious offence.

Piaget believed that both cognitive development (and therefore maturation) and social experience, particularly interactions with the peer group, play a role in the transformation from one stage to the next. In the earlier, heteronomous stage, the child's moral reasoning is influenced by (a) egocentricism (inability to view events from the point of view of others), and (b) dependence on the authority of adults. (See Box 5.1.)

Kohlberg's universal stage model

Building upon Piaget's work, Kohlberg (1969, 1976) attempted to produce a more detailed and comprehensive account of moral development. Like Piaget, Kohlberg focused on an individual's reasoning when presented with a series of moral dilemmas in the form of short stories. Kohlberg's 'moral stories' have been presented to thousands of people of all ages, intelligence levels and socio- economic backgrounds.

Kohlberg sees moral development as occurring at three levels, each of which contains two distinct stages. Figure 5.1 gives a brief description of the six stages. He stated that these stages are fixed and that everyone passes through them in the same order, starting at the lowest level. The end product of progression through these stages is a mature and reasoned sense of justice.

While the ages at which people attain different levels varies, participants' responses to Kohlberg's moral dilemmas indicate that, in general, children in middle childhood are pre-conventional (level 1), younger adolescents (13–16 years) are at the conventional level (level 2), and about half of older adolescents (16–20 years) attain the principled level (level 3). Cross-cultural studies have revealed that the same sequence of stages exists in certain other cultures (Kohlberg, 1969).

Many studies have provided supporting evidence of the links between children's moral reasoning and their stage of cognitive

BOX 5.1
Cognitive v. social learning theory

A basic objection was raised to Piaget's cognitive theory of moral development by Bandura and MacDonald (1963) who doubted the relevance of concepts such as 'stages of development'. In an attempt to explain children's moral judgement through social learning theory they carried out the following experiment.

Groups of children, all of whom had previously taken Piagetian-style tests of moral reasoning, were exposed to a number of conditions in which adult models responded in various ways to similar dilemmas. Results showed that, in general, children imitated their model's responses, even where these responses conflicted with their own usual style of reasoning, as revealed by the earlier Piagetian test. These findings presented a strong challenge to the cognitive approach, which predicts that:

(a) children at a particular stage of development would be unlikely to imitate responses which conflicted with their level of moral reasoning, and
(b) children in a higher stage of development would be unlikely to revert to a lower level of moral reasoning.

Critics of the study have commented on the deficiencies of the experimental design and report, and on Bandura and McDonald's failure to pay attention to children's reasons for their judgements.

Langer (1975), in a replication of the experiment, found that:

1. the moral judgements of half the children remained the same even after viewing the model;
2. where children's choices did change, the explanations they gave did not.

Langer concluded that the techniques used in Bandura and McDonald's experiment confused the children, resulting in imitation of the model without true understanding of the reason for the judgement. Hoffman (1979) suggests that children did not merely imitate the model. They were aware that moral acts may not be intentional, but placed less emphasis on intentions because the stories used, like Piaget's, portrayed more serious consequences for accidental rather than intended acts. Perhaps if consequences for accidental and intended acts had been equal the children's responses would have been different.

FIGURE 5.1

Kohlberg's six stages of moral development

LEVEL 1 – PRECONVENTIONAL

(Middle Childhood)

Stage 1:	Punishment and obedience orientation	Rules are kept in order that punishment may be avoided. The consequences of an action determine the extent to which that action is good or bad. The interests and points of view of others are not considered, i.e. the child is egocentric.
Stage 2:	Instrumental relativist orientation	A 'right' action is one which is favourable to oneself rather than to others. Some consideration is given to the needs of others, but only where the result is favourable to oneself.

LEVEL II – CONVENTIONAL

(Approximate age – 13–16 years)

Stage 3:	'Good boy/girl' orientation	An action is judged as right or wrong according to the intentions of the actor. Socially acceptable standards of behaviour are valued and 'being good' is important.
Stage 4:	'Law and order' orientation	There emerges a profound respect for authority and a belief that society's rules must be kept. Consideration is given to the point of view of the system which makes the rules, in addition to the motives of the individual.

LEVEL III – POST-CONVENTIONAL or PRINCIPLED

(Approximate age – 16–20)

Stage 5:	Social-contract legalistic orientation	What is right is judged in relation to the majority opinion within a particular society. 'The greatest good for the greatest number' is the general rule. It is recognised that moral and legal points of view sometimes conflict with each other.
Stage 6:	Universal principles of conscience	Self-chosen ethical principles now dictate one's actions: the equality of human rights and respect for the dignity of human beings as individuals are of paramount importance. When laws conflict with these principles, one acts in accordance with the principle.

development. However, Kohlberg's theory has also generated much controversy. Debate centres on the main tenets of Kohlberg's theory –

1. moral reasoning is linked to cognitive development;
2. the stage sequence is the same for everyone –

and on the relationship between Kohlberg's stages and moral *behaviour*. A brief discussion of some relevant research follows.

Critique of Kohlberg's theory

Research evidence   Rest (1983) reviewed a dozen cross-sectional and longitudinal studies and reported that participants did generally develop moral reasoning in the direction proposed by Kohlberg's theory. However, some participants showed no improvement in moral reasoning over time and one in 14 participants who were in school actually moved back to an earlier stage. In a strict interpretation of stage theory, participants should continue to move to higher stages and regression to an earlier stage should not occur.

Principled reasoning (level 3) has not been found at all in some groups. Moran and Joniak (1979) showed that scores on moral judgement tests were closely linked to the sophistication of language used. Therefore, those people whose command of language, particularly the use of abstract terms, is poor may be wrongly judged to be operating at a lower level of moral reasoning than they are actually capable of.

Cross-cultural evidence   Kohlberg claimed that the six stages of moral reasoning exist in all cultures. His own study (1969) found that children in Britain, Mexico, Taiwan, Turkey, USA and Yucatan showed similar sequences of development.

Gardner (1982) questioned whether it is appropriate to apply Kohlberg's approach to other cultures, since moral judgements in other cultures may be based on very different values and priorities from those in Western cultures.

In a review of 44 studies completed in 26 different cultures around the world, Snarey (1985) concluded that there is much support for the cross-cultural universality of Kohlberg's theory. Edwards (1986), in a review of a large number of cross-cultural studies, drew similar conclusions.

Moral reasoning and moral behaviour A major criticism of Kohlberg's work concerns the extent to which there is a positive relationship between moral reasoning and moral behaviour. In general, there is evidence of a link between the two. In one study (Milgram, 1974) participants were led to believe that they were administering severe shocks to another person. It was later found that those participants who refused to administer shocks when instructed to do so by an authority figure were more likely to be at the principled level of moral reasoning than were those who did administer shocks. However, these findings might have been the result of other factors not examined in the study, such as intelligence level or naivety about psychological experiments. Many more recent studies have found a positive relationship between moral reasoning as tested by Kohlberg's model, and moral behaviour. However, rarely has a strong link been established (Kutnik, 1986). Richards *et al.* (1992) found that children classified as either Stage 1 or Stage 3 were less likely to be rated by their teachers as exhibiting conduct disorders than those classified as Stage 2. Kohlberg's theory would predict a consistent trend towards better behaviour with increasing moral maturity. The relationship between moral reasoning and moral behaviour is clearly a complex one which further research findings may clarify.

Social contexts of moral development

The family context

Since children's first and most pervasive exposure to moral regulations takes place within the family context, it is to be expected that the beginnings of morality are to be found here. Many researchers have argued that the attachment process in infancy (see Chapter 2) is of crucial importance and have noted that securely attached infants have been found to comply favourably to parents' rules (Speicher, 1994). Observational studies by Kagan (1989) and Dunn and Brown (1994) found that rudimentary moral awareness was apparent in children as young as 21 months and was very closely tied to social interactions within the family. Durkin (1995) argues:

> A serious limitation of both Piaget's and Kohlberg's theories of moral development is that they underestimate the knowledge and abilities of the preschooler, and fail to incorporate the early social

developmental contexts of morality into their models. (Durkin, 1995, p. 489)

Child rearing practices There is a large body of research which suggests that the type of parental discipline administered in childhood affects moral development. In a review of the research, Hoffman (1978) drew attention to two contrasting styles of discipline used by parents:

1. the use of 'inductions', that is discipline techniques which encourage the child to reflect on her/his behaviour and consider the effects of wrong-doing on other people;
2. 'power assertive' discipline, which involves the use of force, threats and withdrawal of privileges.

The central finding was that the frequent use of inductions fosters a personality who behaves morally even when there is no pressure from others to do so, and who is likely to experience strong guilt feelings when she or he does transgress. In contrast, the use of power assertive techniques by parents is associated with individuals who behave morally solely to avoid punishment.

It has been pointed out that most of the studies were correlational, and therefore prevented inferences about a causal link (see Chapter 1) between type of discipline and moral internalisation. However, Hoffman argued that the weight of evidence is such that it must be assumed that style of parental discipline does strongly influence moral development.

Peer influences

Despite its undoubted importance, there has been little research on how interaction with peers affects a child's moral development. Correlational studies have shown a negative relationship between early comfortable and frequent interactions with peers and rates of delinquency during adolescence (Conger and Miller, 1966).

Experimental research reviewed by Hoffman indicates that if a child observes a peer who behaves aggressively and is not punished, there is an increased likelihood of that child also behaving aggressively.

The role of peers in moral socialisation, and the influence of school experiences (an area which has been neglected), await further research.

Eisenberg's model of prosocial reasoning

Kohlberg's moral dilemmas tended to be concerned with misdeeds such as stealing or disobeying laws. They do not investigate children's reasoning in relation to prosocial behaviour (actions that are intended to help or benefit another person). Eisenberg and her colleagues (Eisenberg, 1986; Eisenberg *et al.*, 1987) have examined this issue by asking children to respond to stories in which a choice has to be made between self-interest and helping another person. In a typical story, a child is on his way to a birthday party when he comes upon another child who has fallen and hurt himself. If he stops to help he might miss the party food. What should he do?

Eisenberg found a clear developmental sequence in children's responses to stories like this. Typically, pre-school children were concerned with the implications for themselves rather than with moral considerations. They say things such as 'I wouldn't stop because I might miss the party', or 'I'd stop and help because she might help me sometime'. Eisenberg calls this **hedonistic reasoning.** Gradually, children begin to display what Eisenberg calls **needs-oriented** reasoning. Here the child expresses concern for the well-being of the other person even if the need is in conflict with the child's own wishes. A typical statement might be 'I'd help because she'd feel better'. There is no attempt to express generalised principles or values; the reaction is one of responding to need.

Later, in adolescence, children typically say they will do helpful things because it is expected of them. For example, a typical response might be 'Society would be a better place if we all helped each other'. In general, young people at this stage show that they have developed and internalised clear guiding principles in relation to prosocial behaviour. The pattern here is very similar to that shown at Kohlberg's level 3 (principled reasoning). Eisenberg has reported that similar sequences have been found among children in West Germany, Poland and Italy.

Though there are obvious similarities between the pattern of prosocial reasoning found by Eisenberg's and Kohlberg's levels of moral reasoning, researchers have not found a strong correlation between the two. Though the stages are similar, children seem to move through them at different rates.

Though it has not changed the fundamental principles of Kohlberg's theory, Eisenberg's research has provided for a broader and more complete view of the nature of children's moral and prosocial reasoning.

Gender and morality

An area of controversy currently surrounding Kohlberg's theory concerns the possibility of gender differences in moral reasoning. Archer (1989) argues that to some extent boys and girls develop in different social worlds. They experience different opportunities and different constraints and social expectations. Durkin (1995) asks whether these differences lead to different kinds of morality.

Much research evidence suggests that there are differences between males and females when Kohlbergian measures of moral reasoning are used (Holstein, 1976). For example, findings from a longitudinal study of adolescents by Holstein revealed that the most frequent score for boys was around Stage 4, while girls scores tended to be around Stage 3. One possible interpretation of these findings is that moral reasoning in females is inferior to that of boys. Unsurprisingly, this argument has provoked a heated and emotive debate.

Gilligan's 'moral orientations'

Gilligan (1977, 1982) has challenged the very basis of Kohlberg's theory. She has argued that his focus on the development of concepts of justice is based on male ways of viewing life and therefore his measures of moral reasoning are biased against females.

Gilligan argues that there are two distinct **moral orientations:** justice and care. Each has its own inbuilt assumption – not to behave unfairly towards others (justice) and not to ignore someone in need (caring). Males and females learn both of these principles, Gilligan hypothesises, but boys are more likely to operate from an orientation of justice, while girls are more likely to operate from an orientation of caring. Boys are brought up to be independent and achievement-oriented and are therefore concerned with issues such as equality of treatment and applying abstract principles to resolve conflicts of interest. In contrast, girls are encouraged to be caring and concerned for the well-being of others. These gender differences, Gilligan argues, may result in boys and girls using different criteria when judging moral dilemmas.

Gilligan's model generated a lot of debate and stimulated a number of research studies designed to examine possible gender differences in reasoning about moral dilemmas. Some studies of adults have found that there is a tendency for males to use 'justice' reasoning and females 'care' reasoning (Lyons, 1983). However, this pattern has not been replicated in studies of children. For example, Walker *et al.* (1987) applied Kohlberg's justice scheme and Gilligan's criteria for a care orientation to participants' responses to moral dilemmas. He found no gender differences among children and only adults produced the pattern that would be expected by Gilligan.

Gilligan's proposals are by no means proved. However, the value of her work lies in the fact that a new debate has been opened up about possible gender differences. There is no conclusive evidence that males take a justice orientation in moral reasoning and females a caring orientation. However, this does not mean that there are no differences in the assumptions that males and females bring to moral judgements. Further research might be enlightening.

Self-assessment questions

1. Outline both the psychodynamic and the social learning theory approaches to moral development.
2. According to Piaget, what would be the main differences in moral reasoning between a five-year-old child and a nine-year-old child?
3. Discuss two similarities between the work of Piaget and that of Kohlberg in the area of moral development.
4. Briefly evaluate Kohlberg's theory, referring to relevant research evidence.
5. What are the central findings from research into parental discipline and moral development?
6. In what ways has Gilligan's theory of 'Moral Orientations' challenged the findings from Kohlberg's work?

SECTION II   DEVELOPMENT OF GENDER

The study of how individuals develop a gender role (or sex role) has been a central concern of developmental psychologists for many years. Gender role development has been an important focus of debate within the major theories of psychology, and is a frequent target of the nature–nurture controversy.

The study of gender role development is beset by a proliferation of similar, often confusing terms. 'Sex' and 'gender' are defined in many dictionaries as synonymous and are often used as such. Thus, different researchers may refer to 'sex-role' or 'gender role' and mean essentially the same thing – behaviour considered by society to be appropriate for males and females. Because the term 'sex' has a number of meanings and is usually associated with biological/genital differences, there has been a trend towards using 'gender' to refer to the psychological/cultural aspects of maleness and femaleness. (Huston (1983) has produced a detailed account of sex-role taxonomies and definitions.)

Masculinity and femininity

Throughout history, men and women have been perceived as psychologically different in many important ways. These differences have usually been accepted as 'natural' and closely linked to the roles played by the sexes in society. Over the last two decades, however, following the emergence of the women's liberation movement, a great deal of research has raised doubts about the 'natural' nature of these differences and has questioned why it is that women's roles are typically of lower status than those of men.

Research into differences between the sexes has generally posed one of two types of question. Firstly, what characteristics do typical males and females posses and how do they differ? Secondly, to what extent do individuals perceive themselves to be masculine or feminine? The first question deals with gender-stereotypes. The second deals with gender-identity.

Gender stereotypes

Gender stereotypes refers to rigid beliefs about what males and females are like. Numerous studies have identified characteristics which can be said to form stereotypes of males and females and there appears to be strong agreement between them. One example is a study carried out by Spence *et al.* (1975) in which the researchers used an instrument known as the Personal Attributes Questionnaire with large samples of college men and women. Some of the characteristics attributed to males and females were as follows:

Males	Females
Independent	Emotional
Assertive	Warm to others
Aggressive	Creative
Dominant	Excitable
Like maths and science	Feelings easily hurt
Mechanical aptitude	Need approval

Ruble (1988) suggested that stereotypes of males and females had changed little in the last 20 years, at least among college students, despite the Feminist Movement and growing concern with equality between the sexes. In the USA, Bergen and Williams (1991) found a very high correlation (0.9) between stereotyped perceptions of the sexes in 1972 and those in 1988. Other research, for example Williams and Best (1990), has found that the overall gender stereotypes revealed in American research tend to exist also in countries in Asia, Africa and Europe.

Gender identity

Gender identity refers to people's perceptions of themselves as either masculine or feminine. Early research into gender identity tended to place a high value on sex-typing. An important aim of the research was to look for ways of helping males and females to acquire appropriate sex-typed attitudes and behaviour in order to promote their psychological well-being. Masculinity and femininity were seen as representing opposite ends of a continuum, and it was assumed that an individual would exhibit either masculine characteristics or feminine characteristics, but not both.

More recently, Bem (1974) and others have criticised this bi-polar approach, claiming that both so-called masculine and feminine characteristics may develop in the same individual. For example, a person may be both assertive (a characteristic generally associated with masculinity) and sensitive to the needs of others (thought of as a feminine characteristic) and still function effectively. Bem has used the term **androgynous** to describe people who possess both masculine and feminine characteristics.

Bem's research stimulated a large number of studies which attempted to determine whether androgynous individuals are more psychologically healthy and well-adjusted than are individuals who are rigidly typed as either masculine or feminine. Though there have been a few inconsistencies, most research has confirmed that this is in fact the case. For example, several studies have reported that androgynous individuals score higher on measures of self-esteem than do individuals who are rigidly sex-typed (Bem, 1983). However, several researchers have found weak or no differences between androgynous and masculine-typed individuals on measures such as self-esteem. Also, it has been suggested that masculine characteristics tend to be more highly valued in Western societies than are feminine characteristics and it may be mainly the masculine aspects of an androgynous personality that are positively related to psychological flexibility and adjustment.

Sex differences in behaviour

Many studies have attempted to discover whether commonly held beliefs about the characteristics of men and women are borne out by the way in which people actually behave. A comprehensive review of the literature was published by Maccoby and Jacklin in 1974. They investigated over 2,000 studies of sex differences in personality or intellectual abilities, comparing studies which reported statistically significant sex differences with studies which did not find statistically significant differences. Maccoby and Jacklin reported the existence of sex differences in only four areas: aggressive behaviour, and mathematical, spatial and verbal abilities. Specifically, they observed:

1. From the age of around 8 or 9 girls score higher than boys on tests of verbal ability, whereas boys perform better on mathematical and spatial tasks from puberty onwards
2. Boys are more physically aggressive than girls. This difference is evident at all ages from about two years on, and across many different cultures.

In other areas where sex differences have been claimed, Maccoby and Jacklin could find no reliable supporting evidence.

Maccoby and Jacklin's findings provoked a great deal of controversy, largely centring on the methodology used in their review. A number of points have been made:

- Some of the studies reviewed were methodologically weaker than others, employing smaller sample sizes and less powerful statistical analyses. Such studies are less likely to find true sex differences. Maccoby and Jacklin's approach in giving each study equal weight could lead to an *under*-representation of true sex differences.

• Studies which do detect sex differences are more likely to be published than those which show no significant difference. Therefore an *over*-representation of sex differences could be present in Maccoby and Jacklin's review.

• The way studies were categorised may have obscured sex differences. For example, broad categories such as 'social sensitivity' may include characteristics such as role-taking, nurturance and empathy. So, for example, a large number of studies with a 'no differences' finding in role-taking might obscure a true difference in, say, nurturance or empathy.

Later reviews of sex differences attempted to avoid some of the methodological problems found in Maccoby and Jacklin's review by using a technique called **meta-analysis.** Meta-analysis is a way of aggregating and statistically analysing the results of a number of independent studies in relation to a particular hypothesis. Studies using the technique of meta analysis (for example, Eaton and Enns, 1986) have found reliable sex differences in activity level, aggression, influencability, empathy, mathematical reasoning and spatial ability. Brownmiller (1984) found differences in language ability in favour of females. Generally, however, the sex differences found in research have been very small – accounting for less than 5 per cent of the variance – or they have been confined to studies which used particular methods. It is worth noting also that the more recent meta-analyses of cognitive sex differences have shown females to be performing better relative to males than in earlier studies.

Before we leave the question of whether in reality there are genuine psychological differences between males and females, we should note the possible effect of situational factors in the studies carried out. Particular features of a study may differentially influence the way males and females respond, which could lead to contamination of the results. For example, subtle influences such as the sex of the researcher, the relative number of males and females in the room and the topic under investigation may encourage participants to behave in line with current stereotypes of males and females. And researchers themselves may subconsciously be influenced by their own stereotypic beliefs. For example, it is interesting to note that studies of conformity carried out by women are less likely to find sex differences than those conducted by men (Eagly and Carli, 1981). However, Eagly (1987) discusses this 'sex of researchers' effect and concludes that it is not a robust one.

On the basis of current evidence, little justification can be found for existing gender stereotypes and it seems that males and females are much more similar than has generally been thought. So why has there been so much empirical and theoretical attention given to the development of gender roles and gender identity? One reason is that whether or not basic characteristics of males and females are similar, their roles in society are very different. In general, adult men and women have very different roles and responsibilities in the home, and in the workplace they operate in very different fields of activity: women represent the majority of secretaries, nurses and teachers, while men account for almost all engineers, carpenters and mechanics. In the so-called higher professions of medicine and law, whilst women are gaining ground in terms of their overall representation, they are grossly under-represented in the more prestigious, senior posts.

Gender differentiation

Gender differentiation begins very early on. As young as two or three, boys can be seen playing in different ways from girls: boys are more likely to be found playing with construction toys and to engage in considerable 'rough and tumble' play; girls are more likely to be found playing with dolls or household toys. By adolescence, distinctive roles are established both in behaviour and in interests and occupational choices. So, differentiation between the sexes is pervasive and the study of developmental processes can help us to understand why. And not just to satisfy our scientific curiosity: a knowledge of the processes involved can help our understanding of those factors which may lead to atypical development such as transsexualism. It also informs our ability to make decisions about whether to recommend clinical intervention for an individual who is mentally disturbed. On the other hand we may wish to use our understanding to promote gender equality. Gender differentiation may be seen as wholly unacceptable because it limits the scope of opportunities available to males and females. For example, social sanctions are often imposed on men who want to stay at home to look after their children and on women who do not.

Given that gender differentiation exists from a very early age, what are the factors which cause boys and girls to behave differently and to have particular beliefs about sex-appropriate behaviour? This question has been approached from a number of different theoretical perspectives

Factors which influence gender role development

1. Biological factors

There are two main types of physical characteristics which may play a part in gender role differences and which have been considered by researchers.

- **Chromosomal sex** Males and females differ in one pair of chromosomes. Prenatally, the presence of a Y chromosome in males leads the embryo to develop testes, the absence of the Y chromosome in females results in the development of ovaries.
- **Hormonal differences** Hormones affect prenatal sex differences in anatomy and brain differentiation. Though males and females can produce the same range of hormones, males produce far more androgens than females, the most important androgen being testosterone. Females produce mainly oestrogen and progesterone.

It is thought that these two physical characteristics, chromosomal and hormonal differences, affect the genetic blueprint which determines masculinity and femininity. (There may also be differences between the two sexes in the way the brain is organised, though as yet, there is no firm evidence.)

The question arises as to how far these obvious biological differences also extend to psychological development. What clues can be found about the extent to which biological factors may influence gender role behaviour? One line of enquiry has been to make cross-cultural comparisons

Cross-cultural studies The underlying rationale of this approach is that the sex differences which exist in many different cultures ought to imply that there is a biological basis. In nearly all cultures women are the main caretakers, while men are the warriors and protectors. There is evidence, too, of consistent sex differences across cultures in characteristics such as dominance, aggression and interest in infants.

Though these findings suggest biological influences, caution must be exercised in drawing firm conclusions. Cross-cultural similarities in sex roles might be explained by similarities in socialisation practices across different cultures. Also, there are some notable examples of differences between cultures (see Box 5.2).

BOX 5.2
Gender roles in New Guinea (Mead, 1935)

Probably the best known example of differences in sex role development between cultures is Margaret Mead's study of three primitive tribes in New Guinea (1935). In the **Arapesh** tribe, both males and females exhibited gentle non-aggressive, affectionate characteristics, behaving in ways traditionally associated with femininity in Western cultures. Among the **Mundugumor** tribe, both males and females behaved in what we would call a 'masculine' way – aggressive and assertive. The **Tchambuli** tribe completely reversed sex roles as we know them. Women were assertive, made decisions about the economic organisation of the tribe and looked after the collection of food; men, on the other hand, took few decisions and spent a lot of time following artistic pursuits.

Mead concluded that sex roles are culturally, rather than biologically, determined. However, Mead has been accused of exaggerating the differences between the Arapesh and Mundugumor tribes. Also, in a later book (1939) she adopted the view that there were 'natural' differences between males and females, females being more nurturing and intuitive than males.

Despite the lack of firm evidence from cross-cultural studies, a suggestion does exist of consistent sex differences in aggression and parenting which may result from biological influences, possibly combined with socialisation.

Hormonal influences   Numerous animal studies have provided evidence of the effects of hormones on behaviour. Typically, male and female rats are injected with hormones appropriate to the opposite sex during a sensitive period early in development. Such animals later exhibit behaviour characteristic of the opposite sex. Behaviour studied includes aggression, parenting, rough-and-tumble play and mating behaviour. These findings suggest that hormonal influences in non-human mammals are responsible for the animals behaving in a masculine or feminine manner. However, the effects of hormone manipulations may vary from species to species, and how relevant such findings are to the understanding of sex differences in humans remains a matter for debate.

For obvious ethical reasons, it is not possible experimentally to manipulate the hormonal state of humans. Nevertheless, some studies have been carried out on humans who, for various reasons, develop abnormal hormonal conditions. For example, a foetus can be exposed to unusual hormone levels if a mother receives hormone injections for medical reasons during pregnancy.

Several studies have indicated that females exposed to male hormones before birth often later exhibit more masculine gender-role behaviour than matched control groups of girls who were not exposed to the hormone (Money and Erhardt, 1972; Hines, 1982). This suggests that hormones may control sex-related behaviour in humans as it does in animals. However, the interpretation of these findings is not so straightforward as might appear. Children exposed to abnormal hormones before birth are often born with some abnormality of the genitals. It is possible, therefore, that a girl's more masculine behaviour reflects her own, her parents' and possibly the investigator's reactions to her more masculine appearance. This research highlights the difficulty of separating out the effects of biological factors from socialisation processes.

In general, research into the effects of prenatal hormones in humans suggests that sex hormones may have some effect on behaviour. For example, it is possible that during normal foetal development, sex hormones predispose boys to become more physically active and interested in rough-and-tumble play. However, while it is impossible to conclude that biological factors do *not* play an important part in any thorough explanation of sex differences, they cannot by themselves explain the process of gender role development.

Biosocial theory Money and Erhardt argue that in most cases social learning can override biological processes; gender identity is usually consistent with the sex of rearing rather than genetic sex. Money and Erhardt's argument is often referred to as the **biosocial approach**.

The biosocial approach is based on extensive study of individuals whose genetic endowment is at odds with the way they have been reared. One very striking example of such a case is that of a monozygotic (produced from a single egg) twin boy who was reared as a girl because of an accident to his penis during a circumcision operation (Money and Erhardt, 1972). At 17 months, the child was given surgery to create a vagina and then was given steroids. According to the parents, this reassignment of sex was very success-ful. Studies like this and the many studies where an individual has been born with a genetic abnormality, such as hermaphroditism, suggest that the effects of the socialisation process are very powerful indeed. (Hermaphroditism refers to a condition in which a person has functioning sexual organs of both sexes.) Money and Erhardt suggested that provided a clear and consistent gender assignment is made by around the age of three, there will be no problems of adjustment to gender reassignment.

2. Socialisation influences

Biological factors may predispose males and females to adopt particular gender behaviour. However, most investigators agree that cultural influences and socialisation processes are the main determi-nants of an individual's gender role identity and roles. Debate continues, however, about how the child learns gender identity and when during development this learning occurs. Two theories will be briefly considered:

Freud's Psychoanalytic Theory (see Chapter 4, Section I) suggests that during the phallic stage of development, the child encounters the Oedipus/Electra complex. Satisfactory resolution of the conflict results in the child identifying with the same sex parent. Thus the sex-appropriate attitudes and behaviour of the parent become internalised during the child's socialisation.

As has already been noted, psychoanalytic theory is open to much criticism and controversy and verification of the existence of the Oedipus/Electra complex has not been empirically established.

Social Learning Theorists (see Chapter 4, Section II) maintain that gender role identity and behaviour are, like all behaviour, learned through the processes of **reinforcement** and **modelling**. Children are said to be shaped towards male or female roles. Children learn by being rewarded for sex-appropriate behaviour and punished for inappropriate behaviour, and by imitating the behaviour of male and female models such as their parents (initially). Thus, if we look at reinforcement, boys may receive approval for aggressive beha-viour, whereas girls would be penalised for the same behaviour;

dependency may be encouraged in girls but frowned upon in boys. One problem with this explanation is that although we know that reinforcement does affect behaviour, it is not always easy to know what is reinforcing. Take the example of the toddler who throws a tantrum in the supermarket and is reprimanded by her father. If the child's behaviour is aimed at attention-seeking, then her father's anger will be reinforcing and the behaviour will be repeated.

Huston (1983) claims that there is little firm evidence that children are more likely to imitate a model of the same sex rather than of the other sex. He suggests that the role of observational learning in the development of gender roles may be over-simplified. The modelling process is likely to be affected by such things as the characteristics of the model and the extent to which they reflect the young person's own characteristics (Duck, 1990). The child's perception of the situation and of the importance of gender are also important factors.

There is a wealth of research which indicates that boys and girls receive different socialisation experiences. Below is a selection of that research.

- Maccoby and Jacklin (1974) found little evidence that boys were reinforced for aggression and girls for dependency. They concluded that infant and toddler girls and boys were treated very similarly. However, Maccoby and Jacklin may have failed to detect subtle differences in treatment.
- Smith and Lloyd (1978) have shown that boys are encouraged in more physical activities than are girls. Several other studies have shown that adults are more likely to offer a doll to a child they think is a girl and toys such as trucks or blocks to a child they think is a boy.
- Parke and Suomi (1980) showed that fathers are more likely to engage in physical rough-and-tumble play with their sons than with their daughters
- Fagot (1978) found that parents consistently show more approval when children behave appropriately to their sex and react negatively when girls or boys behave in an inappropriate way.
- Langlois and Downs (1980) found that both boys and girls are put under pressure by parents to behave in gender-appropriate ways, but this is particularly true of fathers. It seems, also, that boys are put under more pressure than girls.

- Eccles-Parsons (1983) argued that many studies show that parents' expectations of achievement, particularly mathematical accomplishment, are lower for girls than for boys.

There is considerable evidence that people do respond differently to boys and girls on the basis of the expectations of what girls and boys are like. In one study by Rubin *et al.* (1974) parents were asked to describe their new-born babies as they would to a close friend. Even though boys and girls were very similar in health and in size and weight, they were described very differently. Boys were generally depicted as more alert, stronger and better co-ordinated than girls. Girls were described as smaller, softer and less attentive than boys.

The media   Development of gender roles, like the acquisition of other complex behaviour, is unlikely to be the result solely of differential treatment and reinforcement. Therefore, many researchers have concerned themselves with how children may learn masculine or feminine behaviour by imitating same-sex models.

Male and female stereotypes abound in the literature and television as well as in the real world. In most areas of television, whether light entertainment programmes or documentaries, males outnumber females seven to three (Durkin, 1995). Males are usually represented in more dominant roles with higher occupational status, while females are often shown in subordinate roles and in traditional feminine occupations, such as housewife, nurse or secretary. In TV commercials, women are more likely to be shown using products, particularly domestic products, while men are generally seen as receiving their services or commenting on the quality of the products. These sorts of findings have been found repeatedly in research in North America, Britain, Australia, Italy and other countries (Davis, 1990; Furnham and Bitar, 1993). And sex stereotypes exist also in other media to which children are exposed, including radio advertisements, the lyrics and style of pop music videos, and the content of teen magazines.

These findings are remarkable, but how influential are these models during gender role development? Is there a relationship between viewing such material and the acquisition of particular behaviour and attitudes? Research findings are not always clear.

Some studies have reported a positive correlation between the amount of television children watch and the likelihood of their subscribing to stereotyped beliefs (Levy, 1989). However, these findings do not present such a clear picture as they appear to. Firstly, in the majority of studies the correlations found were rather small. Also, it should be remembered that the technique of correlation does not imply causation (see Chapter 1). It might be that children who are already strongly sex-typed prefer to watch a lot of television because it supports their own stereotyped beliefs. In Levy's (1989) study, it was found that girls who preferred educational TV programmes showed much more gender role flexibility than other girls.

Interestingly, one investigation, a large-scale field experiment, found that children sometimes change their stereotyped attitudes when they are presented with counter-stereotyped television programmes (Johnson and Ettema, 1982).

It seems that media content might be implicated in gender role development, but the findings of research are by no means conclusive.

3. Cognitive-developmental theory

Social learning theory stresses the influence of external pressures on children's developing gender identity and behaviour and these influences clearly play a major part. However, the effect of these influences cannot be fully understood without a consideration of internal factors within the child. In applying cognitive developmental theory to the development of gender roles and identity, Kohlberg (1966) believed that the most important factor is the child's level of cognitive development.

Kohlberg argued that early in life, the child is labelled as 'boy' or 'girl' and this categorisation leads to the child's perception of him or herself as masculine or feminine. This **gender self-concept** coupled with the child's growing knowledge and understanding of gender, directs and organises his or her activities and ways of thinking. Thus, a girl may in effect say to herself 'I am a girl and I must behave like a girl'. A key stage in the process involves the child's acquisition of **gender constancy**. This refers to the child's knowledge and understanding that gender is a consistent and stable characteristic and that gender is constant even if a person wears opposite-sex clothes or takes part in opposite-sex activities. Though children appear to be able to apply gender labels to themselves and other people from around 2 years old, it is thought that gender constancy is not fully acquired until around 5 or 6 years old. (It is thought to coincide with the child's understanding of the constancy of objects as illustrated in Piaget's conservation tasks.)

A central feature of cognitive-developmental theory is that the child's growing cognitive abilities lie at the heart of gender role development. The theory suggests that as children's conceptual awareness increases, so they are motivated to search for more information about gender role. One way of doing this is to look for models of gender-appropriate behaviour. This aspect of cognitive-developmental theory has something in common with social learning theory in that it suggests that modelling plays an important part. However, unlike social learning theory, the suggestion here is that modelling the behaviour, attitudes and values related to a particular gender role takes place as a result of the child's developing cognitive processes. Information about gender-appropriate attributes is *actively* sought out rather than *passively* acquired (Martin, 1991).

Self-socialisation   A wealth of research supports the claim that children's gender role awareness becomes more accurate and complete with age and that as development proceeds they search for more information and structure their own gender role behaviour accordingly. This process has been referred to as **self-socialisation** (Ruble, 1987). This aspect of cognitive-developmental theory offers a more complete account than has been available previously of the possible role of media in gender role development. It may be important to consider what children themselves bring with them to reading books or TV viewing (including their own stereotypes) rather than simply considering the stereotypes that are to be found there (Calvert and Huston, 1987).

Gender schema processing theory   Another cognitive developmental theory – gender schematic processing theory – also emphasises the child's active processing of gender-related information (Martin, 1991). However, this theory differs from Kohlberg's in an important respect. It is proposed that children do engage in an active process of finding out about their own gender, but this process starts when they discover their own sex rather than when they attain gender constancy as suggested by Kohlberg (Martin and Halverson, 1987).

This theory suggests that once children have a gender identity, they increasingly search the environment for information with which to extend and enhance the relevant **gender schema** – an internal body of knowledge about the characteristics and behaviours associated with a particular gender. The schema enables the child to interpret what is happening in the environment and to select and attend to appropriate kinds of behaviour. In this way, children's perceptions of themselves become sex-typed.

Martin and Halverson explain how gender schematic processing may occur. They propose that initially, children learn which objects and activities are appropriate for each sex. Subsequently, they concentrate on learning more about the activities that are appropriate to their own sex and pay less attention to activities associated with the opposite sex. For example, boys become aware that playing with dolls is 'for girls' so they avoid dolls and learn little more about them. Thus appropriate gender-related behaviour becomes a part of a child's gender schema. Information that is consistent with their schema is taken on board and information that is inconsistent is disregarded or rejected. For example, if children encounter an adult who is taking part in an activity that is associated with the opposite sex, they may fail to take in the information. In support of this idea, a number of experiments have shown that when young children are shown pictures or films of adult engaged in stereotypical opposite-sex activities (such as a female as a doctor and a male as a nurse) they tend to either disregard the information, miss the point or forget it completely, insisting that the woman was the nurse and the man the doctor (Liben and Signorella, 1993).

How important is gender constancy to gender role development? As we have seen, Kohlberg (1966) argued that the acquisition of gender constancy (at around 5 or 6) is a central influence in the development of gender role. This view has been supported by many experimental studies – for example, those by Ruble *et al.* (1981) and Frey and Ruble (1992). In Ruble *et al.*'s (1981) study, the researchers administered a measure of gender constancy to pre-school children and then divided them into 'low' or 'high' levels of gender constancy. The children were subsequently shown a series of TV commercials which presented some attractive toys as either for girls or for boys. It was found that the 'high gender-constancy' children were more likely to respond to the underlying message of the advertisements. This affected their judgement of which sex the toys were appropriate for and whether they were inclined to play with the toys or not.

Self-evaluation Other studies have not found a clear relationship between gender constancy and sex-typing or preferences (Bussey and Bandura, 1984). Bussey and Bandura (1992) argue that gender development starts as a result mainly of external sanctions from parents. Gradually a shift then occurs towards a process of self-regulation which is organised by the child's perceptions of the likely consequences of particular attitudes and behaviour. According to this proposal, the main mechanism to influence this process is **self-evaluation** – judging one's own attitudes and behaviour.

To investigate the relative importance of gender constancy and self-evaluation, Bussey and Bandura (1992) asked pre-school children whether they would feel 'happy' or 'unhappy' if they played with a number of same-sex or opposite-sex toys. The findings were as follows:

- Both boys and girls between the ages of 3 and 4 showed approval for same-sex behaviour and disapproval for opposite-sex behaviour.
- By the age of 4, boys were very happy to play with dump-trucks and robots, but not comfortable with dolls and kitchen sets. Girls' preferences were the opposite of this.
- Across a number of tasks, children's judgements of their own preferences and likely behaviour (self-evaluation) served to predict gender-linked behaviour, whereas gender constancy and gender knowledge scores did not.

Bussey and Bandura concluded that early in life, children learn the sanctions against opposite-sex behaviour and start to organise their own behaviour accordingly. (It is interesting to note that Bussey and Bandura were coming from a social learning theory perspective.)

Some problems with cognitive-developmental theories

Cognitive-developmental approaches are currently the most influential in the study of gender role development. However, they have a number of limitations:

- Like social learning theory approaches, cognitive-developmental theory does not explain *why* the sexes are valued differently (Bem, 1993).
- In contrast to social learning theory, cognitive-developmental theory has little to say about the precise links between the child's

development and the surrounding culture (Bem, 1993). The environment is taken as fixed and the child is thought to acquire information because of developing cognitive processes which are the same for all.

- Lloyd and Duveen (1993) argue that most cognitive-developmental models argue from the basis of **individual social cognition** (see page 148) emphasising the individual's perceptions of what is happening in society. Since we now know that cognitive development itself is influenced by social interactions (see Chapter 3, Section II), there is a need to study gender role knowledge as being acquired in a social context.

- There appears to be a problem with the relationship between cognition and behaviour (Huston, 1985). Huston argues that if cognitions are major determinants of gender role development, then after the early years we would expect to find a positive relationship between gender concepts and sex-typed preferences in behaviour. These relationships do not appear to be strong and there is a marked difference between males and females. For example, both boys and girls appear to develop their gender role cognitions in the same order and at around the same pace. However, boys tend to have stronger gender stereotypes than girls and are less likely to engage in opposite-sex activities. Further, boys increasingly tend to display preferences for masculine activities and masculine self-images throughout childhood, while girls actually move away from feminine preferences and identity during middle childhood (Archer, 1989). Huston argues that there is a need for research to concentrate less on concepts and cognitions and more on behaviour, activities and interests.

Conclusions

It seems clear that no single process is responsible for the development of gender roles and all the major theoretical approaches have something to offer to our understanding. The process probably works something like the following:

- It seems likely that sex hormones and other biological factors predispose young children towards masculine or feminine characteristics.
- It is probable that, at the same time, these naturally occurring differences are heightened by factors such as reinforcement from

adults for gender appropriate behaviour and the presence of
gender-stereotyped models in the family, school and media. And
right from birth, gender-stereotyped expectations are likely to
exert their influences.

- These biological and social factors probably interact at various
points in development and are organised by the child's own
perceptions and growing understanding of gender and their
selective attention to behaviour and attitudes which are relevant
to their own gender.

These are very general conclusions and it is clear that the
acquisition of gender role is a complex process which cannot yet
be fully explained. There is a great deal more to be discovered,
particularly about the importance of the social context in which
children develop a gender role.

Self-assessment questions

1. Explain, giving examples, the terms 'gender stereotypes', 'gender
   identity' and 'androgyny'.
2. Are there psychological differences between males and females?
   Refer to research evidence.
3. Outline the biological explanation of gender role development.
   Evaluate a study that has been used to support the biological
   approach.
4. Briefly describe some research which suggests that the development of gender roles is influenced by (a) parental treatment and
   (b) the media.
5. Outline two cognitive-developmental approaches to the study of
   gender role. What problems are associated with these approaches?
6. Given the available evidence, what conclusions would you draw
   about the development of gender roles?

SECTION III   UNDERSTANDING SELF AND OTHERS

One of the most important areas of research in social cognition is
that concerned with the child's developing understanding of the self.
In the first part of this section, we shall explore the main findings of
research in this area. The second part of the section will be

concerned with the development of the child's understanding of others and in particularly the emergence of a 'theory of mind'. Theory of mind refers to the child's understanding of the thoughts, feelings and beliefs of other people.

The nature of self

One of the most crucial processes of the child's early years is the development of a sense of self. What do we mean by a sense of self? What characteristics exist in the child who has a well-developed sense of self? Gardner (1982) suggests that there a number of factors. Children should:

- be aware of their own body, its appearance, state and size (body image);
- be able to refer to themselves appropriately through language and be able to distinguish descriptions which apply to self and those which do not;
- be aware of their own personal history, experiences they have had, skills and abilities acquired, their own needs and wishes.

Such a knowledge of self involves the ability to see oneself as others do and to develop a sense of self-awareness by taking account of the attitudes and perspectives of others. In addition to these ingredients, a mature sense of self includes a feeling of self-worth or self-esteem – an acceptance of and contentment with what one is like. Self-esteem is that part of the self-concept in which we judge our own competence in comparison to some internalised standard or expectation.

The influence of social factors

Early writers such as Cooley (1902) and Mead (1934) have highlighted the influence on the development of self of interactions with other people. This proposal has been confirmed in more recent research (Fogel, 1993). Through these interactions the child becomes aware of the judgements parents make: for example, 'naughty', 'good', 'bright', 'a bit slow', 'very feminine', 'a real boy'. It is from these labels that children develop a sense of who and what they are – the self-concept. Cooley called this the 'looking glass self' since it reflects what other people think of us.

Kuhn (1960) showed that as a child develops, the sense of self becomes less physically oriented and increasingly influenced by social factors. Groups of children and young adults were asked to respond to the questions 'Who am I?' Only 25 per cent of statements made by seven-year-olds related to social roles such as 'I am a son', compared with 50 per cent of statements made by 24-year-olds.

Developmental trends

In the early months of life, children do not distinguish themselves from the things around them. Gradually, however, they develop an awareness of their own body as an entity separate from the environment. This distinction between 'self' and 'not self' seems to develop gradually from about the third month of life and is well established between 12 and 15 months. Lewis and Brooks-Gunn (1979) described this distinction of oneself from others as the **'existential self'**. This sense of 'separateness' is established tbrough the pattern of interactions the baby has with those around him. Interestingly, Lewis and Brooks-Gunn link this awareness of 'separate self' to the understanding of object permanence as described by Piaget (see page 74).

During the second year of life, a second aspect of 'self' develops – what Lewis (1990) refers to as the more objective 'categorical' self. This refers to the characterisation of oneself in terms of categories such as age, gender, attractiveness, ability, and so on. The categories used may vary between cultures or historical period or they may be universal. Also, they may remain constant over a lifetime or they may change, depending upon an individual's experiences. Meadows (1986) explains these features by describing her own 'categorical self':

> my own categorical self would include the following categories, all relative and not in any order of importance: 'tall', which appeared early, will remain constant and could be universal; 'female', also early, universal and constant, although the defining attributes and connotations of 'female' have undergone historical and cultural changes.

By the age of two, the child appears to have acquired many of the basic components of a sense of self, including the ability to use language appropriately to refer to him or herself. By the time they are three, children are able to refer to a wide range of self-characteristics, including feelings and perceptions, appearance and opinions (Shatz, 1994)

Some of the basic landmarks in this early, very rapid development of the self can be seen in research studies carried out:

(1)   Lewis and Brooks-Gunn (1975) carried out a series of studies of the emergence of a sense of the self in infants. Confronted with pictures of themselves, one-year-old babies generally call themselves 'baby'. Shortly before they reach two, most children start to use their own name and can verbally express their own mental state; by two and a half they can use personal pronouns such as 'I'; by the age of three, almost all children can refer to themselves in pictures using both their names and the correct personal pronouns.

(2)   In addition to using language correctly to refer to oneself as subject (the sense of 'I'), a sense of self involves the ability to recognise oneself as object (the sense of 'me' that is perceived by others) One aspect of the 'me' that has attracted much research attention in relation to infancy is the physical self. Lewis and Brooks-Gunn (1979) investigated infants' reactions to their own reflections in a mirror. A child's nose was secretly coloured with rouge and she was placed in front of the mirror. It was assumed that a child who recognised the reflection as herself might well touch her own nose. The findings were that few 9–12-month-old children touched their own noses, about two-thirds of 21-month to 2-year-old children did so. The older children also acted coy or touched the mirror image. The researchers concluded that an awareness of one's own person emerges around the age of about 18 months.

(3)   Bannister and Agnew (1977) also illustrated children's increasing self-awareness with age. Groups of children of school age were asked a variety of questions about themselves and their home and school lives. The answers were tape-recorded and then re-recorded in different voices to disguise the identity of the original speakers. Four months later, the same children were asked to listen to the recordings and identify which statements were their own and which were not, and to give reasons for their choices. Findings indicated that the children's ability to recognise their own statements increased with age. It was notable, also, that the children's explanations for their decisions reflected a growing knowledge of and confidence in their own feelings and beliefs. Thus, five-year-old children tended to rely on memory and simple clues contained in the statements – for example, 'That girl likes swimming and I swim, so I

ve said that'. Nine-year-olds tended to use more complex s for determining which statements were theirs and which ot. One child insisted that the statement 'I want to be a soldier when I grow up' was not his, because 'I don't think I could kill a human being so I wouldn't say I wanted to be a soldier'.

Adolescence has been recognised by many researchers as a time of particular importance in the development of self. Erikson (1968) described the 'identity crisis' which occurs during the teenage years. Faced with dramatic body changes and pressures arising from the need to make career and other important choices, the adolescent tries out different roles in order to 'find herself'. All the young person's cognitive and emotional capacities are brought to bear on the task of forming a coherent sense of who and what one is. At adolescence, too, many studies have highlighted the special importance of the body image as an aspect of the sense of self. (Development during adolescence will be considered in greater detail in the next chapter.)

Self-esteem

As we saw earlier, self-esteem is that aspect of the self which is concerned with how we evaluate ourselves as people. It has been claimed that a major factor in the development of psychological disorder is some individuals' feelings of inadequacy and unworthiness. The classic work of Coopersmith (1968) has shown marked variations in the behaviour of children who differ in self-esteem.

Coopersmith studied a group of children from the age of 10 until early adult life. Using the results of a battery of tests and self-ratings, the sample was divided into three groups which were labelled 'high', 'medium' and 'low' self-esteem. The findings were as follows:

- **High self-esteem** boys showed themselves to have a positive and realistic view of themselves and their own abilities. They were confident, not unduly worried by criticism and enjoyed participating in things. They were active and expressive in all they did and were generally academically and socially successful.
- **Medium self-esteem** boys had some of these qualities but were more conformist, less confident of their own worth and more in need of social acceptance.

- **Low self-esteem** boys were described by Coopersmith as a sad little group who were self-conscious, isolated, reluctant to participate in activities; they constantly underrated themselves and were oversensitive to criticism.

All the boys came from the same socio-economic background (middle class) and there were no significant differences between the groups in such characteristics as intelligence and physical attractiveness.

A major difference between the three groups arose when the researchers investigated the characteristics and behaviour of the boys' parents.

- In general, **high self-esteem** boys tended to have parents who were also high in self-esteem. These parents, in contrast with the parents of low self-esteem boys, were more affectionate and showed greater interest in and respect for their children as individuals. Parents had higher and more consistent standards than did those in the other groups. Methods of discipline were consistent and relied upon rewards for good behaviour and withdrawal of approval rather than physical punishment for bad behaviour.
- Discipline in the homes of **low self-esteem** boys was inconsistent. It varied between highly punitive and over-permissive styles, and less clear guidance was given to the boys, who were rarely sure where they stood Low self-esteem boys often regarded their parents' behaviour as unfair.

A follow-up of the sample into adult life showed that the high self-esteem boys were more successful than low self-esteem boys, both educationally and in their careers.

Limitations of Coopersmith's study

One must be cautious when drawing conclusions from Coopersmith's study. Self-esteem is notoriously difficult to measure accurately. Asking children questions about how they evaluate themselves is a procedure which is open to biased responses; children may not want to admit they have undesirable characteristics. Also, Coopersmith did not investigate the influence of socio-economic background or sex upon self-esteem; all the participants were boys and from middle-class backgrounds.

However, more recent research – notably Rosenberg (1985) – has tended to support Coopersmith's findings that the key factors which appear to be related to high self-esteem appear to be firm, consistent but reasoned control, positive encouragement of independence and a warm, loving atmosphere.

There is evidence to suggest that children from lower socio-economic backgrounds typically exhibit lower self-esteem than do those from homes higher up the socio-economic scale. In general, too, girls tend to have lower self-esteem than boys. Even in primary schools where they often outshine boys, girls are inclined to under-rate their own abilities. Girls tend, also, to set themselves lower goals in life and to rate themselves lower on written measures of self-esteem than do boys. This is probably the result of cultural factors and the general lower status of women in society (Fontana, 1988).

Domain specificity

A more recent measure of self-esteem contains four sub-scales designed to measure three different aspects of a child's feelings of self-worth – cognitive, social and physical skills together with general feelings of self-esteem (Harter, 1982). Studies which have used this scale reveal that children often rate themselves very differently in these domains. Thus, their evaluation of their physical skills may differ from an evaluation of their cognitive skills. Marsh *et al.* (1991) found that from about the age of 8, children have the cognitive and emotional maturity to be able to integrate information from several different domains of their lives into a general assessment of their self-worth.

Harter (1987) asked children to rate themselves in five areas (scholastic competence, athletic competence, social acceptance, physical appearance, and behavioural conduct) as well as completing a more general assessment of their self-worth. The main findings were as follows:

- Where children made a low assessment of themselves in an area which was important to them, the more likely it was that their general self-esteem would be low; however, where children perceived themselves as not very competent in an area which was relatively unimportant to them, their high self-esteem tended to be maintained. For example, if a child who considers athletic appearance to be relatively unimportant perceives herself as incompetent in this domain, she is unlikely to suffer a serious threat to her general self-esteem. However, in a domain which she considers to be important, for example, mathematical competence, perceived incompetence may adversely affect general feelings of self-worth.

• One domain which appears to be especially important to children is that of physical appearance. Both boys and girls who were unhappy with the way they looked tended to have low self-esteem.

Why should such a relatively superficial aspect of the self, such as external appearance, affect a child's general feeling of self-esteem when aspects such as conduct or competencies may not? To answer this, psychologists point to the importance of the real world social context (Erwin, 1993). For example, good looks are highly valued in most cultures and it seems that conceptions of what constitutes attractive physical appearance are established early in life.

The research findings in relation to domain specificity of self-esteem are important and should be understood by teachers and other people who work with children. Improving children's feelings of self-worth about their athletic competence will not necessarily make them feel good about their academic performance or improve general feelings of self-worth.

Theory of mind

As we saw in Chapter 3, Piaget focused on cognitive development in children. He believed that a special quality of human beings is their scientific and technological potential. Given the enormous scientific and technological advances that have taken place over the past centuries, his assumption would seem to be correct. However, the question has been asked as to whether that potential is the only highly developed human quality, or whether there is some other important quality which is closely linked to our social development.

As human beings we live and interact in groups. A feature of human social behaviour that distinguishes us from many non-human animals and insects, such as ants, who also operate in groups, is our capacity to interact together in work and play in a reciprocal way. This seems to require a capacity to appreciate what other people are thinking and feeling. Such a capacity has become known as a **theory of mind**. Mitchell (1992) asks:

What do we have instead of the ants' instincts that enables us to be such proficient creatures? We have a 'theory of mind' and this could be the most important feature of human cognition.

(Mitchell, 1992, p. 36)

The idea behind possession of a theory of mind is that human beings are natural psychologists who collect evidence about other people's emotions, beliefs and wishes. On the basis of this evidence, they construct a theory which enables them to predict and explain the behaviour of others.

The ability to understand that other people have minds which are similar to our own, but which see the world from their own unique perspective, is something we take for granted. In many of our interactions we are very preoccupied with what is going on in the other person's mind. In a game like chess, a large part of the skill of playing is to try to assess how your opponent is thinking of moving or what he or she is thinking about your play.

So far as young children are concerned, we must not take the possession of a 'theory of mind' for granted. It appears that a theory of mind is not present in the child's repertoire of cognitive abilities until the age of about four.

Consider the following scenario which has been enacted in many experimental situations. Suppose we show to a young child, Jennie, aged 3, a Smarties tube that, in fact, unbeknown to the child, actually contains pencils. If we ask Jennie what is in the tube, it would not be unreasonable to say that she would be sure to answer 'Smarties', since she cannot see inside the tube. We then open the tube and show Jennie that it contains pencils. Next, we tell Jennie that we are going to call her friend Lucy into the room and ask her what is in the Smarties tube. If we ask Jennie to tell us what she thinks her friend Lucy will say when we ask her what is in the Smarties tube, Jennie, at 3 years old, is almost certain to say 'Pencils'. She has not yet developed a theory of mind – the ability to appreciate the perspectives, beliefs and feelings of other people – which would enable her to realise that Lucy will be misled in the way she was herself.

The 'Smarties' procedure and other similar procedures have been used in many studies into theory of mind (Perner *et al.*, 1987; Gopnik and Astington, 1988). Studies found that the great majority of children under four, when asked the question 'What do you think Lucy will say when we ask her what is in the tube?', answered 'Lucy will say "Pencils"'. Children of four and above were quick to appreciate that Lucy would be misled because of the nature of the tube and the fact that she had not seen it before. They were aware that Lucy would have a **false belief** and would give the answer 'Smarties'.

False beliefs

A central feature of a theory of mind is being able to understand that people sometimes entertain false beliefs. If children can appreciate that people can have false beliefs, then they are able to understand that the way someone's mind represents the world may be different from the way the world really is (Mitchell, 1992). In such circumstances, we would conclude that the child had acquired a theory of mind. If, on the other hand, a child was unable to grasp that people can have false beliefs, then it would be assumed that she or he had not yet acquired a theory of mind and thinking was restricted to the way the world really is.

'False belief tasks' as they have come to be called have been of particular interest to developmental psychologists because they have provided a format for discovering whether or not a child possesses a theory of mind. Box 5.3 outlines the rationale which underlies the tasks set for children in many theory of mind experiments.

BOX 5.3

'Theory of mind' experiments

Theory of mind experiments:

- test children's understanding of belief and particularly false belief;
- require that a child attributes a false belief to another person;
- in order to demonstrate that children attribute beliefs to another, must show that they can ascribe to the other beliefs different from their own.

The procedure is as follows:

- A situation is arranged so that the child's beliefs are true and the other's beliefs are false.
- The child is asked what the other person will think or do.

If children can recognise that the other person will act on the basis of his or her own false beliefs, we conclude that they can attribute beliefs to the other.

What these studies show is that while a four-year-old understands that people have beliefs and that these beliefs can be different from the way the world really is, the three-year-old does not.

Theory of mind and egocentrism

You may be thinking that a young child's problem in understanding what is going on in someone else's mind is similar to Piaget's idea that young children are egocentric. Piaget's view of egocentrism was that young children understand their own mental perspective on a situation, but cannot understand that another person's mental perspective of the same situation might be different (see the description of Piaget's Three Mountains Task in Chapter 3). This is similar to the idea that young children cannot appreciate other people's false beliefs and therefore have no theory of mind However, there is an important difference between the two concepts. Egocentrism refers to ignorance about other people, whereas the idea that young children lack a theory of mind implies that they know nothing about minds at all, including their own.

In support of the idea that young children have no notion about their own minds, Gopnik and Astington (1988) carried out a variant of the Smarties experiment. As before, the child was shown a Smarties tube and when asked what was inside it replied 'Smarties'. Then it was revealed that the tube really contained pencils. After closing the lid of the tube, the child was then asked 'When you first saw the tube before we opened it, what did you think was inside?' As before, the large majority of children of about four and above correctly replied 'Smarties', whereas the great majority of children under that age answered 'Pencils'. Moreover, the children who gave this wrong answer were generally the same ones who had given an incorrect answer when they were asked to judge another person's false belief. Astington (1994) argues that three-year-olds simply do not understand that their own beliefs may change: when they find out they are wrong, they are unable to remember their own earlier false beliefs.

Debate in the study of theory of mind: how does theory of mind develop?

There is currently much research interest into how theory of mind develops in children and the age at which a child possesses a theory of mind. This has generated a great deal of debate and sometimes disagreement. Some of the ideas arising from research are outlined below:

(1) Many researchers have proposed that the three-year-old has a conceptual deficit that is overcome at around four. This is known as the 'magic age' view. The 'magic age' view generally reflects a tendency to see the development of a theory of mind as dependent upon cognitive development. It tends to ignore social and environmental influences in the developmental process.

(2) Hobson (1990) has suggested that perhaps the development of a theory of mind is dependent not on innate mechanisms, as might be suggested by linking it to cognitive development, but occurs when a certain level of understanding has been gained through relevant experiences.

(3) Harris (1989) argued that it is children's awareness of their own mental state which enables them to appreciate the mental states of other people. This occurs through the child using an 'as if' or pretence mechanism: being able to understand someone else arises from imagining yourself in their situation.

(4) Leslie (1987) agreed with Harris that pretence is important, but he believes that it is only one example of the child using what he calls second-order representations or **meta-representations**, which emerge at around 18 months.

- A first-order representation involves symbolising something in your own mind, for example a book or a toy or a state such as thirst.
- A second-order representation, or meta-representation, includes children's ability to understand their own representations by adding pretence or imagination. For example, a child playing with a doll will be able to think about the actual doll (a primary representation). In the context of play, the child may pretend that the doll is a real baby and imagine scenarios that are relevant to looking after a baby (meta-representations). Leslie considers that the cognitive ability of meta-representing is the most important factor underlying theory of mind. The ability to meta-represent is observable in a child's pretend play, talking about mental states and understanding false beliefs.

(5) Perner (1991) disagrees with Harris's view on the importance of pretence and uses the term 'meta-representation' rather differently. Perner argues that the ability to meta-represent involves modelling mental states and this does not occur until the child is

four. It is then that they possess a theory of mind and can succeed in false belief tasks.

(6) Lewis and Osborne (1990) argued that it was possible that some of the standard false belief tasks used in earlier experiments demanded too much of a younger child's language skills. For example, when, in the 'Smarties' procedure described on page 192, the child is asked 'What will Lucy say when we ask her what is in the tube?', does the child really understand that this question refers to a time before Lucy finds out what is really in the tube? The researchers set up an experiment using the 'Smarties' procedure. However, they changed the question 'What do you think was in the tube?' to 'What do you think was in the tube *before I took the top off?*' and the question 'What will (friend's name) think is in the tube?' to 'What will (friend's name) think is in the tube *before I take the top off?*'. This amended procedure resulted in a clear improvement in the performance of 3-year-olds. A clear majority of 3-year-olds now gave the correct answer.

Box 5.4 briefly describes a study by Mitchell and Locahee (1991) which examined links between children's understanding of false belief and the reality of the situation.

BOX 5.4

False belief and reality

Mitchell and Locahee (1991) proposed that young children do know about false beliefs, but are loath to acknowledge anything which is not based in reality. By definition, understanding another person's false belief does not have a basis in reality.

The researchers endeavoured to set up an experiment that would provide a false belief with a basis in reality, yet would preserve its 'false' status. A sample of three-year-olds were shown a Smarties tube and asked to mail a picture of what they thought was in the tube in a special post box. All the children posted a picture of Smarties and the pictures were kept in the post box out of sight until after the next stage of the experiment. Next, the children were shown that the tube really contained pencils. The pencils were returned to the tube, the lid was closed and the children were asked the modified question 'When you posted your picture, what did you think was in the tube?'

Tested in this situation a majority of the three-year-olds correctly answered 'Smarties'. The researchers argued that their study showed that young children can understand false belief when it is based in something real (the picture in the post box).

Theory of mind and autism

Autism is quite a rare developmental disorder. It affects about two in every 10,000 people. Autism is usually diagnosed from about 3 years onwards and is very disabling. A characteristic feature of autistic children is a complete disinterest in social contact and interaction; they often play alone, and if they do interact they do so in a rigid stereotyped way as though they were dealing with objects rather than people.

Numerous studies have shown that autistic children appear to be seriously lacking in 'mindreading' skills or theory of mind capabilities and it has been argued that this lack is the cause of the serious deficit they have in social relationships.

Baron-Cohen, Leslie and Frith (1985) carried out a study with the following groups. The first group consisted of 20 autistic children aged 6–16 years. Their mental age was around 5 years as measured by a standard verbal IQ test and about 9 years using a non-verbal IQ test. For comparison, two other groups were used: (i) 27 normal children between 3 and 5 years; (ii) 14 Down's Syndrome children aged 16–17 years, whose IQ ratings were slightly below those of the autistic children – this group was used to act as a control for mental retardation which did not relate to autism.

The researchers used a modified version of the Sally–Anne 'false belief' task originally used by Wimmer and Perner (1983). See Figure 5.2 for a diagramatic illustration of the task.

In this task, there are two dolls, Sally and Anne (see picture 1). As the child watches, the experimenter causes Sally to put a marble into her basket (picture 2). Sally then leaves (picture 3) and Anne moves the marble into her own basket (picture 4). Sally then returns (picture 5). At this point, the experimenter asks the child three questions:

- 'Where is the marble really?' (**reality** question)
- 'Where was the marble in the beginning?' (**memory** question)
- 'Where will Sally look for her marble?' (**belief** question)

The results were quite striking:

- All the children answered the Memory question and the Reality question on both trials. This indicated that they had understood what was happening and had remembered it.

FIGURE 5.2

The Sally–Anne task

Source: Frith (1989).

- Almost all the normal and Downs Syndrome children answered the 'belief' question correctly; this was as expected, particularly for the normal children, since research has shown that children can usually solve a 'false belief' task. However, all but four of the autistic children answered incorrectly. When they were asked 'Where will Sally look for her marble?' they pointed to where the marble really was.

The researchers claimed that these findings supported the view that theory of mind appears to be lacking or seriously impaired in autistic children. Specifically, it was argued that autistic children are unable to appreciate the mental states of other people or assign beliefs to them.

Some criticisms have been made of the procedures used in this experiment:

- de Gelder (1987) pointed out that it is known that autistic children have difficulty with pretend play. Therefore using dolls to represent real people might cause them some difficulties. However, Leslie and Frith (1987) repeated the study using real children and obtained similar findings.
- Another criticism related to the possibility that the three groups of children may not have been well matched for language ability (Boucher, 1989). Despite these criticisms, Baron-Cohen *et al.*'s study has been replicated and the findings supported by many other researchers.

It does seem that theory of mind appears to be lacking or seriously deficient in autistic children, relative to other children However, this deficiency does not apply to all such children, since Baron-Cohen *et al.*'s study showed that 4 out of the 20 autistic children correctly solved the false belief task.

Self-assessment questions

1. What characteristics exist in a child who has a well-developed sense of self?
2. Outline some studies which demonstrate children's increasing self-awareness with age.
3. What factors may influence the level of a child's self-esteem?
4. Explain what is meant by a 'theory of mind'. Outline the findings of some studies into theory of mind in young children.

5. What is meant by the 'magic age' view in relation to the development of a theory of mind? Does research support this view?
6. Explain why researchers believe that sufferers from autism may lack a theory of mind.

Further reading

Archer, J. and Lloyd, B. (1985) *Sex and Gender* (Cambridge: Cambridge University Press).

Astington, J. W. (1994) *The Child's Discovery of the Mind* (London: Fontana).

Durkin, K. (1995) *Developmental Social Psychology: From Infancy to Old Age* (Cambridge, Mass.: Blackwell).

Smith, P. K. and Cowie, H. (1991) *Understanding Children's Development* (Oxford: Blackwell).

"I BLAME MY PARENTS — THEY
NEVER SET ME ANY STANDARDS
WORTH REBELLING AGAINST."

Adolescence and Adulthood 6

At the end of this chapter you should be able to:

1. identify and discuss physical and psychological changes that take place during adolescence;
2. assess alternative views of the factors which influence personality and social development during adolescence;
3. discuss the findings from a range of empirical studies into aspects of adolescence;
4. assess theories and studies of development and change during early, middle and later adulthood;
5. discuss the impact of particular life events during adulthood, for example marriage, parenting, divorce, unemployment, retirement, bereavement and death.

SECTION I ADOLESCENCE

Sometime after the age of 10, humans mature sexually and become capable of reproducing (see Box 6.1). The period of time during which the reproductive processes mature is known as **puberty**. Although the most obvious signs of development during puberty are physical, changes also occur in cognitive functioning, social interactions, emotions and the sense of self. **Adolescence** is a longer period of time, and is generally defined as the period from the onset of puberty up to adulthood.

Adolescence has traditionally been considered a time of conflict and turmoil. G. Stanley Hall, the first person to study adolescence scientifically, described it as a period of 'storm and stress' as well as of great physical, mental and emotional change. Currently, many clinical psychologists and psychoanalytic theorists still describe adolescence as a time of psychological disturbance, though some studies of typical adolescents suggest that the extent of adolescent disturbance has been exaggerated (Conger, 1977).

BOX 6.1
Physical changes during adolescence

During puberty, hormonal secretions from the pituitary gland, which lies at the base of the brain, begin to stimulate the ovaries in females and testes in males, and the adrenal glands in both sexes. In males, reproduction depends upon the production of sperm cells, an event which usually occurs between 12 and 15 years. In females, the onset of the first menstrual flow, usually between the ages of 11 and 14, signals the production of ova.

Certain changes which occur during puberty are known as **primary sexual changes**: ovulation in females is accompanied by an increase in the size of the vagina, clitoris and uterus, while in males enlargement of the penis and testes coincides with the production of sperm. In addition to these primary changes, a number of **secondary sexual changes** occur. These include, for both sexes, the development of pubic hair and changes in the shape and proportions of the body. In females, the breasts develop and in males the voice deepens and facial hair begins to appear. Both sexes experience the 'growth spurt', a substantial and rapid increase in height. The growth spurt in boys generally begins about two years later than it does in girls, and lasts for a longer period of time.

Late and early maturation

As noted above, the age at which young people reach puberty varies. Late or early maturation appears to have few lasting psychological effects in girls. However, in males the picture is different. Boys who mature early are likely, because of their greater strength and size, to have an advantage in sports. They are also likely to develop earlier self-confidence in relationships with girls. The reverse is likely to be true for late-maturing boys. As a result, there are likely to be some personality differences between late and early-maturing males. A large number of studies have indicated that late-maturing males are likely to be more tense and self-conscious, less socially adept and to have greater feelings of inadequacy and rejection. In contrast, early maturers appear to be more self-assured and at ease with themselves. Follow-up studies indicate that these differences can persist into adult life. At age 33, most late maturers appeared to be less self-confident and controlled and more in need of support and help from others (Clausen, 1975).

As we have seen, early maturation seems to be advantageous for boys. However, the impact on girls is less extensive and more variable (Crockett and Peterson, 1987). Initially, early-maturing girls tend to be more dissatisfied with their body image, more moody, listless and discontented and more disorganised when under stress. They are often less popular with their same-sex peers than are late-maturing girls and are more likely to perform poorly in school (Simmons *et al.*, 1983) However, they also appear more independent and are more popular with opposite-sex peers. By late adolescence and adulthood, however, the picture is very different. The formerly discontented early-maturing girl tends to become more popular with her peers of both sexes, is more self-possessed and better at coping.

How can this transformation be explained and why is early maturation clearly more favourable for boys than for girls? Simmons *et al.* (1983) suggests a number of factors may be important, including the following:

- Early-maturing adolescents are in the minority among their peers.
- While society tends to view early maturation in boys favourably, the messages are more ambiguous for females. For boys, greater strength and physical prowess is more socially desirable. Among girls, early maturation may mean being temporarily taller and heavier than their female peers and taller than boys of their own age. In our society, early-maturing girls may also be the target of more conflicting sexual messages than is so for males.

Adolescent identity

Erikson (1968, 1970)

According to Erikson (1968), adolescence is the stage of development during which the individual is searching for an identity (see Section II for an outline of Erikson's Theory of Lifespan Development). The crisis '**identity versus role confusion**', encountered during adolescence, is seen by many psychologists as the central crisis of all development. The major goal of the adolescent at this time is the formation of a secure and enduring **ego-identity**, or sense of self. Ego-identity has three important components:

1. a sense of **unity**, or agreement among one's perceptions of self;
2. a sense of **continuity** of self-perceptions over time; and
3. a sense of **mutuality** between one's perceptions of self and how one is perceived by others.

In order to arrive at a coherent sense of identity, adolescents typically 'try out' different roles without initially committing themselves to any one. Thus, stable attitudes and values, choices of occupation, partner and life-style gradually come together and make sense to oneself and others around.

Failure to achieve a firm, comfortable and enduring identity results in **role-diffusion**, or a sense of confusion over what and who one is. Over-strong pressure from parents and others may cause the young person to become bewildered and despairing, resulting in withdrawing, either physically or mentally, from normal surroundings. In the most extreme cases of role diffusion, adolescents may adopt a negative identity. Convinced that they cannot live up to the demands made by parents, the young people may rebel and behave in ways which are the most unacceptable to the people who care for them. So the son of a local Tory dignitary may join a left-wing group, or the daughter of an atheist may become a devout member of a religious group.

Erikson's views arose mainly from clinical observations of both normal and troubled adolescents.

Marcia (1966, 1980)

Marcia extended and elaborated on Erikson's account of adolescent identity and identified four different kinds of identity status in adolescents:

- **Identity diffusion**: An identity status which is characterised by a lack of commitment and indecision about important life issues such as vocational choices, ideology and religion.
- **Identity foreclosure**: A status of initial commitment and development of values, but overshadowed by a hesitant acceptance of the values of others (for example, parents or teachers) rather than by self-determined goals (for example choosing 'A' level subjects or job options because an adult advises that they are desirable).

- **Moratorium**: A status of extreme identity crisis when an individual rethinks his or her values and goals but has difficulty making firm commitments.
- **Identity achievement**: A status where individuals have resolved their crises and have made firm commitments to particular values or choices in life, for example religious commitment or vocational choice.

Meilman (1979) studied a group of American males aged between 12 and 24 years. He found that there seemed to be a broad age-related trend in relation to the statuses identified by Marcia. For example, younger participants tended to be categorised as experiencing identity diffusion or foreclosure, while from the age of 18 on, increasing numbers of young men were categorised as identity achievers. However, the status of moratorium – the most extreme crisis – was found in only a very small number of participants, whatever their age.

Female identity   An important question arises from Meilman's research and the work of Erikson and Marcia. Are researchers making the assumption, as has so often been done in the past, that male development is the standard against which females are to be judged? The picture of identity development so far as females are concerned is not clear. Though some research has included female participants, there does seem to have been some bias towards issues of male identity. Erikson argued that females develop differently because they postpone their identity development until they have found a male partner, whose name they will accept and whose occupation determines their social status. Marcia (1980) concedes that Erikson's model and the identity status approach can be applied to females 'only more or less' (p. 178).

Parental styles and identity

Parents play a significant part in determining how successful adolescents are in achieving an untroubled and enduring sense of identity. It has been shown that adolescents who are poorly adjusted and suffer a wide range of psychological problems are more likely to have experienced parental rejection or hostility than acceptance and love (Rutter, 1980). In particular, the style of parental control is an important factor in the parent/child relationship. A number of studies have shown the following:

- **Democratic, but authoritative**, parents are most likely to have children who, as adolescents, have high self-esteem and are independent and self-confident. Democratic/authoritative parents, while respecting the young person's right to make decisions, expect disciplined behaviour and give reasons for doing so (Elder, 1980). Such rational explanations are important to adolescents who are approaching cognitive and social maturity and preparing to take responsibility for their own behaviour.
- In contrast, more **authoritarian** parents expect unquestioning obedience from their children and feel no need to explain reasons for their demands. Adolescents with authoritarian parents are likely to be less self-confident and independent, and more likely to regard their parents as unaffectionate and unreasonable in their expectations (Elder, 1980; Conger and Petersen, 1984).

In general, research evidence provides little support for the idea that the majority of adolescents experience a serious identity crisis, though this may be the case for a small minority (Feldman and Elliott, 1990). Hill (1993) suggests that the question of whether everyone experiences a total moratorium remains unanswered. Adams *et al.* (1994) reviewed research findings which point to the influence of family styles on development of a sense of identity. He concluded that youths suffering role diffusion tend to come from rejecting and detached families, while those who achieve a secure sense of identity appear to come from warm, supportive families that encourage independence and initiative. Durkin (1995) argues that what emerges from research in this area is that identity development is not a short-term process but one which extends beyond adolescence and at least into young adulthood and depends heavily on interactions between young people and their social contexts.

Two views of adolescence

The 'traditional' view

The traditional view of adolescence is that of a period of development beset by turmoil and personal upheaval. Adolescence is characterised by extreme physical, emotional and cognitive changes, developing sexual urges, the need to make vocational and other choices, coping with pressure to conform to peer group expectations. All these factors exert pressure and contribute to the turmoil experienced by many young people.

The notion of adolescence as a time of storm and stress is taken for granted in many developmental theories, especially psychoanalytic theories. Anna Freud (1958), for example, described the adolescent as experiencing renewed sexual feelings and strivings. The intensity of inner drives, she believed, leads to excessive emotional upset as the adolescent tries to cope with these impulses and desires. However, this view was challenged in 1939 by the anthropologist Margaret Mead (see Box 6.2).

Sociological theory

Mead's views on the problems experienced by adolescents in Western societies has been reflected more recently in sociological theory. The sociological view of adolescence, like the psychoanalytic approach, involves a belief in the concept of 'storm and stress'. Where these two theoretical approaches differ is in the explanation of the *causes* of the trauma.

Sociological theory suggests that both socialisation and role changes are more significant during adolescence than at any other time during development. Aspects of adolescence such as the increasing independence from parents and other authority figures, greater involvement with peers coupled with a heightened sensitivity to evaluations by other people, all serve to hinder the process of role change from childhood to adulthood. Major environmental changes, such as changing schools, going to university or college, leaving home, or starting a job, all demand the formation of a new set of relationships and this in turn leads to different and often greater expectations and major reassessment of the self. The effects of competing socialisation agencies, including the family, the school, the peer group, the mass media, and so on, present the adolescent with a wide range of values and ideals from which to choose. This may result in uncertainty and conflict (Marsland, 1987). Many of those writing from a sociological perspective believe also that social changes that have occurred since the early 1970s have presented young people with increasingly stressful situations.

BOX 6.2
Adolescence in Samoa

The anthropologist, **Margaret Mead** (1939), challenged the traditional view of adolescence, questioning whether the Western portrayal of adolescence as a troubled and tumultuous time was applicable in other cultures. Mead's study of life among preliterate peoples in the island of Samoa in the South Seas suggests that adolescent turmoil may result from cultural pressures that exist in industrialised, Western societies.

In Samoan life, boys and girls become familiar at an early age with the facts of life, death and sex. Sexuality is treated in an open, casual manner, and, by adolescence, young people freely engage in sexual and love relations. Samoan adolescents therefore experience less guilt and shame than their Western counterparts, and are spared the anxiety and confusion often faced by Western adolescents.

Focusing on the course of adolescence in Samoan girls, Mead describes the process as smooth and natural – in sharp contrast to the adolescent years experienced in Western society. Growing up in Samoa is easier because life in general is less complicated. Emotional relationships are treated casually, child rearing is treated lightly, competitiveness and ambition are almost non-existent. Consequently, adolescence is uneventful. In contrast, Western adolescents experience lives filled with opportunities, ambitions, pressures to achieve, and thus the stresses which accompany such lifestyles. Mead sees the wide range of opportunities and the pressure to make choices as fostering conflict and stress in adolescents of more 'civilised' societies.

Mead did not conclude that we should try to remove the stresses that beset adolescents in our Western society. Rather, we should find ways of more adequately preparing young people for the range of personal and societal choices that they must face.

Mead's study has been criticised by some contemporary anthropologists. Freeman (1983), for example, claimed that her account of life in Samoa was inaccurate and misleading. He attributed her 'errors' to a lack of understanding of the Samoan language and to her decision to live with American ex-patriots on the island rather than with the people she was studying.

Freeman's other argument was that both earlier and later studies provided views of Samoa which conflicted with that of Mead. However, he based his arguments mainly on his own work in Samoa in the 1940s and 1960s. It may be that Samoan society has changed greatly since the 1920s because of the influence of Christian missionaries and American military bases.

Studies of adolescent turmoil

Masterson (1967) found evidence of anxiety in 65 per cent of a sample of normal adolescents aged between 12 and 18 years. Similar findings were reported by Rutter, Tizard and Whitmore (1970). Almost half of their sample of 14- to 15-year-olds showed symptoms of emotional upset, such as depression or extreme misery.

In contrast, some studies failed to find evidence of stress or turmoil in adolescents. For example, Offer (1969) reported that for the majority of adolescents, changes in identity and in relations with parents and peers occurred gradually and without trauma. Dusek and Flaherty (1981) investigated the stability of self-concept in adolescents during a three-year longitudinal study. Responses to self-report questionnaires indicated that adolescent self-concept does not appear to undergo excessive change. The changes that were noted in subjects appeared to occur gradually and uneventfully.

Coleman and Hendry (1990) found that in most situations, peer-group values appeared to be similar to those of important adults rather than in conflict with them.

Overwhelmingly, research into adolescence indicates that though a small minority may show some disturbance, the large majority of teenagers seem to cope well and show no undue signs of stress or turmoil. Coleman (1995) contends that support for this belief can be found in every major study that has appeared in recent years.

Conflict between theory and research

As we have seen, research provides little support for the 'storm and stress' view of adolescence proposed both in psychoanalytic theory and in sociological theory. Coleman (1995) suggests the following reasons for this mismatch

- It has been pointed out by many writers that psychoanalysts and psychiatrists see a very select sample of the population. Their views on adolescence may well be unduly influenced by the experiences of the individuals they meet in clinics or hospitals.
- Sociological theorists may, it has been argued, fail to disentangle the concepts of 'youth' or 'the youth movement' from assumptions about the young people themselves. Youth is frequently seen by sociologists as in the forefront of social changes in the

established values of society. This may lead to a view which confuses radical forces in society with the beliefs of ordinary people (Brake, 1985).

- Some adolescent behaviours such as hooliganism, drug-taking or vandalism are extremely threatening to adults. It may be that the few who are engaged in these anti-social activities therefore attract greater public attention than the majority who do not. Sensational accounts in the mass media may result in adolescent misdeeds being seen as more common than they actually are. The behaviour of the minority comes to be seen as the norm for all young people.

Coleman argues that all three of these factors may contribute to an exaggerated view of the stress and turmoil that may be expected during adolescence, thus leading to the gap between theory and research widening. This does not mean that the two traditional theories have no value. Perhaps the most important contribution made by the theories is that they have provided a framework for an understanding of those young people who do experience problems and a wider knowledge of those who belong to minority groups. Coleman says of the theories:

it must be recognised that they are now inadequate as the basis for an understanding of the development of the great majority of young people. The fact is that adolescence needs a theory, not of abnormality, but of normality.   (Coleman, 1995, p. 61)

He believes that a viable contemporary theory must incorporate the findings of empirical studies.

Aspects of adolescent experience

Cognitive growth

In his theory of cognitive development, Piaget (see Chapter 3) defined a new level of thinking which emerges around puberty – **formal operational thought**. Formal operational thought, you will remember, requires the ability to reason and systematically to test out propositions in the abstract without reference to concrete objects. It is considered by Piaget to be the high point of human development.

According to Piaget, the adolescent, faced with a scientific problem to solve, is capable of reasoning hypothetically and taking account of a wide range of differing alternatives, as well as understanding the underlying scientific law. This change in adolescent thought has been described as a shift of emphasis from the 'real' to the 'possible'. However, many studies have shown that true operational thought is found in Western culture in only a minority of adolescents. For example, Shayer and Wylam (1978), testing a very large sample of British schoolchildren, found that only about 30 per cent of young people aged 15 or 16 had achieved 'early formal operations'. Therefore, Piaget's claims do not seem strictly to apply to the majority of adolescents. It is nonetheless clear that significant cognitive changes do occur during the adolescent years. Adolescent thought processes become more analytical and reflective than in younger people. Adolescents are more likely to use complex techniques as aids to memory, and are more likely to be capable of anticipating and developing strategies to deal with problems, both academically and in relation to social situations.

Kohlberg's work on moral development (see Chapter 5) has drawn attention to the way in which cognitive changes influence moral reasoning during adolescence. Moral values in the young child at the Pre-Conventional Level, are typically linked to external sources such as punishments and rewards. At the Conventional Level, in early adolescence, moral thought is dominated by concern for the family, society or national standards. Older and more experienced adolescents and adults, during the Post-Conventional or Principled Level, characteristically base moral judgements on the dictates of their own conscience. In general, studies have broadly supported Kohlberg's proposal that with increasing age, young people tend to reach higher levels of moral reasoning (Rest, 1983).

Peer relationships

Peers play an important role in socialisation during adolescence. As young people become less influenced by family ties, they develop a greater affinity with others of the same age group. This trend was clearly illustrated in a study by Sorensen (1973). Sixty eight per cent of his sample believed that their personal values were in accord with those of most other adolescents. Also, 58 per cent of the sample was more likely to identify themselves with others of the same age rather than with others of the same gender, community, race or religion.

A classic study by James Coleman (1961) drew attention to the so-called **adolescent sub-culture** which existed in Western societies. Such a subculture, Coleman believed, was substantially different from the adult culture and was responsible for orientating adolescents towards their peers and alienating them from their parents or the academic goals of their school.

More recent observers have been critical of the stereotyped view of adolescent society portrayed by Coleman. McClelland (1982) suggested that while many adolescent groups may distinguish themselves from adults through common tastes in clothing, hairstyles, music and so on, not all these groups are necessarily in revolt against adult norms. According to Hartup (1983), adolescents are more likely to be influenced by parents than peers in such areas as moral and social values. Berndt (1992) concludes that most experts agree that for the majority of teenagers today, peers have far less influence than had previously been believed.

The functions of peer relationships Dunphy (1963) believed that peer relationships during adolescence tend to fall into three main categories:

1. **'Cliques'**, or small, intimate same-sex, and later both-sex, groups tend to be made up of young people of similar age, interests and social backgrounds. The clique is thought to provide the framework for the sorts of intimate personal relationships that formerly existed in the family setting.
2. Around the clique exists the **crowd**, the larger, more impersonal and loosely defined group. The crowd comes together mainly on the basis of similar social interests or future life-expectancies or career orientations. For instance, university-bound or career-minded 'A' level students might loosely constitute one crowd, while students who are training for skilled, manual jobs might constitute another.

As well as belonging to cliques and crowds, adolescents usually have one or two close friends. **Friendships** involve more intense and intimate relationships than do cliques and provide a setting for young people to 'be themselves' and to express their innermost feelings, hopes and fears. Adolescents put a high premium on loyalty and trustworthiness in friends. Of almost equal value, especially for girls, is that a friend will listen and respond sympathetically to confidences. Berndt (1982) believes that adolescent friendships can enhance self-esteem by allowing individuals to feel that others respect and are interested in their ideas and feelings. Also, intimate friendships are likely to enhance *later* periods of development by contributing to the young person's social skills and sense of security.

There is agreement between theorists that the peer group offers the young person a 'safe' environment in which to make the shift from unisexual to heterosexual relationships. The 13- or 14-year-old can practise her new relationship skills within the protected context of the crowd or the clique. When greater confidence is acquired, she can then move towards dating and later the formation of more committed heterosexual pair relationships.

Self-assessment questions

1. Briefly describe the physical changes which take place at puberty. Explain some of the psychological effects of late and early maturation.
2. Outline Erikson's views on the adolescent's search for an identity. Does research evidence support his views?
3. Discuss some different theoretical views on the nature of adolescence.
4. Why do you think there is a conflict between theory and research in relation to the existence of 'storm and stress' during adolescence?
5. What cognitive changes occur during adolescence?
6. In what ways are peer relationships of importance during adolescence?

SECTION II   LIFESPAN DEVELOPMENT: THE STUDY OF ADULTHOOD

Until relatively recently few developmental psychologists paid attention to the course of development during adulthood. Partly because two of the most important thinkers in the field, Piaget and Freud, did not consider the adult years, adolescence was treated as the last major period of development. More recently, however, research has been carried out into the nature and quality of adulthood, particularly old age. Investigations have viewed the adult years as a series of 'phases' linked both to age and to various milestones in life, or 'critical life events' such as marriage, parenting, divorce, unemployment, retirement, bereavement and death.

Few theories of adulthood have been proposed. However, a major theory which has embraced the entire lifespan from birth to old age is that of Erik Erikson (1963). Erikson has written extensively not only on childhood and adolescence, but on the developmental changes that take place during adulthood.

Erikson's theory of psychosocial development

Erikson's (1963) theory attempted to provide a framework within which development throughout the whole lifespan may be viewed. A practising psychoanalyst, Erikson has been strongly influenced by the ideas of Sigmund Freud. However, whereas Freud described psycho*sexual* stages of development, Erikson emphasised the social forces which influence development. He described a sequence of psycho*social* stages which he claimed are applicable to individuals in different cultures and societies. A brief account of Erikson's stages is set out in Figure 6.1. It includes an indication of the approximate ages covered by each stage of the lifespan.

Erikson sees each stage of life as marked by a crisis, or struggle, which the individual must confront and attempt to resolve. (Note that the stages are named in relation to the opposite extremes of the crisis; for example, during the first stage the crisis is 'Trust versus Mistrust', indicating the individual's need to develop a sense of trust in the environment.) The level of success with which the crisis is managed will determine that individual's psychological well-being at a particular time. The person who is unable to deal satisfactorily with a crisis will continue to experience problems in later stages and thus progress will be impaired. However, Erikson believed that it is possible to compensate later for unsatisfactory experiences at a particular stage. Similarly, satisfactory negotiation of a crisis at an early stage could be diminished if the individual suffers deficiencies in later development.

Erikson's claim that the eight psychosocial stages of development are applicable universally to individuals in different societies is open to some doubt. The validity of the crises described at each stage and agreement about what constitutes a desirable outcome may depend heavily upon the norms and values of a particular culture (Booth, 1977). For example, stage 4, industry-v-inferiority, may only apply in cultures, such as ours, which place heavy emphasis on competitiveness and which frown upon children who do not succeed in particular skills at a given time.

Some studies of Erikson's theory

- Central to Erikson's theory is the notion that personality change arises in relation to the different crises that characterise each developmental stage. A study by Ryff and Heinke (1983) asked the question 'Do people perceive their own personality changes in this way?' Perceptions of personality change were studied in three adult groups: young, middle-aged and old-aged. Participants completed a number of personality scales including two which related to the Eriksonian concepts of integrity (related to old age) and generativity (related to middle age). Concurrent, retrospective and prospective self-reports were obtained. Support for Erikson's theory was found in that all age groups perceived themselves as being most generativity-oriented at middle age and having higher integrity at old age.
- A series of studies by Block (1971, 1981) have offered support for Erikson's belief that personality changes occur during the adult years and that adolescence is a critically important time in personality development.
- A longitudinal study by Kahn *et al.* (1985) found support for Erikson's proposition that establishing an identity in adolescence is crucial for later successful intimate relationships. Students' identity scores taken in 1963 were related with their marital status some twenty years later. Interesting sex differences emerged: women with low identity scores were more likely to be divorced or separated; men with low identity scores were found more often to remain single.

A further examination of some of Erikson's views on adulthood will appear in the following sections on young, middle and late adulthood.

Levinson's seasons of a man's life

Levinson (1978, 1986) formulated an influential account of adult development based upon the notion of a series of phases said to occur in each person's life cycle. The account was initially based upon detailed interviews with 40 American men between the ages of

FIGURE 6.1

Erikson's stages of psychosocial development

Life crisis	Favourable outcome	Unfavourable outcome
First Year		
Trust-v-mistrust The child needs consistent and stable care in order to develop feelings of security.	Trust in the environment and hope for the future.	Suspicion, insecurity, fear of the future.
Second and third years		
Autonomy-v-shame and doubt The child seeks a sense of independence from parents. Parental treatment should not be too rigid or harsh.	A sense of autonomy and self-esteem.	Feelings of shame and doubt about one's own capacity for self-control.
Fourth and fifth years		
Initiative-v-guilt The child explores her environment and plans new activities. Sexual curiosity should be sympathetically handled by parents.	The ability to initiate activities and enjoy following them through.	Fear of punishment and guilt about one's own feelings.

Six to 11 years **Industry-v-inferiority** The child acquires important knowledge and skills relating to her culture.	A sense of competence and achievement. Confidence in one's own ability to make and do things.	Unfavourable reactions from others may cause feelings of inadequacy and inferiority.
Adolescence (12–18 yrs) **Identity-v-role confusion** The young person searches for a coherent personal and vocational identity.	Ability to see oneself as a consistent and integrated person with a strong, personal identity.	Confusion over who and what one is.
Young adulthood (20s and 30s) **Intimacy-v-isolation** The adult seeks deep and lasting personal relationships, particularly with a partner of the opposite sex.	The ability to experience love and commitment to others.	Isolation; superficial relationships with others.
Middle adulthood (40–64) **Generativity-v-stagnation** The individual seeks to be productive and creative and to make a contribution to society as a whole.	The ability to be concerned and caring about others in the wider sense.	Lack of growth; boredom and overconcern with oneself
Late adulthood (65+) **Integrity-v-despair** The individual reviews and evaluates what has been accomplished in life.	A sense of satisfaction with one's life and its accomplishments; acceptance of death.	Regret over omissions and missed opportunities; fear of death.

35 and 45. Each participant was asked to review his life so far and to comment on critical choices and their consequences.

From his participants' responses, Levinson proposed four life periods or 'seasons':

- childhood and adolescence;
- early adulthood (approximately 17–45 years);
- middle adulthood (approximately 40–65 years); and
- older adulthood (from 60 onwards).

Levinson claimed that though each individual person is unique, everyone goes through the same basic sequence. Each season has its own character, and a person's life experiences will be influenced by the biological and social changes associated with that phase of life.

Levinson's account of early and middle adulthood described the self-perceptions and social orientations of a group of men. However, he claims that a broadly similar pattern exists for women.

- **Early adulthood** is seen as the stage where the individual seeks independence from parents and becomes the basis for what Levinson calls **the Dream** – a vision of his goals in life which provide motivation and enthusiasm for the future. For example, a man at this stage of his life might anticipate achievement in his career, sporting achievement or the accumulation of personal wealth, and so on. How the individual relates to his Dream is seen by Levinson as crucial, in that if the Dream does not become a part of his life, it may die and he loses his sense of purpose and responsiveness to life.

  Around the age of 28–33, the individual faces the **age 30 transition** when he goes through a period of self-questioning before he finds his niche in life and makes a commitment to a particular career.

  A key feature of the early adulthood season is the existence of a mentor, an older and more experienced colleague or boss who provides help and advice on career advancement.

- **Middle adulthood** is viewed as a time for the consolidation of interests, goals and commitments. Somewhere between the early 30s and about 40, people begin to 'settle down'. Stable commitments are made to family, career, friends or some special interest. The transition to middle life occurs around 40 and lasts for about five years. This transition period forms a link between early and middle adulthood and according to Levinson is a period of crisis when people evaluate themselves. This re-evaluation involves measuring their achievements in the light of earlier goals – the Dream – and where necessary, readjusting these goals. Levinson believed that the individual must come to terms with discrepancies between what was aimed for earlier in life and what the reality is now. If this acceptance is achieved the individual will experience stability during middle adulthood. Levinson notes that qualities such as wisdom and compassion often emerge during middle adulthood.

Levinson's model is useful in that it illustrates the scale and complexity of adult development. However, it was initially based upon the collection of data from a small group of males in a particular country, who were experiencing development within a particular social, economic and political climate. Critics have stressed the need for cross-cultural research and studies into female development. In relation to the latter, subsequent researchers have studied women's lives in order to discover the extent to which Levinson's framework fits.

Seasons of women's lives

Roberts and Newton (1987) have reviewed four studies (unpublished doctoral dissertations) carried out by female investigators with a total sample of 39 females. Their aim was to discover whether Levinson's model of adult development was also applicable to women. A danger, of course, with this kind of research is that attempting to view women's lives through a structure which emerged from a study of men might overlook some important dimension of women's lives or view the developmental progress of women as inferior against a male criterion. However, if anything, the results appear to point to greater complexity in female development.

Roberts and Newton (1987) concluded that in general terms, the age-related developmental progress of women's lives were very similar to that which Levinson found in men. For example, the early adulthood phase involved the same pre-occupation with the 'Dream' and almost all the women experienced an age 30 transition.

However, there were some subtle but important differences:

- For women, the Dream involved different priorities. Very few placed occupational goals as high on the list. Even a group of lawyers who did place importance on their careers, considered them secondary to marriage. Women's Dreams were generally more complex and diffuse than men's and reflected a conflict between their personal goals and their obligations to others. For many participants, part of their Dream was their husbands' success.

- Levinson stressed the crucial role played by a mentor in men's lives. Roberts and Newton suggested that for women, such a person was difficult to find. Even women who had professional careers and who did identify role models, tended not to find a mentor from whom they could receive advice and support in relation to career development.
- The age 30 transition was found to be as important in women's lives as it was for the men in Levinson's study. However, the nature of this transition tended to be influenced by what had gone before. For example, women who had in their twenties placed more emphasis on marriage and motherhood, tended now to develop more individualistic goals. Those who had been career oriented during their twenties, now focused on marriage and starting a family.
- The thirties seemed to be less clearly defined for women and few saw this as a time for 'settling down'. Durkin (1995) suggests that for women the establishment of seniority in a career may be more uncertain, thus providing a less objective basis for 'settling down'.

As with Levinson's research, the studies described by Roberts and Newton are based upon a small sample drawn from an American population. However, in general, women do seem to experience the 'seasons' of adult life described by Levinson. However, the priorities of women's lives are often different from those of men's. Greater emphasis is placed on relationships than on careers and there seems to be a greater willingness to orient their goals and dreams around other people.

Self-assessment questions

1. Briefly outline Erikson's theory of lifespan development. How far do you think his model can be applied to all human beings?
2. Outline and evaluate Levinson's model in relation to the study of early and middle adulthood.
3. How far do Levinson's 'Seasons' of adulthood apply to the development of females?

SECTION III   YOUNG ADULTHOOD

Growth trends

Following the sometimes turbulent and uncertain period of adolescence, the young adult is usually preoccupied with self-growth in the context of society and relationships with others. According to Sheehy (1976) the central concern of 'Who am I?' during adolescence, shifts to questions such as 'How do I put my aspirations into effect?' or 'Where do I go from here?' during adulthood.

White (1975) identified five 'growth trends' observed during young adulthood:

1. **Stabilisation of ego-identity** Ego-identity – one's feelings about oneself – is more firmly embedded than any previous time during development. The ego cannot be seriously damaged, as it might have been during childhood or adolescence, by being called a failure, for example. Greater commitment to social roles, such as occupational role, and to other people, helps the individual to define and maintain a stable and consistent sense of self.
2. **Freeing of personal relationships** Development of a stable view of themselves results in young adults becoming less concerned about themselves and able to develop strong personal relationships with others. This freedom allows them to be more responsive to another person's needs.
3. **Deepening of interests** Young adults develop more commitment, and consequently achieve greater satisfaction, from interests such as hobbies, study, occupation, or personal relationships than do younger people.
4. **Humanising of values** During this period young adults increasingly view moral and ethical problems in the light of life experiences. They are therefore more likely to be aware of the human aspects of values and the way these values apply in society.
5. **Expansion of caring** A much more general concern for the wellbeing of others develops during early adulthood. This concern extends not only to particular individuals known personally to them, but in the wider sense to the deprived and suffering in society at large.

White emphasises that these growth trends represent the ideal goals of development during youth and young adulthood. Most people make some progress through the dimensions, though it is doubtful whether everyone fulfils all these goals.

Life events

Another way of considering adult development is to look at the way in which people adjust to important life events. A life event can be any 'happening', or phase, in the life of an individual which requires that individual to change the pattern of life. Some life events, such as marriage or starting a job, are experienced by most adults. Others, such as imprisonment or suffering a disabling accident, are experienced by relatively few people. Life-event theory suggests that all life events, whether good or bad, can induce stress and therefore require some psychological adjustment. (See 'Stressful life events' in the next section.)

Lowenthal, Thurber and Chiriboga (1975) found that, as might be expected, young adults are in general exposed to more life events than are middle-aged and older adults. The latter two groups report more negative stresses, while young adults report more positive stresses. Lowenthal *et al*. point out that the impact of a life event on an individual is not determined simply by the actual occurrence of the event. The critical factor in assessing the level of stress appears to be the individual's perception of the event. Two people might experience a similar life event, divorce, for example, but perceive it in very different ways. One person might feel bereft, while another might feel liberated.

Marriage

In modern Western societies, over 90 per cent of adults marry at least once. Although there is an increasing tendency for younger people not to enter into formal marriage, the majority of people who do not legally marry still enter into long-term pair-bonding relationships which resemble those of a husband and wife (Reibstein and Richards, 1992).

There are many different kinds of marriage, each of which may sustain different roles for the husband and wife. Duberman (1973) has identified three main types of marriage:

1. The **traditional marriage** operates on the assumption that the husband is the main force and decision-maker. While the wife may have authority over such matters as child-care and domestic matters, all other areas are controlled by the husband.
2. In the **companionship marriage** the emphasis is on equality and companionship. Male and female roles are not differentiated and either partner may make decisions and assume responsibilities in any area.
3. The **colleague marriage** is similar to the companionship marriage in that heavy emphasis is placed upon sharing and personal satisfaction. However, role differences are accepted, and each partner becomes responsible for different areas of married life, according to their interests and abilities.

Companionship and colleague-type marriages are becoming increasingly common among middle-class couples. Many marriages, of course, do not fit neatly into any of these categories, and many features overlap.

Marital adjustment Many studies have examined the changes and adjustments that people undergo when they marry. Vincent (1964) found that in a group of married people significant changes occurred in such traits as dominance and self-acceptance. Traditionally, greater adjustments to marriage have been made by women. Women often relinquish a career to become housewives and mothers and this may result in less contentment in marriage for women than for men. Unger and Crawford (1992) found that more women report dissatisfaction with their marriages than do men. Marriage appears, however, to have a beneficial effect on men. Veroff and Feld (1970) found that married men reported that they were happier than single men. They were also healthier and lived longer. Teachman *et al.* (1994) found that in the USA, married men spent less time unemployed than single men and were more likely to take a job than single men.

As with all relationships, marriage is not static (Reibstein and Richards, 1992). Both partners develop and change and the nature of the relationship changes as a result. For some couples this change is for the worse though for others marital satisfaction is maintained or increased throughout life. Bengston *et al.* (1990) found that in general, patterns of marital satisfaction tended to follow a U-shaped curve, high in the early and later stages but dropping in the middle.

Marital roles   Current social pressures regarding roles in marriage are less rigid than they were. Far more young people subscribe to the idea of shared roles in marriage, as compared with their parents' generation. As more women work outside the home, their husbands make greater contributions to household chores and child-care. Bahr (1973) reported that husbands of working wives perform significantly more household chores than husbands of non-working wives. However, Walker (1970) compared the work activity of husbands and wives in the home and showed that women spent far more time on household tasks than men (five hours a day compared with one and a half hours a day). Presland and Antill (1987) found that where both partners were working, there is a slight increase in the amount of time men spend on housework and a more substantial decrease in the amount of time women devote to it. However, women tend generally to retain the overall responsibility for household chores. Matlin (1993) argues that traditionally in marriages, women and men generally divide up the household tasks according to how much physical strength may be required and whether the tasks are performed inside or outside the home. For example, women have tended to do the cooking, cleaning and baby-tending, while men have washed the car, done the gardening and taken out rubbish.

A study by Booth (1977) showed that husbands of working women tended to be happier and under less stress than husbands whose wives were full-time homemakers. It is interesting that Wright *et al.* (1992) found that Swedish men were considerably more involved in housework than American men. This suggests that deliberate social policy changes have influenced domestic gender behaviour. Since the 1970s, the Swedish government has pursued a policy of commitment to gender equality in areas such as tax systems and child-care provision, family support which has not been paralleled in America and in other European countries.

Divorce

Recent statistics indicate that more than one in three marriages will end in divorce. Most of these divorces will occur during the first seven years of marriage (Reiss, 1980). Teenage marriages are almost twice as likely to end in divorce as marriages that take place in the 20s.

The fact that marriages that break down tend to do so in the early years, and that teenage marriages are more likely to end in divorce, suggests that there may be some underlying developmental cause. One or the other of the marriage partners may not have firmly established a coherent identity independent of parents, or have succeeded in making a commitment to an occupation.

Adjustment to divorce Studies suggest that divorce is highly stressful and ranks second only to the death of a spouse in terms of the readjustments which the individual must make in his or her life (Holmes and Rahe, 1967). Emotional reactions to divorce will vary according to the events that preceded the break (Kelly, 1982). For the unsuspecting, previously contented person, the reaction may be shock; the person who has suffered years of conflict and misery may well experience relief. However, evidence suggests that both will suffer distress and will experience a period of 'mourning' for the relationship.

Wiseman (1975) reports that many divorced people experience an identity-crisis as they reorganise their lives. This is particularly true for a woman who married young and whose identity was dominated by that of her husband.

Bohannon (1985a, 1985b) proposes that there are six components involved in the process of divorce. These components are not sequential and may overlap. Bohannon suggests that it is important to understand these components in order to cope with the emotional chaos which divorce may bring:

- **Emotional divorce** This component typically begins before the decision is made to divorce. It is characterised by a failing marriage and involves a wide range of negative feelings and behaviours, including betrayals, accusations and lack of affection and support.
- **Legal divorce** This relates to the legal process of severing the civil ties of marriage. Many couples are unprepared for the complexities of divorce and the amount of psychological energy needed to cope.
- **Economic divorce** Decisions must be made about how couples will divide up their money and possessions. Invariably, this process involves resentment, anger and hostility

- **Coparental divorce**   Where there are children, the courts will decide which parent will receive custody. This is done on the basis of what is best for the children. Access rights for the parent not given custody must also be determined. During this stage, worry and distress is often expressed about the effects of the divorce on the children.
- **Community divorce**   This relates to the changes which occur in a divorced person's status in the surrounding neighbourhood. Many divorced people feel isolated and lonely and may experience some social disapproval. Sometimes, relationships with friends are changed and some divorced people regret that divorcing a spouse involves also a 'divorce' from their in-laws.
- **Divorce from dependency**   The shift from being part of a couple to becoming single requires considerable psychological adjustment. As might be expected, those individuals who maintained a high degree of independence in their marriages are likely to become autonomous more quickly than those marriage partners who were dependent upon one another.

Bohannon's components should not be seen as a precise and rigid framework that is the same for everyone who is going through divorce. As noted previously, reactions to divorce may vary from person to person, depending upon the events that went before. However, the main value of Bohannon's work is that it highlights the complexity of divorce and provides a framework which helps us to understand the changes that people face when going through this painful process.

Parenting

In Erikson's model of psychosocial development, the young adult experiences the crisis of **intimacy-v-isolation**. The need to feel love for and make a commitment to another person is the main goal of this stage. Following the resolution of this crisis, the first stirrings of the crisis of **generativity** occurs as couples confront feelings and make decisions about parenthood. Generativity – the desire to care for others and contribute to the growth and well-being of future generations – may be achieved through having children.

Fertility motivation   Many factors influence a couple's decision to have children. Researchers on **fertility motivation** – people's motives for having or not having children – have cited a number of factors which may contribute to the decision: social pressure, particularly from their own parents; a need for the emotional security that offsprings may give in later life; a desire to pass down one's own characteristics and values; a love of children for their own sake.

Parenthood as a developmental process Many researchers believe that, for both parents, having a child contributes to the developmental process in that it allows them to relive the earlier developmental crises through which they themselves have passed. Erikson (1968) believes that pregnancy allows a woman to use the 'productive inner space' which lies at the centre of female fulfilment. Benedek (1959), a psychoanalyst, suggests that a woman's maternal instinct arises from her early identification with her own mother. Memory traces retained from her own childhood allow her to re-experience the pleasures and problems of infancy as she looks after her own child. Dinnerstein (1976), however, believes that a woman's feelings about mothering would be different if child-care were shared more evenly with the father.

Adjusting to parenthood A major task of parenthood is to socialise the infant. The parents, in turn, are socialised by the child. As the parents help the child to acquire good eating, toilet and social habits, they learn how to respond to the child and make it comfortable and secure.

Parenthood has been described as a crisis point in the life of a couple. In a study of over 2,500 adults, Dohrenwend *et al.* (1978) found that the birth of the first child was rated the sixth most stressful life event in a list of 102 possible events. This may be at least in part because people receive little preparation for parenthood from society.

Many studies have indicated that marital satisfaction tends to decrease with the arrival of the first child (Reibstein and Richards, 1992). Schulz (1972) found that young parents talk to each other only about half as much as couples without children, and then the conversation is often about the child. In some marriages, however, particularly if children are planned, they can strengthen the marital relationship.

Parenthood invariably leads to the couple relating to society in a new way. New mothers enjoy the company of other new mothers;

young parents seek out the company of their own parents for advice and emotional support – and for babysitting. Social institutions which previously have had little significance in the lives of the couple will be re-evaluated. Parks, libraries and schools will be assessed, and active involvement may occur in causes such as the promotion of road safety or opposition to TV violence (Brodzinsky *et al.*, 1986).

There is strong evidence that the quality of the relationship which existed between the parents before the child was born is important. Their relationship has implications firstly for how the parents will meet the challenge of parenthood and secondly for the quality of their interactions with the child (Cox *et al.*, 1989; Heinicke and Guthrie, 1992). Heinicke and Guthrie found that parents who showed the most positive pre-birth interactions and who were able to deal with any conflicts in a mutually respectful way were more likely to adjust well to the birth of a child. Cox *et al.* (1989), reviewing the literature concluded that the extent to which couples establish a confiding relationship was related to maternal warmth and the husband's feelings about his role as a father.

Attachment behaviour in parents   We saw in Chapter 2 that typical behaviour indicating attachment in infants included wanting to stay close to the attachment figure, distress at absence, and feelings of security in the presence of the attachment figure. These character-istics are also to be found in the new parent who experiences a close attachment to the child (Newman and Newman, 1988). However, the parents' experience of attachment has some additional features: for example, a strong sense of responsibility for the child's well-being, satisfaction on meeting the child's needs and anxiety and stress when those needs do not appear to be met. Also, the parent experiences a new social capacity: the opportunity and obligation to exert authority. How this is incorporated into family life has important implications for the child's development and the par-ent–child relationship. There appears, also, to be a sense of continuity in attachment relationships. Feeney *et al.* (1994) and Main (in press) found that new parents' reports of their own personal attachment histories were closely related to the attachment types found in their own infants. These findings offer some support for Benedek's (1959) views referred to earlier on the implications of a woman's identification with her own mother.

Self-assessment questions

1. Describe White's account of development during young adulthood.
2. What do you understand by the term 'life events' as used in psychological literature?
3. Discuss some of the research carried out into the impact of either marriage or divorce.
4. What psychological adjustments must be made during parenthood? To what extent are parents socialised by the child?

SECTION IV   MIDDLE ADULTHOOD

There are two conflicting interpretations of the nature of middle age. One view is that it is a time of conflict and crisis. Researchers have used the term 'mid-life crisis' to describe the time when middle-aged people become conscious of, and often depressed about, the changes which are taking place in their lives, such as the physical and psychological effects of ageing, occupational adjustments and the departure of children from the home. A more optimistic view emphasises that middle age is a time when people are more accepting of themselves and are ready to approach life with renewed vigour.

Which of these two interpretations is adopted by middle-aged people depends upon how they perceive themselves and their lives. So, too, does the timing of the advent of middle age. Some people perceive themselves to be young or middle-aged well into their 60s, whereas others consider themselves middle-aged at 35.

Does the midlife crisis exist?

As was noted in Section I, Levinson reported that men of between 40 and 45 experienced a crisis as they moved through the transition period from young to middle adulthood. He believed that these feelings of turbulence and self-evaluation are a normal part of development and allow the individual to reach a new stability in life.

- As a result of Levinson's work, the notion of a 'midlife crisis' was widely taken up by newspapers both in the USA and in the UK. It was not always remembered that Levinson's sample was small and restricted to particular kinds of men in just one society. Subsequent research has raised doubts about how far Levinson's findings can be generalised to everyone: Vaillant (1977) argued that most periods of life are experienced as difficult by some people.

- Baruch *et al.* (1983) found that doubt about the direction of one's life and the value of achievements is often experienced in early career, rather than during middle age.
- Several studies found that large numbers of middle-aged people actually feel more *positive* about this stage of their life than earlier ones (Long and Porter, 1984).
- Farrell and Rosenberg (1981), using larger samples than Levinson, found that while many people report that they experienced some re-evaluation during middle age, only about 12 per cent felt that they had experienced a crisis.

To summarise, the mid-life crisis does not seem to be as widespread as Levinson indicated. Durkin (1995) suggests that the time and degree to which people experience uncomfortable self-evaluations is likely to vary depending upon personality and social context:

Overall, midlife is a period of change and readjustment but . . . the nature and consequence of the changes are integrally interwoven with the individual's social relationships and roles.

(Durkin, 1995, p. 638)

Personality and social development

A leading question that has been addressed by researchers is, do aspects of personality, such as values and beliefs, change systematically as people move from young adulthood to middle and old age, or is personality stable throughout? Unfortunately, the answer to this question is not easy to obtain. Personality is a very complex aspect of human beings, and not easy to measure accurately over time. However, in general, empirical evidence supports the notion of stability of personality in adulthood.

Longitudinal studies, in particular, note that some of the most stable characteristics include values (social, political, economic, religious and aesthetic) and vocational interests. Neugarten (1977) reported that in cross-sectional studies the findings are less clear-cut, with some studies, though not others, finding differences between age groups in personality characteristics such as rigidity, cautiousness, conservatism and self-concept. (See Chapter 1 for an indication of the strengths and limitations of longitudinal and cross-sectional studies.)

Studies of personality over time have distinguished between **relative stability** and **absolute stability**.

- Relative stability refers to the rank order of personality scores of a sample of subjects over a period of time. A personality dimension would be relatively stable if the rank order among subjects remained similar from one period to another, irrespective of whether there was an overall increase or decrease in the scores.
- Absolute stability refers to whether participants maintain the same score on a personality dimension from one occasion to another. For example, it is known that people increase their level of self-awareness between childhood and middle age. The absolute stability of this personality dimension is therefore low.

Stability of personality over time

Haan and colleagues (1986) carried out a major longitudinal study of personality and physical and mental health in several cohort groups from adolescence to middle age. Participants' personality ratings were correlated across the adolescent, young adult and middle adult years. Results showed the following.

1. Generally, personality dimensions were relatively stable, that is, participants rated high on particular dimensions on one occasion tended to be rated high on a later occasion.
2. Greater stability existed between adolescence and young adulthood, and between young adulthood and middle adulthood, than between adolescence and middle adulthood.
3. Those personality dimensions most concerned with the self, for example self-confidence, tended to be the most stable.
4. Women's personalities tended to be more stable than men's.
5. Men's personalities changed most during the period from adolescence to young adulthood, as they developed careers and financial independence.
6. People increased in cognitive investment, openness to self, nuturance towards others and self-confidence from adolescence to old age; that is, there was a low degree of absolute stability in these dimensions.

Conclusions

It seems that while some developmental change does occur, adult personality is not subject to large and pervasive changes in relation to beliefs, attitudes and values. Haan *et al.* (1986) suggest that transformations in personality that do occur probably arise from circumstances that force a person to change. This supports the idea suggested in the last section that people adjust their personalities in response to life events such as marriage or parenting.

Developmental theories of middle adulthood

Erikson (1963) considered the central conflict of the middle years to be that of **generativity versus stagnation** (see Section II). The individual becomes concerned with contributing to and guiding the next generation. Erikson explains that this drive does not always necessarily relate to one's own children, but may take the form of creative contributions or guidance and counselling with young people. The person who does not achieve generativity will experience a sense of personal impoverishment and an excessive concern with self.

Peck (1968) described four major psychological adjustments which face middle-aged people.

1. They must learn to value wisdom more than physical power and attractiveness. This involves accepting as inevitable the decline in physical powers and gaining satisfaction from the wisdom that comes from experience, knowledge and mental ability.
2. Men and women must value each other as individual personalities rather than as primarily sex objects.
3. They must develop the capacity to shift their emotional investment from one person or activity to another. Emotional flexibility is particularly important in middle age. As children leave home, relatives or friends die and certain activities such as strenuous sport are no longer possible, it is important to be able to focus on and gain satisfaction from different people or activities.
4. It is important at middle age to remain mentally flexible and receptive to new ideas and ways of doing things.

Levinson (1978, 1986), as we saw in Section I, suggested that from the age of approximately 40–45, an individual moves through a midlife transition which forms a bridge between early and middle adulthood. A major task of middle adulthood is to evaluate success or failure in meeting the goals established during young adulthood. This self-appraisal arises from a heightened awareness of one's own mortality and a desire to use the remaining time wisely. A second task of middle adulthood is to take steps to adjust the more negative elements of one's life and establish the basis of a new life structure. The amount of change made at this time will vary greatly from person to person. For some, a drastic change may occur, such as divorce or a major change in occupation. Some individuals may experience change in their social outlook, personal values or inner convictions.

These three theorists each describe a different facet of middle age. A common theme exists in that each agrees that middle adulthood is a period of significant challenge, during which individuals must adjust to changes both within and outside of themselves.

Stressful life events

A factor in the lives of middle-aged adults which has received attention from researchers is the question of stress and its effects on health and psychological well-being. A study by Theorell and Rahe (1974) indicated a positive relationship between the incidence of heart attacks and the number and type of stressful life events such as death of a spouse, loss of job, or divorce.

Measuring life stress

Psychologists have developed ways of measuring the level of stress associated with particular life events as well as the overall level of stress experienced by the individual. Figure 6.2 shows one such measure, the **Social Readjustment Rating Scale (SRRS)**, which was developed by Holmes and Rahe (1967). Subsequent studies which have employed this measure report that the higher the level of stress experienced by individuals, the greater the incidence of health problems.

FIGURE 6.2

Social readjustment rating scale (from Holmes and Rahe, 1967)

Life event	Mean value
Death of spouse	100
Divorce	73
Marital separation	65
Jail term	63
Death of close family member	63
Personal injury or illness	53
Marriage	50*
Dismissal from work	47
Marital reconciliation	45
Change in health of family member	44
Pregnancy	40
Sex difficulties	39
Gain of new family member	44
Business readjustment	39
Change in financial state	38
Death of a close friend	37
Change in number of arguments with spouse	35
Foreclosure of mortgage or loan	30
Change in responsibilities at work	29
Son or daughter leaving home	29
Trouble with in-laws	29
Outstanding personal achievement	28
Spouse begins or stops work	26
Begin or end school/college	26
Change in living conditions	25
Revision of personal habits	24
Trouble with boss	23
Change in work hours or conditions	20
Change in residence	20
Change in schools	20
Change in recreation	19
Change in church activities	19
Change in social activities	18
Change in sleeping habits	16
Change in number of family gatherings	15
Change in eating habits	15
Holiday	13
Christmas	12
Minor violations to the law	11

*Marriage was arbitrarily assigned a stress value of 50. No event was found to be any more than twice as stressful. Here the values are reduced proportionally and range up to 100.

An individual's level of stress is calculated in the following way.

1. The subject is asked to described specific life events experienced during a particular period of time, for example the past two years.
2. The appropriate stress value for each life event is assigned to the person and a total stress index is arrived at by adding together all the stress values the person has received.

Criticisms of SRRS

Rating scales such as SRRS have been criticised on a number of counts:

- It has been suggested that they are too primitive and crude a measure of the impact of stressful life events. For example, Brown *et al.* (1973) pointed out that people vary in their responses to stressful events. What is traumatic for one person may actually be beneficial to another. Brown suggested also that individuals should be interviewed to work out their level of 'contextual threat', a measure of the circumstances surrounding a stressful life event.
- Lazarus (1966) suggested that **daily hassles** were more likely to cause stress than were life events. Day-to-day problems may accumulate and cause the individual to feel unable to cope.
- Factors other than the stress caused by life events may be the cause of ill health. For example, the death of her spouse may cause a woman to change her lifestyle, to adopt an inadequate diet or to drink or smoke more.
- A correlation between two variables does not necessarily indicate a *causal* relationship. It is possible that changes in physical health may be the *cause* rather than the effect of a stressful life event. For example, a health problem may cause an individual to experience difficulties at work, rather than the other way round.

Unemployment

Unemployment is an extremely stressful occurrence for adolescents and adults of all ages. However, the unemployment rates caused by recession are likely to have more serious outcomes for older adults. Middle-aged and older adults, once unemployed are likely to remain so for up to 70 per cent longer than younger workers (Entine, 1976). The psychological consequences for middle-aged adults are also likely to be serious. Family responsibilities will probably be very demanding and the need to save and build up financial security for old age is likely to be at its most pressing.

Unemployed adults appear to progress through four psychological stages during a prolonged period of unemployment:

- **Relaxation and relief** occurs after the initial shock. Individuals experience a feeling of contentment with their new, more relaxed status. Feelings of hope and confidence in their ability to find new employment lead to phase 2.
- A **concerted effort** is made to secure a new job. At this stage, most are becoming bored with their increased leisure time, but are still optimistic about job prospects. As efforts to find work are continually frustrated, the jobless person enters a third phase.
- **Vacillation and doubt**   The individual begins to experience self-doubt and efforts to find work are irregular. Relations with family and friends become strained.
- **Malaise and cynicism**   The last phase is characterised by feelings of apathy and listlessness. Many of the people studied claimed that they felt helpless and inadequate and had difficulty in imagining themselves ever working again.

Studies of the psychological impact of unemployment   An in-depth study of the lives of unemployed men was carried out by Marsden in 1975. Marsden found that the men were beset by difficulties in sleeping, by loss of appetite and by tiredness during the day. As the length of unemployment grew, they tended to lose a sense of meaning in their lives and often their sense of identity.

It was difficult to be sure from Marsden's study how typical these experiences were of unemployed people in general. However, in the 1980s a major programme of research into the psychological consequences of unemployment was set up by Peter Warr of the Social and Applied Psychology Unit at Sheffield (Warr, 1982). The studies showed that unemployment led to increasing levels of psychological distress among men. It could be argued that it was not possible to disentangle cause and effect in the studies. However, a longitudinal study by Warr and Jackson (1985) indicated that once people were re-employed, there was a noticeable improvement in their psychological well-being, suggesting that unemployment was the causal factor.

Research by Gallie and Vogler (1994) showed that the currently unemployed had a lower level of psychological well-being than any labour market group, other than currently non-active people who had been unemployed previously or who had an unemployed partner.

There has been markedly less research interest into the psychological consequences of unemployment for women. However, Kelvin and Jarrett (1985) have suggested that women's experiences of unemployment may differ from those of men in the following ways:

- In general, women are typically to be found in less-skilled and less-well-paid work, with fewer opportunities for career enhancement. Thus, many women may perceive their work as less enriching and therefore the loss of a job is not so traumatic.
- Many women often bear the double burden of a job and domestic work. The loss of paid employment doubtless eases this demanding workload.
- The domestic role many women play may offer an alternative set of activities and source of identity, which shields them from some of the worst effects of unemployment.

Jahoda's thesis   While there appears to be agreement about the damaging psychological effects of unemployment, there is less of a consensus on the mechanisms that may bring this about. Probably the most influential account of the processes which underlie the link between unemployment and psychological well-being has been proposed by Jahoda (1982). Jahoda suggests that employment, however difficult, fulfils a number of important functions:

- It gives people a clear time-structure to the day and provides a compulsory pattern of activity.
- It provides a source of social contacts outside the home.
- It allows people to experience a feeling of participation in a wider collective purpose.
- It is a source of identity and social status.

Jahoda's account focuses on the importance of a life-structure and of ties with the community. She argued that in an advanced capitalist society, it is only through employment that such experiences can be provided.

Jahoda's explanation stimulated a sustained debate in the literature and a number of possible inadequacies were pointed out. For example:

- Fraser (1981) argued that Jahoda greatly underestimated the significance of sheer financial hardship.
- Gallie *et al.* (1994) argued that Jahoda's proposals do not adequately address the possible differences between men's and

women's experiences or whether other roles outside employment can provide compensatory benefits for the loss of employment-based experiences.

A small-scale study by Miles (1983) has provided some support for Jahoda's thesis. However, it focused only on men in one particular region (Brighton), the sample was not randomly selected and there was only a very small control group of employed people.

Following Jahoda's thesis, Gershuny (1994) examined two aspects of unemployment: firstly whether unemployment does cause psychological distress through changes in the individual's environment other than those brought about by financial loss; secondly, the extent to which different patterns of sociability and domestic situation may alleviate the effects of unemployment. His provisional conclusions are as follows:

- The categories of experience described by Jahoda do seem to be strongly associated with paid employment.
- There is a significant, though small, relationship between opportunities to experience these categories and levels of psychological adjustment. This applies both to men and women, though the relationship is rather smaller for women.
- Activities outside of employment can to some extent provide experiences of the kind that Jahoda saw as vital for psychological health. However, in general, they do not appear to be an adequate substitute for employment itself.

Self-assessment questions

1. What do you understand by the term 'mid-life crisis'? Does it exist?
2. What conclusions would you draw from research carried out to investigate the stability of personality over time? Distinguish between absolute and relative stability.
3. Outline one developmental theory of middle adulthood.
4. For what purpose is the Social Re-adjustment Rating Scale used? In what way has this scale been criticised?
5. Briefly discuss Jahoda's (1982) thesis in relation to the psychological impact of unemployment. How far is the thesis supported by research evidence?

SECTION V LATE ADULTHOOD

Old age is the last phase of the lifespan. Gerontologists (gerontology is the name for the scientific study of the elderly) have attempted to define when exactly the period of old age begins. Some distinguish between 'elderly' and 'advanced' old age. Early old age is said to occur between the ages of 65 and 74, and late old age from 75 on. However, a chronological definition of ageing can be misleading. The adage 'You are as old as you feel' is subscribed to by many older adults. This implies that subjective or psychological factors are more important in defining whether or not a person is old, than is noting the number of years lived.

The study of older adults has gathered momentum over the last 20 years or so. As life expectancy increases, older people have become the focus of attention by psychologists, medical practitioners, urban planners and politicians. Among gerontologists, many disagreements arise about late adulthood. Some find that intellectual ability declines with age; others refuse to accept that this is so. Some believe that successful adjustment to old age is brought about by the individual's disengagement from society; others believe that continued activity actually enhances adjustment in later years.

Senescence

Senescence, or primary ageing, refers to the period of life when the degenerative processes of ageing set in. It is a normal part of growing older and usually occurs gradually. The timing and effects of senescence vary from person to person.

Researchers have identified many different aspects of senescence. These include physiological, biochemical and behavioural changes. As people age there is a loss of neural tissue; the heart, lungs and nervous system become less efficient; and the body's resistance to disease breaks down. Older people are thus more likely to become ill and have greater difficulty in recovering. Many of the external signs of senescence begin to appear during middle age: grey hairs, skin wrinkles, weight gain, diminishing muscle strength and agility, and sight and hearing difficulties are all outward manifestations of the changes which occur with increasing age.

Attitudes towards the elderly

Cultural variations

Attitudes to increasing age vary considerably across cultures. In many traditional societies, chronological age is not an important factor, partly because the years are not counted. Historical and anthropological evidence reviewed by Fry (1985) and Tout (1989) showed that, in many societies, elderly people retain their status, authority and social involvement. However, Keith (1990) found that in advanced industrial nations, chronological age promotes social differentiation.

Even within Western societies whose economic status is similar, policies and attitudes towards the elderly vary. For example, in Greece there is a general view that people retain their vigour well into their later 70s and should be cared for and involved in the family (Amira, 1990). In Denmark, there is a policy of state-funded institutional support which ensures the care of the elderly, but which also results in their separation from relatives and greater problems of loneliness (Jamieson, 1990).

Stereotypes of the elderly

In British and American societies, attitudes toward the elderly are somewhat paradoxical. On the one hand, we respect the wisdom and experience of many professional people, such as judges and politicians, who are past the normal age of retirement. On the other hand, there are many negative attitudes associated with ageing and stereotypes abound in many areas of life. Schmidt and Boland (1986) found a range of different stereotypes, from 'perfect grandparent' at the positive end to 'bag lady' and 'vagrant' at the negative.

Stereotypes of the elderly tend to contain some negative components, whatever the age-group of the perceivers (even older people themselves!). However, the most negative stereotypes appear to be held by children and adolescents (Goldman and Goldman, 1981). Over 800 children aged 5–15 from Australia, England, Sweden and the USA were interviewed about their perceptions of old age. Though there were some variations among interviewees, there were two general patterns of response:

1. Children of all ages were more likely to say negative things about the elderly than positive; this kind of response was more likely as the age of the respondents increased. Over 90 per cent of 15-year-olds described elderly people in negative terms.
2. The researchers commented on the revulsion and often disgust expressed about old age. Remarks about physical attributes (wrinkled skin, feebleness, sickness, etc.) and psychological characteristics (bad-tempered, slow to react or understand, etc.) were common.

There may be many reasons why old age is perceived in such a negative way. Jackson (1992) suggests that diminishing physical attractiveness may be one reason. Attractiveness is highly prized in many societies. Durkin (1995) proposes that another reason may be the older person's changing status both within the family and in the world of work. When people retire, they no longer have a clear economic role, their income is reduced and their authority diminished.

As we have seen, there is compelling evidence that stereotypes exist in relation to the elderly. However, on a positive note, it seems that few people extend the stereotypes to all the people that they actually *know*. For example, most studies find that grandparents are generally valued and described in positive terms by children and adolescents (Werner, 1991).

Cognitive functioning in late adulthood

Certain aspects of intelligence appear to decline with age.

- **IQ** – Longitudinal studies indicate that performance on IQ tests is relatively stable up to the age of around 60. After this, a steady decline is often noticeable in areas which measure psycho-motor skills, attention, memory, inductive reasoning and quickness of response. However, social knowledge, verbal-conceptual ability and mathematical reasoning do not appear to be affected by the ageing process (Horn and Donaldson, 1980).

   Decreases in intellectual functioning do not seem to be experienced equally by all people. A study by Schulz, Kaye and Hoyer (1980) found that those who had kept themselves mentally active throughout their lives, experienced little, if any, decline. Shaie

(1983, 1990) found that older people who continue actively to use a skill or ability often perform better than younger people who have had less practice.

- **Memory** – Studies of memory processes during old age indicate that short-term memory, that is the recall of immediate information that is still being attended to, suffers some decline. There appears to be little difference between older and younger adults in the number of items that can be held in short-term memory. The older adult, however, is likely to be more susceptible to distraction and less able to recall memorised information in a different form.

So far as long-term memory is concerned, research indicates that older people have more problems remembering material that they have ceased actively to focus upon, though they will have little difficulty remembering knowledge and experiences that they recall frequently.

As with general intellectual functioning, well-educated and mentally active individuals do not experience the same memory decline as those people who do not exercise their minds.

Many researchers stress that although some aspects of cognitive functioning do show decline, this should not lead to an overly pessimistic view of old age. As people age, deficits in physical and mental functioning are often compensated for by greater wisdom arising from experience and breadth of knowledge.

The cognitive quality of **wisdom** incorporates such characteristics as intuitiveness, experience, introspection, empathy, understanding, patience and gentleness. Clayton and Birren (1980) note that most adults associate these characteristics with old age.

Pratt *et al.* (1987) compared young, middle-aged and older adults' responses to moral dilemmas and found no decline with age but noted evidence of increasingly complex reasoning among 60- to 75-year-olds.

Theories of personality development and adjustment

Late adulthood is seen by many theorists as a time of continuing psychological growth. The developmental tasks of the older adult include adjusting to declining physical powers and health, coping with retirement and limited income, and adjusting to the death of a marriage partner.

Erikson's theory

During old age, according to Erikson (1968), the individual must resolve the crisis he describes as **ego-integrity-v-despair**. As people approach the end of their lives they tend to look back and evaluate the decisions they have made and the actions which have influenced their lives. This review should ideally lead to feelings of satisfaction and acceptance that the life one has lived is meaningful and important. Such feelings lead to high ego-integrity. The person whose life review reveals feelings of regret and disappointment that life has been unsatisfactory and unfulfilling will experience despair.

While most people will experience both these psychological states at various times, the person who achieves a greater degree of integrity over despair will experience a feeling of well-being and a sense of purpose even in the face of death.

Peck's theory

Peck (1968) believes that continued psychological growth during late adulthood depends upon how well individuals cope with three major developmental tasks:

1. They must come to terms with **vocational retirement**. This involves developing feelings of self-worth and satisfaction in areas other than the job of work which has been a central influence in earlier stages of life. People able to express their personalities in ways not connected with their work-role are more likely to lead happy, interesting and well-adjusted lives in later years.
2. **Physical decline** is inevitable in old age. People who have relied upon physical well-being for satisfaction and pleasure may become very preoccupied with the state of their bodies and depressed about their declining physical powers. Peck believes that it is important that older people should shift their attention away from bodily concerns and learn to value satisfying relationships with others and creative mental activities.
3. The final adjustment that older adults must make is related to **human mortality**. Each individual must recognise and accept that death is inevitable. Such acceptance should include the knowledge that their lives can be significant after death through children, through friendships and through contributions they have made to society.

Successful adjustment to ageing

What constitutes successful adjustment to old age has been the subject of some debate. There are two prevalent, largely conflicting theories: disengagement theory and activity theory:

Disengagement theory proposes that as individuals approach their last years of life, they gradually withdraw from social contacts and activities. They also become less concerned with the problems of the outside world and detach themselves from complicated emotional interactions with other people.

Studies suggest that older people increasingly take less part in family and community activities (Neugarten, 1977). This does not mean that friends and social relationships are not important to them. In fact, friendships can often provide valuable support and compensate for losses experienced in old age. Therefore, friendship and social interaction can help the adjustment process during ageing (Tesch, 1983).

Disengagement theory was first proposed by Cumming and Henry (1961) who maintain that the gradual disengagement of the individual from society will lead to psychological well-being and contentment. However, premature disengagement caused by ill health or early retirement is likely to lead to problems in adjustment.

Activity theory developed by Maddox *et al.* (1964) suggests that successful adjustment during old age is brought about by the individual remaining productive and active. Psychological well-being is maintained where an individual can find substitute activities for those that are ending. For example, retirement from work will require the individual to find new interests and activities to fill the gap.

Activity theory has received little empirical support and has been criticised as an over-simplification of the issues involved. Some individuals clearly prefer to maintain a high level of involvement in social activities and relationships, while others are more contented with disengagement.

Studies by Reichard, Livson and Peterson (1962) indicate that personality factors are important determinants of whether a person will adjust successfully to old age. Therefore, they argue that neither disengagement nor activity theories alone can adequately explain successful ageing.

Also, factors other than personality or the ageing process may partially determine whether an individual disengages from society or continues to lead an active life. Lack of money, reduced mobility, societal attitudes towards old people may all militate against an individual leading an active, independent life in old age.

Durkin (1995) argues that two factors stand out as being critical to well-being and satisfaction in later years: personal control and social involvement. These are the same factors which are important throughout the lifespan from infancy onwards. Pratt and Norris (1994) found that higher self-efficacy (seeing oneself as having control over one's life) is associated with well-being among the elderly. When asked to identify the most important factors to affect the quality of life, older people consistently tend to place relationships, social networks and health at the top of the list (Ferris and Branston, 1994).

Retirement

Most people retire from full-time work during their 60s. The exact age at which people retire is usually determined by our social security system which decrees that 60 for a woman and 65 for a man are the appropriate ages. However, there is an increasing tendency for people to retire earlier. This, coupled with the fact that life expectancy is increasing, means that the proportion of retired people in the general population will steadily increase. By the beginning of the next century, it is expected that a person will generally live another 25 years after retirement. While some people approach retirement with pleasurable anticipation and relief, others consider themselves not yet ready to relinquish what is often a meaningful and important part of their lives.

Psychological impact of retirement

Because of the emphasis placed on the importance of work in our culture, retirement presents most people with a substantial sense of loss. It involves moving from a role which is clearly defined and economically productive to one which is more ambiguous and economically unproductive (Ransom *et al.*, 1991). Loss of identity, social role, financial security and prestige require that significant psychological adjustments are made. However, research has indicated that, contrary to popular belief, retirement is not generally associated with decline in health and psychological well-being. For example, Streib and Schneider (1971) observed that, except for people who are compulsorily retired, it does not appear to lead to low morale. Troll (1982) noted that for many people, health improves in the early post-retirement years. Bosse (1991) found that for those men and women who were forced to retire for reasons of poor health or redundancy or whose health or financial circumstances deteriorated, retirement became a stressful experience.

The retirement process

Retirement is often thought of as a life event which happens suddenly, usually in late adulthood. However, some researchers view retirement as a developmental process which takes place gradually over a period of time.

Atchley (1982; 1991) suggests that the process of retirement involves seven phases (see Figure 6.3), though not all people necessarily pass through every stage.

- **Phase 1** The **remote phase** usually occurs during middle adulthood. At this time most working adults are fully immersed in their jobs and may have only vague thoughts about retirement. Little or no preparation for retirement is made at this time.
- **Phase 2** As the time for retirement approaches, people enter the **near pre-retirement phase**. At this time much active thought and planning for retirement occur. The individual gradually disengages from some of the duties and responsibilities of the job.

FIGURE 6.3
Atchley's 'phases of retirement'

	Retirement Event					End of Retirement Role
Remote phase	Near phase	Honeymoon phase	Disenchantment phase	Re-orientation phase	Stability phase	Terminal phase
PRE-RETIREMENT		POST-RETIREMENT				

- **Phase 3**   The actual retirement is often accompanied by feelings of pleasure and anticipation – the **honeymoon phase**. Many of the activities previously planned can now be engaged in.
- **Phase 4**   Retirement activities often prove to be less satisfying than expected. When this happens the individual enters the **disenchantment phase** and feels depressed and 'let down'.
- **Phase 5**   Disenchantment is usually followed by a **re-orientation phase** during which people face up to the reality of retirement. The individual contemplates the future and attempts to develop a realistic view of its alternatives.
- **Phase 6**   There next follows what Atchley terms the **stability phase** when people settle to the routines of retirement with realistic awareness of their own capabilities and limitations. In the stability phase, people can be said to have fully adjusted to the role of the retired person.
- **Phase 7**   The **terminal phase** occurs when for one reason or another the retirement role ends. This may happen because individuals become ill or disabled and can no longer care for themselves. For some people the role of retiree is terminated when they seek out employment once again.

Atchley's phases of retirement may not apply in the same form and sequence to everyone. Individual differences in personality, variations in the age at which people retire and the reasons why they retire will all influence the process of retirement. However, his model aids our understanding of the developmental tasks which are faced by most older people who are making the transition from the role of worker to that of non-worker.

Death and bereavement

In Western cultures the subject of death is a sensitive issue which, in the past, has been frequently avoided. Metaphors such as 'passed away' or 'no longer with us' have been used to describe the occurrence of death. Over the past two decades there has been a considerable shift in attitudes towards dying. Doctors and psychologists have attempted to view death not as a distinct event which terminates life but as an important **process** in the life cycle.

Previously, doctors and family members have tended to withhold the truth from a dying person, on the basis that it was kinder to do so. Today, however, most doctors recognise that a dying person needs to be aware of his or her condition in order that the necessary psychological adjustments and practical arrangements may be made (Schulz, 1978).

Kübler-Ross's Stages in the Dying Process

Kübler-Ross (1969) studied over 200 terminally ill people. On the basis of her observations and interviews with the patients, she proposed that the dying process consists of five stages through which the dying person passes as death approaches:

1. **Denial** Most people, on learning that they are terminally ill, react with shock followed by a sense of disbelief. They may assert that there has been an error in diagnosis and that the doctors are incompetent. Denial can be observed in almost all patients and is considered to be a fairly healthy way of coping with the initial shock.
2. **Anger** As denial becomes difficult to sustain, the dying person typically experiences anger at his or her condition and resentment of the healthy. 'Why me?' is a common cry. Kübler-Ross believes that it is important for the person's caretaker to understand why and how the anger originates, and to empathise with the patient.
3. **Bargaining** At this stage the person adopts a different approach and attempts to bargain with God for an extension of life or a period of time without pain and discomfort. A patient may promise, for example, a life dedicated to the church, or donation of organs to medical research in return for a postponement of death.
4. **Depression** When terminally ill patients can no longer deny their illness and when more severe physical symptoms occur or hospitalisation is necessary, a sense of deep loss is experienced. Kübler-Ross distinguishes between two kinds of depression which occur at this time: (i) **reactive depression** results from the loss already suffered, for example, loss of physical strength or job; (ii) **preparatory depression** relates to the loss that is to come, for example, loss of loved ones and treasured possessions. Kübler-Ross believes that encouragement and reassurance are helpful to people suffering reactive depression. However, patients suffering preparatory depression must be allowed to express emotions and prepare for impending loss.

5. **Acceptance**   In this final stage, the dying person accepts death. If they have been allowed time to work through the earlier stages and have been given some assistance to do so, they will feel no anger or depression. Quietness and gentle companionship are appreciated and they appear emotionless and detached.

Not all terminally ill people move through the stages described by Kübler-Ross. For example, a person may die in the anger stage because he or she is psychologically incapable of moving beyond it, or because the rapid progression of the illness does not allow the time to do so.

Care of the dying

One important outcome of Kübler-Ross's study of dying people is the realisation by doctors and other medical workers that dying persons need sensitive care as they prepare for death. Many terminally ill patients face death alone in a sterile and impersonal hospital ward without the support and companionship of family and friends.

A more humane approach towards the care of the dying is slowly gaining ground with the emergence of the **hospice** movement. A hospice is an establishment which provides a homelike and emotionally supportive setting for terminally ill people. The emphasis is on keeping the patient comfortable and free from pain and providing companionship as the patient prepares for death. Family and friends are encouraged to help with the care of the patient. The hospice movement arose from the work of the British doctor, Cicely Saunders in the 1960s.

Bereavement

Bereavement is the condition or state of loss and is most often experienced when someone close to us dies. However, bereavement may result from other losses such as loss of a close relationship through divorce or the loss of a job because of redundancy.

Grief is a person's emotional response to bereavement. The grieving process involves psychological suffering. However, it has been suggested that it is a necessary process and people who do not grieve are unlikely to recover from their loss.

Clayton *et al.* (1971) identified the 'symptoms' most commonly associated with the grieving process. In a study of 109 recently bereaved widows, the most common symptoms reported by more than 80 per cent of the respondents included crying, depression and insomnia. Over half suffered from loss of appetite and had difficulty concentrating. It is generally recognised among researchers that loss of a spouse during later adulthood provides one of the most serious threats to the health and well-being of the surviving partner (Wortman and Silver, 1990).

The loss of a child is also traumatic and parental bereavement is just as powerful for young parents as it is for those in their 60s. Their dreams and plans may be as strong for a young baby as they are for an adult or teenage offspring. Loss during pregnancy, too, promotes intense grief among parents (Smart, 1992).

Research indicates that bereavement can produce changes in nervous, hormonal and respiratory systems and can weaken the immune system (National Academy of Sciences, 1984). Bereaved persons are therefore at greater risk of suffering physical or mental illness.

Stages of bereavement

Bowlby (1980) identified five stages in the grieving process:

1. concentration on the deceased person;
2. anger towards the deceased or other people;
3. appeals to others for help;
4. despair, withdrawal, disorganisation;
5. reorganisation and focus on a new object of interest.

Kavanagh (1974) suggests seven stages of bereavement:

1. shock;
2. disorganisation;
3. violent emotions;
4. guilt;
5 loneliness and loss;
6 relief;
7 re-establishment.

Coping with grief

Coming to terms with complex feelings and the many demands and pressures of bereavement results in a wide range of behaviours. Some of these will be helpful and constructive; others will not and will only increase the psychological distress of the bereaved person. Crosby and Jose (1983) discuss functional (helpful) and dysfunctional (unhelpful) ways of coping.

Dysfunctional methods of coping Three different kinds of behaviour have been observed:

- **Avoidance** This is often known as the 'keep busy' strategy. Though many people believe that avoidance is therapeutic and helpful, if it is adopted over a prolonged period, it often becomes dysfunctional in that it encourages the denial of a loved one's death and prevents the bereaved person from coping. Similarly, getting away from home on a trip too soon after the death may result in the bereaved person failing to come to terms with the first stages of grief. Returning home is then more difficult to cope with and the grief process has been disrupted.
- **Obliteration** This is a process which goes beyond avoidance and denial. It involves an attempt to totally erase all memories of the deceased person. This may involve disposing of all clothing, pictures, hobbies and other possessions.
- **Idolisation** This is the opposite of obliteration. Here, the survivor glorifies the memory of the deceased person, who is perceived to be impossibly perfect. This appears to be an attempt to hold on to the belief that the deceased is still present.

Functional methods of coping Crosby and Jose see the key process here as good communication within an accepting and positive network of support. The bereaved person's energies need to be directed at the actual loss, as experienced collectively and individually. There should be no scapegoating, blaming and feelings of guilt about the deceased. Within this network, survivors should feel free to express their feelings but should recognise that feelings are often the result of irrational or illogical internalised beliefs. Thus, they should also be prepared to challenge their own beliefs and the beliefs of others.

Open communication allows unlimited opportunities for grief reduction. Where feelings are shared, survivors can often be helped to see the sometimes irrational assumptions they make about their own role in events that were actually far beyond their control. Often, survivors reason that if they had done something differently, the death would never have happened. This then leads to prolonged grieving, where grief becomes mixed up with guilt.

Self-assessment questions

1. What has research told us about attitudes towards the elderly in different cultures?
2. To what extent does cognitive functioning decline with age?
3. Outline two theories of personality development during late adulthood.
4. Contrast two theories concerned with successful adjustment to late adulthood.
5. Discuss research which has investigated the psychological impact of retirement.
6. In what ways can the findings of psychological research be of help to those who care for the dying?
7. Discuss some of the physical and psychological effects of bereavement.

Further reading

Bromley, D. B. (1988) *Human Ageing* (3rd edn) (Harmondsworth: Penguin).

Coleman, J. C. and Hendry, B. (1990) *The Nature of Adolescence* (2nd edn) (London and New York: Routledge).

Sugarman, L. (1990) *Lifespan Development* (London and New York: Routledge).

Durkin. K. (1995) *Developmental Social Psychology: From Infancy to Old Age* (Cambridge, Mass.: Blackwell).

Turner, J. S. and Helms, D. R. (1995) *Lifespan Development* (5th edn) (Orlando, FL: Harcourt Brace College Publishers).

Bibliography

Adams, G. R., Gullotta, T. P. and Markstrom-Adams, C. (1994) *Adolescent Life Experiences* (3rd edn) (Pacific Grove, Calif.: Brooks/Cole).

Ainsworth, M. D. S. (1967) *Infancy in Uganda: Infant Care and the Growth of Love* (Baltimore, Md: Johns Hopkins University Press).

Ainsworth, M. D. S. (1969) 'Object relations, dependency and attachment: a theoretical review of the infant–mother relationship', *Child Development*, **40**, 969–1025.

Ainsworth, M. D. S. (1989) 'Attachments beyond infancy', *American Psychologist*, **44**, 709–16.

Ainsworth, M. D. S. and Wittig, B. A. (1969) 'Attachment and exploratory behaviour of one-year-olds in a strange situation', in B. M. Foss (ed.), *Determinants of Infant Behaviour*, vol. 4 (London: Methuen).

Ainsworth, M. D. S., Bell, S. M. and Stayton, D. J. (1974) 'Infant–mother attachment and social development: "socialisation" as a product of reciprocal responsiveness to signals', in M. P. M. Richards (ed.), *The Integration of a Child into a Social World* (Cambridge: Cambridge University Press).

Ainsworth, M. D. S., Blehar, M. C., Waters, E. and Wall, S. (1978) *Patterns of Attachment: a Psychological Study of the Strange Situation* (Hillsdale, NJ: Erlbaum).

Amira, A. (1990) 'Family care in Greece', in A. Jamieson and R. Illsely (eds), *Contrasting European Policies for the Care of older People* (Aldershot: Avebury).

Anastasi, A. (1958) in R. M. Lerner (1986) *Concepts and Theories in Human Development* (2nd edn) (New York: Random House).

Antonucci, T. C. and Levitt, M. J. (1984) 'Early prediction of attachment security: a multivariate account', *Infant Behaviour and Development*, **7**, 1–18.

Archer, J. (1989) 'Childhood gender roles: structure and development', *The Psychologist: Bulletin of the British Psychological Society*, **9**, 367–70.

Archer, J. and Lloyd, B. (1985) *Sex and Gender* (Cambridge: Cambridge University Press).

Astington, J. W. (1994) *The Child's Discovery of the Mind* (London: Fontana).

Atchley, R. C. (1982) 'Retirement: Leaving the world of work', *Annals of the American Academy of Political and Social Science*, **464**, 120–31.

Atchley, R. C. (1991) *Social Forces and Aging: An Introduction to Social Gerontology* (6th edn) (Belmont, CA: Wadsworth).

Bahr, S. (1973) 'Effects of power and division of labor in the family', in L. Hoffman and G. Nye (eds), *Working Mothers* (San Francisco: Jossey-Bass).

Baltes, P. B., Reece, H. W. and Lippsitt, L. P. (1980) 'Life-span developmental psychology', *Annual Review of Psychology,* **31**, 65–110.

Bandura, A. (1965) 'Influence of model's reinforcement contingencies on the acquisition of imitative responses', *Journal of Personality and Social Psychology,* **1**, 589–95.

Bandura, A. (1977) *Social Learning Theory* (2nd edn) (Englewood Cliffs, NJ: Prentice-Hall).

Bandura, A. and MacDonald, F. J. (1963) 'Influence of social reinforcement and the behaviour of models in shaping children's moral judgements', *Journal of Abnormal and Social Psychology,* **67**, 274–81.

Bandura, A., Ross, D. and Ross, S. (1963) 'Imitation of film mediated aggressive models', *Journal of Abnormal and Social Psychology,* **66**, 3–11.

Bannister, D. and Agnew, J. (1977) 'The child's construing of self', in A. W. Landfield (ed.), *Nebraska Symposium on Motivation 1976* (University of Nebraska Press).

Baron-Cohen, S., Leslie, A. M. and Frith, U. (1985) 'Does the autistic child have a theory of mind?', *Cognition,* **21**, 37–46.

Baruch, G., Barnett, R. and Rivers, C. (1983) *Lifeprints* (New York: McGraw-Hill).

Bateson, P. P. G. (1964) 'Effect of similarity between rearing and testing conditions on chicks', following and avoidance responses', *Journal of Comparative and Physiological Psychology,* **57**, 100–3.

Bayley, N. (1969) *Bayley Scales of Infant Development* (New York: Psychological Corporation).

Bayley, N. (1970) 'Development of mental abilities', in Mussen P. H (ed.), *Carmichael's Manual of Child Psychology,* vol. 1 (3rd edn) (New York: Wiley), 163–209.

Bee, H. (1989) *The Developing Child* (6th edn) (New York: Harper & Row).

Bee, H. (1995) *The Developing Child* (NY : HarperCollins).

Belsky, J. and Rovine, M. (1987) 'Temperament and attachment security in the Strange Situation: a rapprochement', *Child Development,* **58**, 787–95.

Belsky, J. and Rovine, M. (1988) 'Nonmaternal care in the first year of life and the security of infant-parent attachment', *Child Development,* **58**, 787–95.

Belsky, J. and Steinberg, L. D. (1978) '*The effects of day care: a critical review',* Child Development, 49, 929–49.

Bem, S. (1974) 'The measurement of psychological andogyny', *Journal of Consulting and Clinical Psychology,* **42**, 155–62.

Bem, S. (1993) *The Lenses of Gender: Transforming the Debate on Sexual Inequality* (New Haven, Conn.: Yale University Press).

Bem, S. L. (1983) 'Gender schema theory and its implications for child development: raising gender aschematic children in a gender-schematic society', *Signs: Journal of Women in Culture and Society* 8, 598–616.

Benedek, T. (1959) 'Parenthood as a developmental phase', *American Psychoanalytic Association Journal,* 7, 389–417.

Bengston, V. L., Rosenthal, C. and Burton, L. (1990) 'Families and aging: diversity and heterogeneity', in R. H. Binstock and L. K. George (eds), *Aging and the Social Sciences* (3rd edn) (San Diego: Academic Press).

Bennett, N. and Dunne, E. (1989) 'Implementing cooperative groupwork in classrooms', paper presented at EARLI conference, Madrid.

Bergen, D. J. and Williams, J. E. (1991) 'Sex stereotypes in the USA revisited', *Sex Roles*, **24**, 413–23.

Berndt, T. J. (1982) 'The features and effects of friendships in early adolescence', *Child Development*, **53**, 1447–60.

Berndt, T. J. (1992) 'Friendship and friends', influence in adolescence', *Current Directions in Psychological Science*, **1**, 156–9.

Betancourt, H. and Lopez, S. R. (1993) 'The study of culture, ethnicity and race in American psychology', *American Psychologist*, **48**, 629–37.

Binet, A. and Simon, T. (1905) 'Methodes nouvelles pour le diagnostic du niveau intellectuel des anormaux', *L'Annee Psychologique*, **11**, 191–244.

Birch, A. and Hayward, S. (1994) *Individual Differences* (Basingstoke: Macmillan).

Block, J. (1971) *Lives Through Time* (Berkeley, California: Bancroft Books).

Block, J. (1981) 'Some enduring and consequential structures of personality', in Rabin, A. I., Aronoff, J., Barclay, A. M. and Zucker, R. A (eds), *Further Explorations in Personality* (New York: Wiley).

Bloom, K. (1979) 'Evaluation of infant vocal conditioning', *Journal of Experimental Child Psychology*, **27**, 60–70.

Bloom, L. (1970) *Language Development: Form and Function in Emerging Grammars* (Cambridge, Mass.: MIT Press).

Bodmer, W. F. (1972) 'Race and IQ: the genetic background', in K. Richardson and D. Spears (eds), *Race, Culture and Intelligence* (Harmondsworth: Penguin).

Bohannon, P. (1985a) *All the Happy Families: Exploring the Varieties of Family Life* (New York: McGraw-Hill).

Bohannon, P. (1985b) 'The six stations of divorce', in L. Cargan (ed.), *Marriage and Family: Coping with Change* (Belmont, CA: Wadsworth).

Booth, A. (1977) 'Wife's employment and husband stress: a replication and refutation', *Journal of Marriage and the Family*, **39**, 645–50.

Booth, T. (1975) *Growing Up in Society* (London: Methuen).

Bornstein, M. H. and Lamb, M. E. (1988) *Developmental Psychology: an Advanced Textbook* (2nd edn) (Hillsdale, NJ: Erlbaum).

Bosse, R. (1991) 'How stressful is retirement? Findings from the Normative Aging Study', *Journal of Gerontology: Psychological Sciences*, **46** (1), P9–P14.

Bouchard, T. J. and McGue, M. (1981) 'Familial studies of intelligence: a review', *Science*, **22**, 1055–9.

Boucher, J. (1989) 'The theory of mind hypothesis of autism: explanation, evidence and assessment', *British Journal of Disorders of Communication*, **24**, 181–98.

Bower, T. G. R. (1981) 'Cognitive Development', in M. Roberts and J. Tamburrini (eds), *Child Development 0–5* (Edinburgh: Holmes McDougall).

Bowlby, J. (1944) 'Forty-four juvenile thieves: their characters and home life', *International Journal of Psycho-Analysis*, **25**, 19–52 and 107–27.

Bowlby, J. (1951) *Maternal Care and Mental Health* (Geneva: World Health Organisation).

Bowlby, J. (1953) *Child Care and the Growth of Love* (Harmondsworth: Penguin).

Bowlby, J. (1969) *Attachment and Loss, vol. 1: Attachment* (London: Hogarth).

Bowlby, J. (1973) *Attachment and Loss, vol. 2: Separation* (London: Hogarth).

Bowlby, J. (1980) *Attachment and Loss, vol. 3: Loss, Sadness and Depression* (Harmondsworth: Penguin).

Bowlby, J. (1988) *A Secure Base: Parent–Child Attachment and Healthy Human Development* (New York: Basic Books).

Brake, M. (1985) *Comparative Youth Subcultures* (London: Routledge & Kegan Paul).

Bremner, J. G. (1988) *Infancy* (Oxford: Blackwell).

Bremner, J. G. (1994) *Infancy* (2nd edn) (Oxford: Blackwell).

Bretherton, I. (1992) 'The origins of attachment theory: John Bowlby and Mary Ainsworth', *Developmental Psychology*, **28**, 759–75.

British Psychological Society (1990) *Ethical Principles for Conducting Research with Human Participants* (Leicester: British Psychological Society).

Brodzinsky, D., Gormly, A. and Amron, S. (1986) *Lifespan Human Development* (3rd edn) (New York: HRW International Editions).

Bromley, D. B. (1988) *Human Ageing* (3rd edn) (Harmondsworth: Penguin).

Bronfenbrenner, U. (1979) *The Ecology of Human Development* (Cambridge, Mass.: Harvard University Press).

Brown, A. L. and Palenscar, A. S. (1989) 'Guided, cooperative learning and individual knowledge acquisition', in L. B. Resnick (ed.), *Knowing, Learning and Instruction* (Hillsdale, NJ: Erlbaum).

Brown, G. W., Harris, T. O. and Peto, J. (1973) 'Life events and psychiatric disorders, Part 2: Nature of causal link', *Psychological Medicine*.

Brown, R. and Bellugi, U. (1964) 'Three processes in the child's acquisition of syntax', in E. H. Lenneberg (ed.), *New Directions in the Study of Language* (Cambridge, Mass.: MIT Press).

Browne, K. (1989) 'The naturalistic context of family violence and child abuse', in J. Archer and K. Browne (eds), *Human Aggression: Naturalistic Approaches* (London: Routledge).

Brownmiller, S. (1984) *Femininity* (New York: Linden Press).

Bruner, J. S. (1964) 'The course of cognitive growth', *American Psychoanalytic Association Journal*, **19**, 1–15.

Bruner, J. S. (1966) 'On cognitive growth', in J. S. Bruner, R. R. Olver and P. M. Greenfield (eds), *Studies in Cognitive Growth* (New York: Wiley).

Bruner, J. S. (1983) *Child's Talk* (New York: Norton).

Bruner, J. S. (1986) *Actual Minds: Possible Worlds* (Cambridge, Mass.: Harvard University Press).

Bruner, J. S. and Kenney, H. (1966) *The Development of the Concepts of Order and Proportion in Children* (New York: Wiley).

Bruner, J. S., Jolly, A. and Sylva, K. (1976) *Play: Its Role in Development and Evolution* (Harmondsworth: Penguin).

Bryant, B., Harris, M. and Newton, D. (1980) *Children and Minders* (London: Grant McIntyre).

Bryant, P. (1974) *Perception and Understanding in Young Children* (London: Methuen).

Bryant, P. (1982) 'Piaget: issues and experiments', *British Journal of Psychology*, Special Issue vol. 73.

Burks, B. S. (1928) 'The relative influence of nature and nurture upon mental development: A comparative study of foster parent–foster child resemblance and true parent-true child resemblance', *Yearbook of the National Society for the Study of Education*, **27**, 219–316.

Burt, C. (1955) 'The evidence for the concept of intelligence', *British Journal of Educational Psychology*, **25**, 158–77.

Burt, C. (1958) 'The inheritance of mental ability', *American Psychologist*, **13**, 1–15.

Burt, C. (1966) 'The genetic determination of intelligence: a study of monozygotic twins reared together and apart', *British Journal of Psychology*, **57**, 137–53.

Bussey, K. and Bandura, A. (1984) 'Influence of gender constancy and social power on sex-linked modelling', *Journal of Personality and Social Psychology*, **47**, 1292–302.

Bussey, K. and Bandura, A. (1992) 'Self-regulatory mechanisms governing gender-development', *Child Development*, 63, 1236–50.

Butterworth, G. (1987) 'Some benefits of egocentrism', in J. S. Bruner and H. Haste (eds), *Making Sense* (London: Methuen).

Calvert, S. L. and Huston, A. C. (1987) 'Television and gender schemata', in L. S. Liben and M. L. Signorella (eds), *Children's Gender Schemata* (San Francisco: Jossey-Bass).

Campos, J. J., Barrett, K. C., Lambe, M. E., Goldsmith, H. H. and Sternberg, C. (1983) 'Socioemotional Development', in M. M. Haith and J. J. Campos (eds), *Handbook of Child Psychology, Vol. 2: Infancy and Developmental Psychobiology* (New York: Wiley).

Carlson, V., Cicchetti, D., Barnett, D. and Braunwald, K. (1989) 'Disorganized/disoriented attachment relationships in maltreated infants', *Developmental Psychology*, **25**, 525–31.

Carver, R. P. (1990) 'Intelligence and reading ability in grades 2–12', *Intelligence*, **14**, 449–55.

Case, R. (1978) 'Intellectual development from birth to adulthood: a neo-Piagetian interpretation', in R. Siegler (ed.), *Children's Thinking: What Develops?* (Hillsdale, NJ: Erlbaum).

Case, R. (1985) *Intellectual Development: Birth to Adulthood* (New York: Academic Press).

Cavanagh, R. E. (1974) *Facing Death* (Baltimore: Penguin).

Cazden, C. (1965) 'Environmental assistance to the child's acquisition of grammar', unpublished doctoral dissertation, Harvard University.

Chomsky, N. (1968) *Language and Mind* (New York: Harcourt Brace).

Christie, J. F (1986) 'Training of symbolic play', in P. K. Smith (ed.), *Children's Play: Research, Development and Practical Applications* (London: Gordon & Breach).

Clark, A. M. and Clark, D. B. (1976) *Early Experience: Myth and Evidence* (London: Open Books).

Clarke-Stewart, A. (1989) 'Infant day care. Maligned or malignant?', *American Psychologist*, **44**, 266–73.

Clausen, J. A. (1975) 'The social meaning of differential physical; and sexual maturation', in S. E. Dragastin and G. H. Elder, Jr (eds), *Adolescence in the Life Cycle* (New York: Halsted).

Clayton, P. J., Halikes, H. A. and Maurice, W. L. (1971) 'Bereavement of the widowed', *Diseases of the Nervous System*, **32**, 594–604.

Clayton, V. and Birren, J. E. (1980) 'Age and wisdom across the lifespan: theoretical perspectives', in P. B. Baltes and O. G. Brim, Jr (eds), *Lifespan Development and Behaviour*, Vol. 1 (New York: Academic Press).

Cohen, D. (1987) *The Development of Play* (London: Croom Helm).

Cohen, L. J. and Campos, J. J. (1974) 'Father, mother and stranger as elicitors of attachment behaviour in infancy', *Developmental Psychology*, **10**, 146–54.

Coleman, J. C. (1995) 'Adolescence', in P. E. Bryant and A. M. Colman (eds), *Developmental Psychology* (London: Longman).

Coleman, J. C. and Hendry, B. (1990) *The Nature of Adolescence* (2nd edn) (London and New York: Routledge).

Coleman, J. C. with the assistance of J. W. C. Johnston and K. Johanasson (1961) *The Adolescent Society: The Social Life of the Teenager and its Impact on Education* (New York: Free Press).

Colombo, J. (1993) *Infant Cognition: Predicting Later Intellectual Functioning* (Newbury Park, CA: Sage).

Conger, J. J. (1977) *Adolescence and Youth* (New York: Harper & Row).

Conger, J. J. and Miller, W. C. (1966) *Personality, Social Class and Delinquency* (New York: Wiley).

Conger, J. J. and Petersen, A. (1984) *Adolescence and Youth: Psychological Development in a Changing World* (3rd edn) (New York: Harper & Row).

Connolly, J. A. and Doyle, A. B. (1984) 'Relation of social fantasy play to social competence in preschoolers', *Developmental Psychology*, **20**, 797–806.

Cooley, C. H. (1902) *Human Nature and the Social Order* (New York: Scribner).

Coopersmith, S. (1968) 'Studies in self-esteem', *Scientific American*, February.

Cowie, H. and Ruddock, J. (1988) *Learning Together, Working Together* (London: BP Publications).

Cowie, H. and Ruddock, J. (1990) 'Learning from one another: the challenge', in H. C. Foot, J. Morgan and R. H. Shute (eds), *Children Helping Children* (Chichester: Wiley).

Cowie, H. and Ruddock, J. (1991) *Cooperative Group Work in the Multi-ethnic Classroom* (London: BP Publications).

Cox, M. J., Owen, M. T., Lewis, J. M. and Henderson, K. V. (1989) 'Marriage, adult adjustment and early parenting', *Child Development*, **60**, 1015–24.

Crockett, L. J. and Petersen, A. C. (1987) 'Pubertal status and psychosocial development: Findings from the early adolescent study', in R. M. Lerner and T. T. Foch (eds), *Biological and Psychosocial Interactions in Early Adolescence: A Life-span Perspective* (Hillsdale, NJ: Erlbaum).

Crosby, J. F. and Jose, N. L., 'Death: Family adjustment to loss', in C. R. Figley and H. I. McCubbin (eds), *Stress and the Family* (New York: Brunner/Mazel).

Cumming, E. and Henry, W. (1961) *Growing Old: A Process of Disengagement* (New York: Basic Books).

Darlington, R. B. (1986) 'Long-term effects of preschool programs', in U. Neisser (ed.), *The School Achievement of Minority Children* (Hillsdale, NJ: Erlbaum).

Davidson, J. E. and Sternberg, R. J. (1984) 'The role of insight in intellectual giftedness', *Gifted Children Quarterly*, **28**, 58–64.

Davis, D. M. (1990) 'Portrayals of women in primetime network television: some demographic characteristics', *Sex Roles*, **23**, 325–32.

Davis, K. (1947) 'Final note on a case of extreme isolation', *American Journal of Sociology*, **52**, 432–7.

De Gelder, B. (1987) 'On not having a theory of mind', *Cognition*, **27**, 285–90.

De Villiers, P. A. and De Villiers, J. (1979) *Early Language* (London: Fontana).

DeLoache, J. S. and Brown, A. L. (1987) 'Differences in the memory-based seaching of delayed and normally developing young children', *Intelligence*, **11**, 277–89.

Dinnerstein, D. (1976) *The Mermaid and the Minotaur: Sexual Arrangements and Human Malaise* (New York: Harper & Row).

Dodd, B. (1972) 'Effects of social and vocal stimulation on infant babbling', *Developmental Psychology*, **7**, 80–3.

Dohrenwend, B., Krasnoff, L., Askenasy, A. and Dohrenwend, D. (1978) 'Exemplification of a method for scaling life events', *Journal of Health and Social Behaviour*, **19**, 205–29.

Donaldson, M. (1978) *Children's Minds* (London: Fontana).

Duberman, L. (1973) 'Step-kin relationships', *Journal of Marriage and the Family*, **35**, 283–92 .

Duck, J. M. (1990) 'Children's ideals: the role of real-life versus media figures', *Australian Journal of Psychology*, **42**, 19–29.

Dunn, J. (1984) *Sisters and Brothers* (London: Fontana).

Dunn, J. and Brown, J. (1994) 'Affect expression in the family, children's understanding of emotions and their interactions with others', *Merrill-Palmer Quarterly*, **40**, 120–37.

Dunn, J. and Kendrick, C. (1982) *Siblings: Love, Envy and Understanding* (Oxford: Basil Blackwell).

Dunphy, D. C. (1963) 'The social structure of urban adolescent peer groups', *Sociometry*, **26**, 230–46.

Durkin, K. (1995) *Developmental Social Psychology: From Infancy to Old Age* (Cambridge, Mass.: Blackwell).

Dusek, J. B. and Flaherty, J. F. (1981) 'The development of the self-concept during the adolescent years', *Monographs of the Society for Research in Child Development*, 46 (Serial No. 191).

Eagly, A. H. (1987) *Sex Differences in Social Behaviour: a Social-role Interpretation* (Hillsdale, NJ: Erlbaum).

Eagly, A. H. and Carli, L. L. (1981) 'Sex of researchers and sex-typed communication as determinants of sex differences in influenceability: a meta-analysis of social influence', *Psychological Bulletin*, **90**, 1–20.

Eames, D., Shorrocks, D. and Tomlinson, P. (1990) 'Naughty animals or naughty experimenters? Conservation accidents revisited with video-stimulated commentary', *British Journal of Developmental Psychology*, **8**, 25–37.

Eaton, W. O. and Enns, L. R. (1986) 'Sex differences in human motor activity level', *Psychological Bulletin*, **100**, 19–28.

Eccles-Parsons, J. (1983) 'Expectancies, values and academic behaviors', in J. T. Spence (ed.), *Achievement and Achievement Motives* (San Francisco: Freeman).

Edwards, C. P. (1986) 'Cross-cultural research on Kohlberg's stages: the basis for consensus', in D. Wagner and H. Stevenson (eds), *Cultural Perspectives in Child Development* (San Francisco: W. H. Freeman).

Eisenberg, N. (1986) *Altruistic Emotion, Cognition and Behaviour* (Hillsdale, NJ: Erlbaum).

Eisenberg, N., Shell, R., Pasternak, J., Lennon, R., Beller, R. and Mathy, R. M. (1987) 'Prosocial development in middle childhood: a longitudinal study', *Developmental Psychology*, **23**, 712–18.

Elder, G. H. Jr (1980) *Family Structure and Socialisation* (New York: Arno Press).

Elliott, C., Murray, D. J. and Pearson, L. S. (1983) *The British Ability Scales* (rev. edn) (Windsor: Nelson-NFER).

Emde, R. N. and Harmon, R. J. (1972) 'Endogenous and exogenous smiling systems in early infancy', *Journal of the American Academy of Child Psychiatry*, **11**, 177–200.

Entine, A. D. (1976) 'Midlife counselling: prognosis and potential', *Personnel and Guidance Journal*, **55** (3), 112–14.

Erikson, E. H. (1963) *Childhood and Society* (New York: Norton).

Erikson, E. H. (1968) *Identity: Youth and Crisis* (New York: Norton).

Erikson, E. H. (1970) 'Reflections on the dissent of contemporary youth', *International Journal of Psychoanalysis*, **51**, 11–22.

Erwin, P. (1993) *Friendship and Peer Relations in Children* (Chichester: Wiley).

Estes, W. K. (1970) *Learning Theory and Mental Development* (New York: Academic Press).

Eysenck, H. and Wilson, G. D. (1973) *The Experimental Study of Freudian Theories* (London: Methuen).

Fagot, B. I. (1978) 'The influence of sex of child on parental reactions to toddler children', *Child Development*, **49**, 459–65.

Falbo, T. and Polit, D. F. (1986) 'Quantitative review of the only child literature: research evidence and theory development, *Psychological Bulletin*, **100**, 176–89.

Farrell, P. and Rosenberg, S. D. (1981) *Men at Midlife* (Boston: Auburn House).

Feeney, J. A., Noller, P. and Hanrahan, M. (1994) 'Assessing Adult Attachment', in M. B. Sperling and W. H. Brown (eds), *Attachment in*

Adults: Clinical and Developmental Perspectives (New York: Guildford Press).

Feldman, S. S. and Elliott, G. (1990) *At the Threshold: The Developing Adolescent* (London: Harvard University Press).

Ferris, C. and Branston, P. (1994) 'Quality of life in the elderly: a contribution to its understanding', *Australian Journal of Ageing*, **13**, 120–3.

Fisher, S. and Greenberg, R. (1977) *The Scientific Credibility of Freud's Theories and Therapy* (Brighton: Harvester Press).

Fogel, A. (1993) *Developing through Relationships: Origins of Communication, Self and Culture* (New York: Harvester Wheatsheaf).

Fonagy, P. (1981) 'Experimental research in psychoanalytic theory', in F. Fransella (ed.), *Personality* (London: Methuen).

Fonagy, P. and Higgitt, A. (1984) *Personality Theory and Clinical Practice* (London: Methuen).

Fontana, D. (1988) *Psychology for Teachers* (2nd edn) (Leicester/Basingstoke: British Psychological Society/Macmillan).

Foot, H. C., Morgan, M. J. and Shute, R. H. (1990) *Children Helping Children* (Chichester: John Wiley).

Fox, N. (1977) 'Attachment of Kibbutz infants to mother and metapalet', *Child Development*, **48**, 1228–39.

Frankenhauser, M., Lundberg, U. and Chesney, M. (1991) *Women, Work and Health: Stress and Opportunities* (New York: Plenum).

Franz, C. E., McClelland, D. C. and Weinberger, T. (1991) 'Childhood antecedents of conventional social accomplishment in midlife adults: a 36 year prospective study', *Journal of Personality and Social Psychology*, **60**, 586–95.

Fraser, C. (1981) 'The Social Psychology of Unemployment', in M. Jeeves (ed.), *Psychology Survey No. 3* (London: Allen and Unwin).

Fraser, E. D. (1959) *Home Environment and the School* (London: University of London Press).

Freeman, D. (1983) *Margaret Mead and Samoa: the Making and Unmaking of an Anthropological Myth* (Cambridge, Mass.: Harvard University Press).

Freud, A. . (1936) *The Ego and the Mechanisms of Defence* (London: Chatto and Windus).

Freud, A. (1958) 'Adolescence', in R. S. Eisler, A. Freud, H. Hartman and M. Kris (eds), *Psychoanalytic Study of the Child*, Vol. 13 (New York: International Universities Press).

Freud, A. and Dann, S. (1951) 'An experiment in group upbringing', *The Psychoanalytic Study of the Child*, Vol. VI.

Freud, S. (1923) 'The ego and the id', in *Standard Edition of the Complete Psychological Works of Sigmund Freud* 19 (London: Hogarth Press).

Frey, K. S. and Ruble, D. N. (1987) 'What children say about classroom performance: sex and grade differences in perceived competence', *Child Development*, **58**, 1066–78.

Frey, K. S. and Ruble, D. N. (1992) 'Gender constancy and the "cost" of sex-typed behaviour: A test of the conflict hypothesis', *Developmental Psychology*, **28**, 714–21.

Frith, U. (1989) *Autism: Explaining the Enigma* (Oxford: Basil Blackwell).
Fry, C. (1985) 'Culture, behaving and aging in a comparative perspective', in J. E. Birren and K. W. Schaie (eds), *Handbook of the Psychology of Aging* (2nd edn) (New York: Van Nostrand).
Furnham, A. and Bitar, N. (1993) 'The stereotyped portrayal of men and women in British television advertisements', *Sex Roles*, **29**, 297–310.
Gallie, D. and Vogler, C. (1994) 'Labour Market Deprivation, Welfare and Collectivism', in D. Gallie, C. Marsh and C. Vogler (1994) (eds), *Social Change and the Experience of Unemployment* (Oxford: Oxford University Press).
Gallie, D., Marsh, C. and Vogler, C. (eds) (1994) *Social Change and the Experience of Unemployment* (Oxford: Oxford University Press).
Galton, F (1869) *Heredity Genius: An Inquiry into its Laws and Consequences*, 2nd edn, reprinted 1978 (London: Julian Friedmann).
Gardner, A. R. and Gardner, B. (1969) 'Teaching sign language to a chimpanzee', *Science*, **165**, 664–72.
Gardner, H. (1982) *Developmental Psychology* (Boston: Little, Brown & Co.).
Gardner, H. (1983) *Frames of Mind: The Theory of Multiple Intelligences* (London: Heinemann).
Gardner, H. and Feldman, D. (1985) 'Project Spectrum', Annual Report submitted to the Spencer Foundation. Unpublished.
Garvey, C. (1977) *Play* (London: Fontana/Open Books).
Garvey, C. (1991) *Play* (2nd edn) (London: Fontana/Open Books).
Gelman, R. and Shatz, M. (1977) 'Appropriate speech adjustments: the operation of conversational constraints on talk to two-year olds', in M. Lewis and L. A. Rosenblum (eds), *Interaction, Conversation and the Development of Language* (New York: Wiley).
Gershuny, J. (1994) 'The Psychological Consequences of Unemployment: an Assessment of the Jahoda Thesis', in Gallie, D., Marsh, C. and Vogler, C. (1994) *Social Change and the Experience of Unemployment* (Oxford: Oxford University Press).
Gilligan, C. (1977) 'In a different voice: women's conception of the self and of morality', *Harvard Educational Review*, **47**, 481–517.
Gilligan, C. (1982) *In a Different Voice: Psychological Theory and Women's Development* (Cambridge, Mass.: Harvard University Press).
Ginsburg, H. (1972) *The Myth of the Deprived Child: Poor Children's Intellect and Education* (Englewood Cliffs, NJ: Prentice-Hall).
Glassman, W. E. (1995) *Approaches to Psychology* (Buckingham, Phil.: Open University Press).
Goldfarb, W. (1943) 'The effects of early institutional care on adolescent personality', *Journal of Experimental Education*, **12**, 106–29.
Goldman, R. J. and Goldman, J. D. G. (1981) 'How children view old people and ageing: a developmental study of children in four countries', *Australian Journal of Psychology*, **3**, 405–18.
Goldman-Eisler, F. (1948) 'Breast feeding and character formation', *Journal of Personality*, **17**, 83–103.
Gopnik, A. and Astington, J. W. (1991) 'Theoretical explanations of children's understanding of the mind', *British Journal of Developmental Psychology*, **9**, 77–31.

Gopnik, A. and Astington, J. W. (1988) 'Children's understanding of representational change and its relation to the understanding of false belief and the appearance–reality distinction', *Child Development*, **59**, 26–37.

Gould, S. J. (1981) *The Mismeasure of Man* (London: Penguin).

Grossman, K. E., Grossman, K., Huber, F. and Wartner, U. (1981) 'German children's behaviour towards their mothers at 12 months and their fathers at 18 months in Ainsworth's "strange situation"', *International Journal of Behavioural Development*, **4**, 157–81.

Haan, N., Millsap, R. and Hartka, E. (1986) 'As time goes by: Change and stability in personality over 50 years', *Psychology and Aging*, **1**, 220–32.

Hale, S., Fry, A. F. and Jessie, K. A. (1993) 'Effects of practice on speed of information processing in children and adults: Age sensitivity and age invariance', *Developmental Psychology*, **29**, 880–92.

Harlow, H. (1958) 'The nature of love', *American Psychologist*, **13**, 637–85.

Harlow, H. and Harlow, M. (1969) 'Effects of various mother-infant relationships on rhesus monkey behaviours', in B. M. Foss (ed.), *Determinants of Infant Behaviour*, vol. 4 (London: Methuen).

Harris, P. L., Johnson, C. N., Hutton, D., Andrews, G. and Cooke T. (1989) 'Young children's theory of mind and emotion', *Cognition and Emotion*, **3**, 379–400.

Harter, S. (1982) *The Perceived Competence Scale for Children* (Denver, Col.: University of Denver).

Harter, S. (1987) 'The determinants and mediational role of global self-worth in children', in N. Eisenberg (ed.), *Contemporary Topics in Developmental Psychology* (New York: Wiley).

Hartup, W. W. (1983) 'Peer relations', in E. M. Hetherington (ed.), *Handbook of Child Psychology, Vol IV: Socialisation, Personality and Social Development* (New York: Wiley).

Harwood, R. L. and Miller, J. G. (1991) 'Perceptions of attachment behavior: a comparison of Anglo and Puerto Rican mothers', *Merrill-Palmer Quarterly*, **37**, 583–99.

Hebb, D. O. (1949) *The Organization of Behaviour* (New York: Wiley).

Heinicke, C. H. and Guthrie, D. (1992) 'Stability and change in husband–wife adaptation and the development of the positive parent–child relationship', *Infant Behaviour and Development*, **15**, 109–27.

Herman, R. (1984) 'The genetic relationship between identical twins', *Early Child Development*, **16**, 265–75.

Herriot, P. (1970) *An Introduction to the Psychology of Language* (London: Methuen).

Hill, A. B. (1976) 'Methodological problems in the use of factor analysis: a critical review of the experimental evidence for the anal character', *British Journal of Medical Psychology*, **49**, 145–59.

Hill, P. (1993) 'Recent advances in selected areas of adolescent development', *Journal of Child Psychology and Psychiatry*, **34**, 69–90.

Hines, M. (1982) 'Prenatal gonadol hormones and sex differences in human behaviour', *Psychological Bulletin*, **92**, 56–80.

Hobson, R. P. (1990) 'On acquiring knowledge about people and the capacity to pretend: response to Leslie (1987)', *Psychological Review*, **97**, 114–21.

Hodges, J. and Tizard, B. (1989) 'IQ and behavioural adjustment of ex-institutional adolescents; and social and family relationships of ex-institutional adolescents', *Journal of Child Psychology and Psychiatry*, **30**, 53–75; 77–98.

Hoffman, M. L. (1978) 'Empathy, its development and prosocial implications', in C. B. Keasey (ed.), *Nebraska Symposium on Motivation*, Vol. 25 (Lincoln: University of Nebraska Press).

Hoffman, M. L. (1979) 'Identification and imitation in children', *ERIC Reports*, ED 175 537.

Hoffman, M. L. (1984) 'Moral Development', in M. H. Bornstein and M. H. Lamb (eds), *Developmental Psychology: An Advanced Textbook* (Hillsdale, NJ: Erlbaum).

Holmes, D. S. (1974) 'Investigations of repression: differential recall of material experimentally or naturally associated with ego threat', *Psychological Bulletin*, **81**, 632–53.

Holmes, T. H. and Rahe, R. H. (1967) 'The Social Readjustment Rating Scale', *Journal of Psychosomatic Research*, **11**, 213–18.

Holstein, C. B. (1976) 'Irreversible, stepwise sequence in the development of moral judgment: a longitudinal study of males and females', *Child Development*, **47**, 51–61.

Honzik, M. P. (1986) 'The role of the family in the development of mental abilities: a 50-year study', in N. Datan, A. L. Greene and H. W. Reese (eds), *Life-span Developmental Psychology: Intergenerational Relations* (Hillsdale, NJ: Erlbaum).

Horn, J. L. and Donaldson, G. (1980) 'Cognitive development in adulthood', in O. G. Brim, Jr and J. Kagan (eds), *Constancy and Change in Human Development* (Cambridge, Mass.: Harvard University Press).

Horn, J. M., Loehlin, J. L. and Willerman, L. (1979) 'Intellectual resemblance among adoptive and biological relatives: the Texas adoption project', *Behaviour Genetics*, **9**, 177–207.

Horowitz, F. D. (1987) *Exploring Developmental Theories: Toward a Structural/Behavioural Model of Development* (Hillsdale, NJ: Erlbaum).

Horowitz, F. D. (1990) 'Developmental models of individual differences', in J. Colombo and J. Fagen (eds), *Individual Differences in Infancy: Reliability, Stability, Prediction*, pp. 3–18 (Hillsdale, NJ: Erlbaum).

Howarth, E. (1982) 'Factor analytical examination of Kline's scales for psychoanalytic concepts', *Personality and Individual Differences*, **3**, 89–92.

Hughes, M. (1975) *Egocentrism in pre-school children* Edinburgh University: unpublished doctoral dissertation.

Huston, A. C. (1983) 'Sex-typing', in E. M. Hetherington (ed.), 'Social Development', in P. H. Mussen (general editor) *Carmichael's Manual of Child Psychology* (4th edn) (New York: Wiley).

Huston, A. C. (1985) 'The development of sex-typing: themes from recent research', *Developmental Review*, **5**, 1–17.

Hutt, C. (1966) 'Exploration and play in children', *Symposia of the Zoological Society of London*, **18**, 61–81.

Hutt, C. and Bhavnani, R. (1972) 'Predictions from play', *Nature*, **237**, 171–2.

Irvine, S. H. (1966) 'Towards a rationale for testing attainments and abilities in Africa', *British Journal of Educational Psychology*, **36**, 24–32.

Jackson, B. and Jackson, S. (1979) *Childminder: A Study in Action Research* (London: Routledge & Kegan Paul).

Jackson, L. A. (1992) *Physical Appearance and Gender: Sociobiological and Sociocultural Perspectives* (Albany, NY: State University of New York Press).

Jahoda, G. (1983) 'European "lag" in the development of an economic concept: a study in Zimbabwe', *British Journal of Developmental Psychology*, **1**, 113–20.

Jahoda, M. (1982) *Employment and Unemployment: A Social-Psychological Analysis* (Cambridge: Cambridge University Press).

Jamieson, A. (1990) 'Informal care in Europe', in A. Jamieson and R. Illsley (eds), *Contrasting European Policies for the Care of Older People* (Aldershsot: Avebury).

Jarvis, P. A. and Creasey, G. L. (1991) 'Parental stress, coping and attachment in families with an 18-month-old infant', *Infant Behaviour and Development*, **14**, 383–95.

Jensen, A. R. (1969) 'How much can we boost IQ and scholastic achievement?', *Harvard Educational Review*, **39**, 1–123.

Johnson, J. and Ettema, J. S. (1982) *Positive Images: Breaking Stereotypes with Children's Television* (Beverly Hills and London: Sage).

Johnson, J. E., Erschler, J. and Lawton, J. T. (1982) 'Intellective correlates of preschoolers' spontaneous play', *Journal of Genetic Psychology*, **106**, 115–22.

Kagan, J. (1989) *Unstable Ideas: Temperament, Cognition and Self* (Cambridge, Mass.: Harvard University Press).

Kahn, S., Zimmerman, G. Csikszentmihaly, M. and Getzels, J. W. (1985) 'Relations between identity in young adulthood and intimacy at midlife', *Journal of Personality and Social Psychology*, **49**, 1316–22.

Kail, R. and Park, Y. (1992) 'Global developmental change in processing time', *Merrill-Palmer Quarterly*, **38**, 525–41.

Kamin, L. J. (1977) *The Science and Politics of IQ* (Potomac, MD: Erlbaum).

Kavanagh, R. E. (1974) *Facing Death* (Baltimore: Penguin).

Kaye, K (1984) *The Mental and Social Life of Babies* (London: Methuen).

Kaye, K. and Marcus, J. (1981) 'Infant imitation: the sensorimotor agenda', *Developmental Psychology*, **17**, 258–65.

Keating, D. P. (1980) 'Thinking processes in adolescence', in J. Adelson (ed.), *Handbook of Adolescent Psychology* (New York: Wiley).

Keith, J. (1990) 'Age in social and cultural context: anthropological perspectives', in R. H. Binstock and L. K. George (eds), *Aging and the Social Sciences* (3rd edn) (San Diego: Academic Press).

Kelly, J. B. (1982) 'Divorce: the adult perspective', in B. Wolman (ed.), *Handbook of Developmental Psychology* (Englewood Cliffs, NJ: Prentice-Hall).

Kelvin, P. and Jarrett, J. E. (1985) *Unemployment: Its Social Psychological Effects* (Cambridge: Cambridge University Press).

Kiminyo, D. M. (1977) 'A cross-cultural study of the development of mass, weight, and volume among Kamba children', in P. R. Dasen (ed.), *Piagetian Psychology* (New York: Gardner Press).

Kline, P. (1972) *Fact and Fantasy in Freudian Theory* (London: Methuen).

Kline, P. (1981) *Fact and Fantasy in Freudian Theory* (2nd edn) (London: Methuen).

Kline, P. (1984) *Psychology and Freudian Theory: An Introduction* (London: Methuen).

Kline, P. and Storey, R. (1977) 'A factor analytical study of the oral character', *British Journal of Social and Clinical Psychology*, **16**, 317–28.

Klinnert, M. D. (1984) 'The regulation of infant behaviour by maternal facial expression', *Infant Behaviour and Development*, **7**, 447–65.

Kohlberg, L. (1966) 'A cognitive-developmental analysis of children's sex-role concepts and attitudes', in E. E. Maccoby (ed.) *The Development of Sex Differences* (California: Stanford University Press).

Kohlberg, L. (1969) 'The cognitive-developmental approach', in D. A. Goslin (ed.), *Handbook of Socialisation Theory and Research* (Chicago: Rand McNally).

Kohlberg, L. (1976) 'Moral stages and moralisation', in T. Linkons (ed.), *Moral Development and Behaviour* (New York: Holt, Rinehart and Winston CBS College Publishing).

Kotelchuk, M. (1976) 'The infant's relationship to the father: experimental evidence', in M. E. Lamb (ed.), *The Role of the Father in Child Development* (New York: Wiley).

Kübler-Ross, E. (1969) *On Death and Dying* (New York: Macmillan).

Kuhn, H. H. (1960) 'Self attitudes by age, sex and professional training', *Social Quarterly*, **11**, 39–55.

Kutnik, P. (1986) 'The relationship of moral judgement and moral action: Kohlberg's theory, criticism and revision', in S. Modgil and C. Modgil (eds), *Lawrence Kohlberg: Consensus and Controversy* (Philadelphia: Falmer Press).

Lamb, M. E. (1977) 'The development of mother-infant and father-infant attachments in the second year of life, *Developmental Psychology*, **13**, 637–48.

Lamb, M. E. (1987) 'Introduction: the emergent American father', in M. E. Lamb (ed.), *The Father's Role: Cross-Cultural Perspectives* (Hillsdale, NJ: Erlbaum).

Lamb, M. E. and Sutton-Smith, B. (1982) *Sibling Relationships: Their Nature and Significance across the Lifespan* (Hillsdale, NJ: Erlbaum).

Lamb, M. E., Thompson, R. A., Gardner, W. P., Charnov, E. L. and Estes, D. (1984) 'Security of infantile attachment as assessed in the "strange situation": its study and biological interpretation, *Behavioural and Brain Sciences*, **7**, 127–71.

Langer, J. (1975) 'Interactional aspects of cognitive organisation', *Cognition*, **3**, 9–28.

Langlois, J. H. and Downs, A. C. (1980) 'Mothers, fathers and peers as socialisation agents of sex-typed play behaviours in young children', *Child Development*, **51**, 1237–47.

Lazare, A., Klerman, G. I. and Armor, D. J. (1966) 'Oral, obsessive and hysterical personality patterns: an investigation of psychoanalytic concepts by means of factor analysis', *Archives of General Psychiatry*, **14**, 624–30.

Lazarus, R. S. (1966) *Psychological Stress and the Coping Process* (New York: McGraw-Hill).

Leahy, A. M. (1935) 'Nature-nurture and intelligence', *Genetic Psychology Monograph*, **17**, 235–308.

Lee, V. E., Brooks-Gunn, J. and Schnur, E. (1988) 'Does Head Start work? A 1-year follow-up comparison of disadvantaged children attending Head Start, no preschool, and other preschool programmes', *Developmental Psychology*, **24**, 210–22.

Lenneberg, E. H. (1967) *Biological Foundations of Language* (New York: Wiley).

Leslie, A. M. (1987) 'Pretense and representation: the origins of "theory of mind"', *Psychological Review*, **94**, 412–26.

Leslie, A. M. and Frith, U. (1987) 'Metarepresentation and autism: how not to lose one's marbles', *Cognition*, **27**, 291–4.

Levinger, G. and Clark, J. (1961) 'Emotional factors in the forgetting of word associations', *Journal of Abnormal and Social Psychology*, **62**, 99–105.

Levinson, D. J. (1978) *The Seasons of a Man's Life* (New York: Ballantyne).

Levinson, D. J. (1986) 'A conception of adult development', *American Psychologist*, **41**, 3–13.

Levitt, M. J. (1991) 'Attachment and close relationships: a lifespan perspective', in J. L. Gewirtz and W. M. Kurtines (eds), *Intersections with Attachment* (Hillsdale, NJ: Erlbaum).

Levy, D. J. (1989) 'Relations among aspects of children's environments, gender schematisation, gender role knowledge and flexibility', *Sex Roles*, **21**, 803–24.

Lewis, C. and Osborne, A. (1990) 'Three-year-olds problems with false belief: conceptual deficit or linguistic artefact?', *Child Development*, **61**, 1514–19.

Lewis, C. C. (1981) 'How adolescents approach decisions: Changes over grades seven to twelve and policy implications', *Child Development*, **52**, 538–44.

Lewis, M. (1990) 'Social knowledge and social development', *Merrill-Palmer Quarterly*, **36**, 93–116 .

Lewis, M. and Brooks-Gunn, J. (1979) *Social Cognition and the Acquisition of Self* (New York: Plenum Press).

Lewis, M. and Brooks-Gunn, J. (1975) 'Infants' reaction to people', in M. Lewis and L. Rosenblum (eds), *The Origins of Fear* (New York: Wiley).

Lewis, M., Feiring, C. McGuffoy, C. and Jaskir, J. (1984) 'Predicting psychopathology in six-year-olds from early social relations', *Child Development*, **55**, 123–36.

Lewis, S. N. C. and Cooper, C. L. (1988) 'The transition to parenthood in dual-earner couples', *Psychological Medicine*, **18**, 477–86.

Liben, L. S. and Signorella, M. L. (1993) 'Gender schematic processing in children: the role of initial interpretation of stimuli', *Developmental Psychology*, **29**, 141–9.

Lloyd, B. and Duveen, G. (1993) 'The development of social representations', in C. Pratt and A. F. Garton (eds), *Systems of Representation in Children: Development and Use* (Chichester: Wiley).

Lock, A. (1980) *The Guided Reinvention of Language* (London: Academic Press).

Long, J. and Porter, K. L. (1984) 'Multiple roles of midlife women: a case for new direction in theory, research and policy', in G. Baruch and J. Brooks-Gunn (eds), *Women in Midlife* (New York: Plenum Press).

Lore, R. K. and Schultz, L. A. (1993) 'Control of human aggression: A comparative perspective', *American Psychologist*, **48**, 16–25.

Lorenz, K. Z. (1935) 'The companion in the bird's world', *Auk*, **54**, 245–73.

Lowenthal, M. F, Thurber, M. and Chiriboga, D. (1975) *Four Stages of Life: A Comparative Study of Women and Men Facing Transitions* (San Francisco: Jossey-Bass).

Lyons, N. P. (1983) 'Two perspectives: On self, relationships and morality', *Harvard Educational Review*, **53**, 125–157.

Maccoby, E. E. and Jacklin, C. N. (1974) *The Psychology of Sex Differences* (Stanford, Calif.: Stanford University Press).

Mackenzie, B. (1984) 'Explaining the race difference in IQ: the logic, the methodology and the evaluation', *Journal of American Psychologist*, **39**, 1214–33.

Maddox, G. L. (1964) 'Disengagement theory: a critical evaluation', *The Gerontologist*, **4**, 80–3.

Maddox, G. L. (1968) 'Retirement as a social event in the United States', in B. L. Neugarten (ed.), *Middle Age and Aging* (Chicago: University of Chicago Press).

Main, M (ed.) (in press) *A Typology of Human Attachment Organisation Assessed in Discourse, Drawings and Interviews* (Cambridge: Cambridge University Press).

Main, M. and Cassidy, J. (1988) 'Categories of response to reunion with the parent at age 6: predictable from attachment classifications and stable over a 1-month period', *Developmental Psychology*, **24**, 415–26.

Main, M. and Solomon, J. (1986) 'Discovery of a disorganised disoriented attachment pattern', in T. B. Brazelton and M. W. Yogman (eds), *Affective Development in Infancy* (Norwood, NJ: Ablex).

Main, M. and Weston, D. R. 'Avoidance of the attachment figure in infancy: descriptions and interpretations', in C. M. Parkes and J. Stevenson-Hinde (eds), *The Place of Attachment in Human Behaviour* (London: Tavistock).

Main, M., Kaplan, K. and Cassidy, J. (1985) 'Security in infancy, childhood and adulthood: a move to the level of representation', in I. Bretherton and E. Waters (eds), *Growing Points of Attachment Theory and Research*, Monographs of the Society for Research in Child Development, **50** (1–2), no. 209.

Malim, T. and Birch, A. (1997) *Research Methods and Statistics* (Basingstoke: Macmillan).

Malim, T., Birch, A. and Hayward, S. (1996) *Comparative Psychology: Human and Animal Behaviour: A Sociobiological Approach* (Basingstoke: Macmillan).

Marcia, J. (1966) 'Development and validation of ego-identity status', *Journal of Personality and Social Psychology*, **3**, 551–8.

Marcia, J. (1980) 'Identity in adolescence', in J. Adelson (ed.), *Handbook of Adolescent Psychology* (New York: Wiley).

Markman, E. M., Cox, B. and Machida, S. (1981) 'The standard object sorting task as a measure of conceptual organisation', *Developmental Psychology*, **17**, 115–17.

Marquis, D. P. (1931) 'Can conditioned responses be established in the newborn infant?', *Journal of Genetic Psychology*, **39**, 479–92.

Marsden, D. (1975) *Workless* (2nd edn 1982) (London: Croom Helm).

Marsh, H. W., Craven, R. G. and Debus, R. (1991) 'Self-concepts of young children 5 to 8 years of age: measurement and multidimensional structure', *Journal of Educational Psychology*, **83**, 377–92.

Marsland, D. (1987) *Education and Youth* (London: Falmer).

Martin, C. L. (1991) 'The role of cognition in understanding gender effects', *Advances in Child Development and Behaviour*, **23**, 113–49.

Martin, C. L. and Halverson, C. F., Jr. (1987) 'The roles of cognition in sex role acquisition', in D. B. Carter (ed.), *Current Conceptions of Sex Roles and Sex Typing: Theory and Research* (New York: Praeger).

Martin, C. L. and Halverson, C. F., Jr. (1981) 'A schematic processing model of sex typing and stereotyping in children', *Child Development*, **52**, 1119–34.

Masterson, J. F. (1967) *The Psychiatric Dilemma of Adolescence* (Boston: Little, Brown).

Matlin, M. W. (1993) *The Psychology of Women* (2nd edn) (Fort Worth, TX: Harcourt Brace Jovanovich).

Mayall, B. and Petrie, P. (1977) *Minder, Mother and Child* (Windsor: NFER).

Mayall, B. and Petrie, P. (1983) *Childminding and Day Nurseries: What Kind of Care?* (London: Heinemann Educational Books).

McClelland, K. (1982) 'An exploration of the functions of friends and best friends', unpublished doctoral dissertation (Rutgers University, New Jersey).

McGarrigle, J. and Donaldson, M. (1974) 'Conservation accidents', *Cognition*, **3**, 341–50.

McGurk, H. (1975) *Growing and Changing* (London: Methuen).

McNeill, D. (1966) 'Developmental Linguistics', in F. Smith and G. Miller (eds), *The Genesis of Language* (Cambridge, Mass.: MIT Press).

Mead, G. H (1934) *Mind, Self and Society* (Chicago: University of Chicago Press).

Mead, M. (1935) *Sex and Temperament in Three Primitive Societies* (New York: Morrow).

Mead, M. (1939) *From the South Seas: Studies of Adolescence and Sex in Primitive Societies* (New York: Morrow).

Meadows, S. (1986) *Understanding Child Development* (London: Routledge).

Meadows, S. (1995) 'Cognitive Development', in P. E. Bryant and A. M. Coleman (eds), *Developmental Psychology* (Harlow: Longman).

Mehler, J., Bertoncini, J., Barrier, J. and Jassik-Gerschenfeld, D. (1978) 'Infant recognition of mother's voice', *Perception*, **7**, pp. 491–7.

Meilman, P. W. (1979) 'Cross-sectional age changes in ego identity status during adolescence', *Developmental Psychology*, **15**, 230–1.

Melhuish, E. C. (1990) 'Research on day care for young children in the United Kingdom', in E. C. Melhuish and P. Moss (eds), *Day Care for Young Children: International Perspectives* (London: Routledge).

Meltzoff, A. N. (1985) 'Cognitive foundations and social functions of imitation and intermodal representation in infancy', in J. Mehler and R. Fox (eds), *Neonate Cognition: Beyond the Booming, Buzzing Confusion* (Hillsdale, NJ: Erlbaum).

Miles, I. (1983) *Unemployment: Cause and Cure* (Oxford: Martin Robertson).

Milgram, S. (1974) *Obedience to Authority* (New York: Harper & Row).

Mitchell, P. (1992) *The Psychology of Childhood* (London: Falmer Press).

Mitchell, P. and Locahee, H. (1991) 'Children's early understanding of false belief', *Cognition*, **39**, 207–27.

Miyake, K., Chen, S. J. and Campos, J. J. (1985) 'Infant temperament, mother's mode of interaction and attachment in Japan: an interim report', in I. Bretherton and E. Waters (eds), Growing Points of Attachment Theory and Research, *Monographs of the Society for Research in Child Development*, 50, 276–97.

Money, J. and Erhardt, A. A. (1972) *Man and Woman; Boy and Girl* (Baltimore: John Hopkins University Press).

Moran, J. J. and Joniak, A. F. (1979) 'Effect of language on preference for response to a moral dilemma', *Developmental Psychology*, 337–8.

Moss, P. (1987) *A Review of Childminding Research* (University of London, Thomas Coram Research Unit).

National Academy of Sciences, Institutes on Medicine. (1984) *Bereavement, Reaction, Consequences and Care* (Washington DC: National Academy of Sciences).

Neimark, E. D. (1975) 'Intellectual development during adolescence', in F. D. Horowitz (ed.), *Review of Child Development Research*, Vol. 4 (Chicago: University of Chicago Press).

Nelson, K., Carskaddon, G. and Bonvillian, J. D. (1973) 'Syntax acquisition: impact of experimental variation in adult verbal interaction with the child', *Child Development*, **44**, 497–504.

Neugarten, B. L (1973) 'Personality change in late life: a developmental perspective', in C. Eisdorfter and M. P. Lawton (eds), *Psychology of Adult Development and Aging* (Washington DC: American Psychological Association).

Neugarten B. L. (1977) 'Personality and aging', in J. E. Birren and K. W. Shaie (eds), *Handbook of the Psychology of Aging* (New York: Van Nostrand Reinhold).

Newman, H. H., Freeman, F. N. and Holzinger, K (1937) *Twins: A Study of Heredity and Environment* (Chicago: University of Chicago Press).

Newman, P. R. and Newman, M. M. (1988) 'Parenthood and adult development', in R. Palkovitz and M. B. Sussman (eds), *Transitions in Parenthood* (New York: Haworth).

Newson, J. (1979) 'Intentional behaviour in the young infant', in D. Schaffer and J. Dunn (eds), *The First Year of Life* (Chichester: Wiley).

Novak, M. A. and Harlow, H. F. (1975) 'Social recovery of monkeys isolated for the first years of life. I: Rehabilitation and therapy', *Developmental Psychology,* **11**, 453–65.

Nyiti, R. M. (1976) 'The development of conservation in the Meru children of Tanzania', *Child Development,* **47**, 1622–9.

Offer, D. (1969) *The Psychological World of the Teenager: A Study of Normal Adolescence* (New York: Basic Books).

Olweus, D. (1989) 'Bully/victim problems among schoolchildren: basic facts and effects of a school based intervention program', in K. Rubin and D. Pepler (eds), *The Development and Treatment of Childhood Aggression* (Hillsdale, NJ: Erlbaum).

Parke, R. D. and O'Leary, S. (1976) 'Father-mother-infant interaction in the newborn period: some findings, some observations and some unresolved issues', in K. Riegel and J. Meacham (eds), *The Developing Individual in a Changing World, vol. 2, Social and Environmental Issues* (The Hague: Moulton).

Parke, R. D. and Suomi, S. J. (1980) 'Adult male–infant relationships: Human and non-human evidence', in K. Immelman, G. Barlow, M. Main and L. Petrinovitch (eds), *Behavioral Development: The Bielefeld Interdisciplinary Project* (New York: Cambridge University Press).

Parkes, C. M., Stevenson-Hinde, J. and Marris, P. (eds) (1991) *Attachment Across the Life Cycle* (London: Tavistock/Routledge).

Parkin, A. J., Lewinsohn, J. and Folkard, S. (1982) 'The influence of emotion on immediate and delayed retention: Levinger and Clark reconsidered', *British Journal of Psychology,* **73**, 389–93.

Parten, M. B. (1932) 'Social participation among preschool children', *Journal of Abnormal and Social Psychology,* **27**, 243–69.

Pavlov, I. (1927) *Conditioned Reflexes* (New York: Oxford University Press).

Peck, R. (1968) 'Psychological development in the second half of life', in B. L. Neugarten (ed.), *Midlife and Aging* (Chicago: University of Chicago Press).

Perner, J. (1991) *Understanding the Representational Mind* (Cambridge, Mass.: Bradford Books/MIT Press).

Perner, J., Leekam, S. R. and Wimmer, H. (1987) 'Three-year-olds' difficulty with false beliefs: the case for a conceptual deficit', *British Journal of Developmental Psychology,* **5**, 125–37.

Piaget, J. (1932/1977) *The Moral Judgement of the Child* (Harmondsworth: Penguin).

Piaget, J. (1936/1952) *The Origin of Intelligence in the Child* (London: Routledge & Kegan Paul).

Piaget, J. (1951) *Play, Dreams and Imitation in Childhood* (London: Routledge & Kegan Paul).

Piaget, J. and Inhelder, B. (1956) *The Child's Conception of Space* (London: Routledge & Kegan Paul).

Pollack, J. M. (1979) 'Obsessive-compulsive personality: a review', *Psychological Bulletin,* **86**, 225–41.

Popper, K. (1959) *The Logic of Scientific Discovery* (London: Hutchinson).

Pratt, M. W. and Norris, J. E. (1994) *The Social Psychology of Aging* (Oxford: Blackwell).

Pratt, M. W., Golding, G. and Kerig, P. (1987) 'Lifespan differences in adult thinking about hypothetical and personal moral issues: reflection or regression? *International Journal of Behavioural Development*, **10**, 359–75.

Premack, A. J. and Premack, D. (1972) 'Teaching language to an ape', *Scientific American*, **222** (4), 92–9.

Presland, P. and Antill, J. K. (1987) 'Household division of labour: the impact of hours worked in paid employment', *Australian Journal of Psychology*, **39**, 273–91.

Radin, N., Oyserman, D. and Benn, R. (1991) 'Grandfathers, teen mothers and children under two', in P. K. Smith (ed.), *The Psychology of Grandparenthood: An International Perspective* (London: Routledge).

Ramey, C. T. (1992) 'High-risk children and IQ: altering intergenerational patterns', *Intelligence*, **16**, 239–56.

Ramey, C. T. (1993) 'A rejoinder to Spitz's critique of the Abecedarian experiment', *Intelligence*, **17**, 25–30.

Ransom, R. L., Sutch, R. and Williams, S. H. (1991) 'Retirement: past and present', in A. H. Munnell (ed.) *Retirement and Public Policy: Proceedings of the Second Conference of the National Academy of Social Insurance* (Dubuque, IA: Kendall/Hunt).

Reibstein, J. and Richards, M. (1992) *Sexual Arrangements: Marriage and Affairs* (London: Heinemann).

Reichard, S., Livson, F. and Peterson, P. G. (1962) *Aging and Personality* (New York: Wiley).

Reiss, I. L. (1980) *Family Systems in America* (3rd edn) (New York: Holt, Rinehart and Winston).

Rest, J. R. (1983) 'Morality', in J. Flavell and E. Markman (eds), *Cognitive Development* in P. Mussen (general editor) *Carmichael's Manual of Child Psychology* (4th edn) (New York: Wiley).

Rheingold, H. L. and Eckerman, C. O. (1973) 'Fear of the stranger: a critical examination', in H. W. Reese (ed.), *Advances in Child Development and Behaviour*, vol. 8 (New York: Academic Press).

Rheingold, H., Gewirtz, J. L. and Ross, H. W. (1959) 'Social conditioning of vocalisation in the infant', *Journal of Comparative and Physiological Psychology*, **52**, 68–73.

Richards, H. C. Bear, G. G. Stewart, A. L. and Norman, A. D. (1992) 'Moral reasoning and classroom conduct: evidence of a curvilinear relationship', *Merrill-Palmer Quarterly*, **38**, 176–90.

Roberts, P. and Newton, P. M. (1987) 'Levinsonian studies of women's adult development', *Psychology and Aging*, **2**, 154–63.

Robinson, W. P. (1981) 'Language development in young children', in D. Fontana, *Psychology for Teachers* (Basingstoke: Macmillan/BPS).

Rosenthal, M. (1985) 'Identity: Summary', in G. K. Brookings and W. R. Allen (eds) *Beginnings: The Social and Affective Development of Black Children* (Hillsdale, NJ: Erlbaum), 231–6.

Rosenthal, R. and Jacobson, L. (1968) *Pygmalion in the Classroom: Teacher Expectation and Pupils' Intellectual Development* (New York: Holt, Rinehart and Winston).

Rovee-Collier, C. (1993) 'The capacity for long-term memory in infancy', *Current Directions in Psychological Science*, **2**, 130–5.

Rubin, J. S., Provenzano, F. J. and Luria, Z. (1974) 'The eye of the beholder: parents' view on sex of newborns', *American Journal of Orthopsychiatry*, **5**, 353–63.

Ruble, D. N. (1987) 'The acquisition of self-knowledge: a self-socialization perspective', in N. Eisenberg (ed.), *Contemporary Topics in Developmental Psychology* (New York: Wiley).

Ruble, D. N. (1988) 'Sex-role development', in M. H. Bornstein and M. E. Lamb, *Developmental Psychology: an Advanced Textbook* (Hillsdale, NJ: Erlbaum).

Ruble, D. N., Balaban, T. and Cooper, J. (1981) 'Gender constancy and the effects of sex-typed television toy commercials', *Child Development*, **52**, 667–73.

Rutter, M. (1972) *Maternal Deprivation Reassessed* (Harmondsworth: Penguin).

Rutter, M. (1980) *Changing Youth in a Changing Society: Patterns of Adolescent Disorder* (Cambridge, Mass.: Harvard University Press).

Rutter, M. (1981) *Maternal Deprivation Reassessed* (2nd edn) (Harmondsworth: Penguin).

Rutter, M. and Rutter, M. (1993) *Developing Minds: Challenge and Continuity across the Lifespan* (Harmondsworth: Penguin).

Rutter, M, Tizard, J. and Whitmore (eds). (1970) *Education Health and Behaviour* (London: Longman).

Ryff, C. D. and Heinke, S. G. (1983) 'Subjective organisation of personality in adulthood and ageing', *Journal of Personality and Social Psychology*, **44**, 807–16.

Sagi, A. and Lewkowicz, K. S. (1987) 'A cross-cultural evaluation of attachment research', in L. W. C. Tavecchio and M. H. van Ijzendoorn (eds), *Attachment in Social Networks: Contributions to the Bowlby–Ainsworth Attachment Theory* (Amsterdam: North-Holland).

Salmon, P. and Claire, H. (1984) *Classroom Collaboration* (London: Routledge & Kegan Paul).

Scarr, S. and McCartney, K. (1983) 'How people make their own environments: a theory of genotype-environmental effects', *Child Development*, **54**, 24–35.

Scarr, S. and Weinberg, R. A. (1976) 'Intellectual similarities within families of both adopted and biological children', *Intelligence*, **1**, 170–91.

Scarr-Salapatek, S. (1971) 'Social class and IQ', *Science*, **174**, 28–36.

Schachter, F. F. (1982) 'Sibling identification and split-parent identification: a family trend', in M. Lamb and B. Sutton-Smith (eds), *Sibling Relationships* (Hillsdale, NJ: Erlbaum).

Schaffer, H. R. (1977) *Mothering* (London: Fontana/Open Books).

Schaffer, H. R. and Emerson, P. E. (1964) 'The development of social attachments in infancy', *Monographs of Social Research in Child Development*, **29**, No. 74.

Schaie, K. W. (1983; 1990) 'The Seattle Longitudinal Study: a twenty-one year exploration of psychometric intelligence in adulthood', in K. W.

Schaie (ed.), *Longitudinal Studies of Adult Psychological Development* (New York: Guilford).

Schiff, M., Dyne, M., Dumaret, A., Stewart, J., Tomkiewicz, S. and Fenigold, J. (1978) 'Intellectual status of working-class children adopted early into upper-middle class families', *Science*, **200**, 1503–4.

Schmidt, D. F. and Boland, S. M. (1986) 'Structure of perceptions of older adults: evidence for multiple stereotypes', *Psychology and Aging*, **11**, 255–60.

Schultz, D. A. (1972) *The Changing Family: Its Function and Future* (Englewood Cliffs, NJ: Prentice-Hall).

Schulz, N. R., Kaye, D. B. and Hoyer, W. J. (1980) 'Intelligence and spontaneous flexibility in adulthood and old age', *Intelligence*, **4**, 219–31.

Schulz, R. (1978) *The Psychology of Death, Dying and Bereavement* (New York: Addison-Wesley).

Selman, R. L. (1976) 'Social cognitive understanding: a guide to educational and clinical practice', in T. Likona (ed.), *Moral Development and Behaviour: Theory, Research and Social Issues* (New York: Holt, Rinehart and Winston).

Shackleton, V. and Fletcher, C. (1984) *Individual Differences: Theories and Applications* (London: Methuen).

Shatz, M. (1994) *A Toddler's Life: Becoming a Person* (New York: Oxford University Press).

Shayer, M. and Wylam, H. (1978) 'The distribution of Piagetian stages of thinking in British, middle and secondary school children: II', *British Journal of Educational Psychology*, **48**, 62–70.

Sheehy, G. (1976) *Passages: Predictable Crises of Adult Life* (New York: E. P. Dutton).

Shields, J. (1962) *Monozygotic Twins Brought Up Apart and Brought Up Together* (Oxford: Oxford University Press).

Shuey, A. M. (1966) *The Testing of Negro Intelligence* (3rd edn) (New York: Social Science Press).

Siegler, R. S (1981) 'Developmental sequences within and between concepts', *Monographs of the Society for Research in Child Development*, 46 (2, Serial No. 189).

Simmons, R. G., Blyth, D. A. and McKinney, K. L. (1983) 'The social and psychological effects of puberty on white females', in J. Brooks-Gunn and A. C. Petersen (eds), *Girls at Puberty: Biological and Psychological Perspectives* (New York: Plenum Press).

Simon, B. (1971) *Intelligence, Psychology and Education – A Marxist Critique* (London: Lawrence and Wishart).

Skeels, H. M. (1966) 'Adult status of children with contrasting early life experiences', *Monographs of the Society for Research in Child Development*, 31 (whole no. 3).

Skinner, B. F (1938) *The Behaviour of Organisms* (New York: Appleton-Century-Crofts).

Skinner, B. F. (1957) *Verbal Behaviour* (New York: Appleton-Century-Crofts).

Slavin, R. E ((1987) 'Developmental and motivational perspectives on cooperative learning: a reconciliation', *Child Development*, **58**, 1161–7.

Sluckin, A. (1981) *Growing up in the Playground: The Social Development of Children* (London: Routledge & Kegan Paul).

Sluckin, W. (1965) *Imprinting and Early Experiences* (London: Methuen).

Smart, L. S. (1992) 'The marital helping relationship following pregnancy loss and infant death', *Journal of Family Issues*, **13** (1), 81–98.

Smilansky, S. (1968) *The Effects of Sociodramatic Play on Disadvantaged Preschool Children* (New York: Wiley).

Smith, C. and Lloyd, B. (1978) 'Maternal behaviour and perceived sex of infant: revisited', *Child Development*, **49**, 1263–5.

Smith, P. K. and Cowie, H. (1991) *Understanding Children's Development* (Oxford: Blackwell).

Smith, P. K., Dalgleish, M. and Herzmark, G. (1981) 'A comparison of the effects of fantasy play tutoring and skills tutoring in nursery classes', *International Journal of Behavioural Development*, **4**, 421–41.

Snarey, J. R. (1985) 'Cross-cultural universality of social-moral development: a critical review of Kohlbergian Research', *Psychological Bulletin*, **97**, 202–32.

Snow, C. (1977) 'The development of conversation between mothers and babies', *Journal of Child Language*, **4**, 1–22.

Sorensen, R. (1973) *Adolescent Sexuality in Contemporary American Society* (Ithaca, NY: Cornell University Press).

Speicher, B. (1994) 'Family patterns of moral judgement during adolescence and early adulthood', *Developmental Psychology*, **30**, 624–32.

Spence, J. T., Helmreich, R. L. and Stapp, J. (1975) 'Ratings of self and peers on sex role attributes and their relation to self-esteem and concepts of masculinity and femininity', *Journal of Personality and Social Psychology*, **32**, 29–39.

Spitz, R. A. (1965) *The First Year of Life* (New York: International Universities Press).

Sternberg, R. J. (1984) 'What should intelligence tests test? Implications of a triarchic theory of intelligence for intelligence testing', *Educational Researcher*, **13** (1), 5–15.

Sternberg, R. J. (1985) *Beyond IQ: A Triarchic Theory of Human Intelligence* (Cambridge University Press).

Sternberg, R. J. (1988) *The Triarchic Mind: A New Theory of Human Intelligence* (New York: Viking).

Sternberg, R. J. (1990) *Metaphors of Mind: Conceptions of the Nature of Intelligence* (Cambridge University Press).

Stott, D. H. (1978) *Helping Children with Learning Difficulties* (London: Ward Lock).

Streib, G. F. and Schneider, C. (1971) *Retirement in American Society* (Ithaca, NY: Cornell University Press).

Sugarman, L. (1990) *Lifespan Development* (London and New York: Routledge).

Sylva, K. D., Roy, C. and Painter, M. (1980) *Childwatching at Playgroup and Nursery School* (London: Grant McIntyre).

Takahashi, K. (1986) 'Examining the Strange Situation procedure with Japanese mothers and 12-month old infants', *Developmental Psychology*, **22**, 265–70.

278 Bibliography

Takahashi, K. (1990) 'Are the key assumptions of the "Strange Situation", procedure universal? A view from Japanese research', *Human Development*, **33**, 23–30.

Teachman, J. D., Call, V. A. and Carver, K. P. (1994) 'Marital status and the duration of joblessness among white men', *Journal of Marriage and the Family*, **56**, 415–28.

Tesch, S. A. (1983) 'Review of friendship development across the life span', *Human Development*, **26**, 266–76.

Theorell, T. and Rahe, R. H. (1974) 'Psychosocial factors and myocardial infarction. I: an inpatient study in Sweden', *Journal of Psychosomatic Research*, **15**, 25–31.

Thomas, R. M. (1992) *Comparing Theories of Child Development* (3rd edn) (Belmont, Calif.:Wadsworth).

Thompson, R. A. and Lamb, M. E. (1983) 'Continuity and change in socioemotional development during the second year', in R. Emde and R. Harmon (eds), *Emotions in Early Development* (New York: Academic).

Thorndike, E. L. (1913) *Educational Psychology* (New York: Columbia University Press).

Tinsley, B. J. and Parke, R. D. (1984) 'Grandparents as support and socialization agents', in M. Lewis (ed.), *Beyond the Dyad* (New York: Plenum).

Tizard, B. and Hodges, J. (1978) 'The effect of early institutional rearing on the development of eight-year old children', *Journal of Child Psychology and Psychiatry*, **12**, 99–118.

Tobias, P. (1974) 'IQ and the nature–nurture controversy', *Journal of Behavioural Science*, **2**, 24.

Tout, K. (1989) *Aging in Developing Countries* (Oxford: Oxford University Press).

Townsend, P. (1957) *The Family Life of Old People* (London: Routledge & Kegan Paul).

Trevarthen, C. (1974) 'Conversations with a two-month-old', *New Scientist*, **62**, 320–3.

Troll, L. E. (1982) *Continuations: Adult Development and Aging* (Monterey, CA: Brooks/Cole).

Turner, J. S. and Helms, D. R. (1995) *Lifespan Development* (5th edn) (Orlando, FL: Harcourt Brace College Publishers).

Turner, P. J. (1993) 'Attachment to mother and behaviour with adults in preschool', *British Journal of Developmental Psychology*, **11**, 75–89.

Unger, R. and Crawford, M. (1992) *Women and Gender: A Feminist Psychology* (New York: McGraw-Hill).

Vaillant, G. E. (1977) *Adaptation to Life: How the Best and Brightest Came of Age* (Boston: Little, Brown).

van Ijzendoorn, M. H. and Kroonenberg, P. M. (1988) 'Cross-cultural patterns of attachment: a meta-analysis of the Strange Situation', *Child Development*, **59**, 147–56.

Vernon, P. A (ed.) (1987) *Speed of Information-Processing and Intelligence* (Norwood, NJ: Ablex).

Vernon, P. A. and Mori, M. (1992) 'Intelligence, reaction times and peripheral nerve conduction velocity', *Intelligence*, **16**, 273–88.

Vernon, P. E. (1969) *Intelligence and Cultural Environment* (London: Methuen).

Veroff, J. and Feld, S. (1970) *Marriage and Work in America: a study of motives and roles* (New York: Van Nostrand Reinhold).

Vincent, C. E. (1964) 'Socialisation data in research on young marrieds', *Acta Sociologica*, August.

Vygotsky, L. (1967) 'Play and the role of mental development in the child', *Soviet Psychology*, **5**, 6–18.

Vygotsky, L. S. (1978) *Mind in Society*, edited by M. Cole, V. John-Steiner, S. Scribner and E. Souberman (Cambridge, Mass.: Harvard University Press).

Wadeley, A. (1991) *Ethics in Psychological Research and Practice* (Leicester: British Psychological Society).

Wadeley, A., Birch, A. and Malim, T. (1997) *Perspectives in Psychology* (2nd edn) (Basingstoke: Macmillan).

Walker, K. (1970) 'Time spent by husbands in household work', *Family Economics Review*, **14**, 8–11.

Walker, L. J., de Vries, B. and Trevethan, S. D. (1987) 'Moral stages and moral orientations in real-life and hypothetical dilemmas', *Child Development*, **58**, 842–58.

Walker, S. (1984) *Learning Theory and Behaviour Modification* (London: Methuen).

Warburton, F. W. (1951) 'The ability of the Gurkha recruit', *British Journal of Psychology*, **42**, 123–33.

Warr, P. B. (1982) 'A national study of non-financial employment commitment', *Journal of Occupational Psychology*, **55**, 297–312.

Warr, P. B. and Jackson, P. (1985) 'Factors influencing the psychological impact of prolonged unemployment and of re-employment', *Psychological Medicine*, **15**, 795–807.

Wartner, U. G., Grossman, K., Fremmer-Bombik, E. and Suess, G. (1994) 'Attachment patterns at age six in South Germany: predictability from infancy and implications for preschool behaviour', *Child Development*, **65**, 1014–27.

Waters, E. (1978) 'The reliability and stability of individual differences in infant-mother attachment', *Child Development*, **49**, 483–94 .

Watson, J. B. and Rayner, R. (1920) 'Conditioned emotional reactions', *Journal of Experimental Psychology*, **3**, 1–14.

Wells, C. G. (1985) *Language Development in the Preschool Years* (Cambridge: Cambridge University Press).

Werner, E. (1991) 'Grandparent–grandchild relationships amongst US ethnic groups', in P. K. Smith (ed.), *The Psychology of Grandparenthood: An International Perspective* (London: Routledge).

Werner, E. E. (1986) 'A longitudinal study of perinatal risk', in D. C. Farran and J. C. McKinney (eds), *Risk in Intellectual and Psychosocial Development* (Orlando, FL: Academic Press), pp. 3–28.

White, R. (1975) *Lives in Progress* (3rd edn) (New York: Holt, Rinehart and Winston).

Wilcox, J. and Webster, E. (1980) 'Early discourse behaviour: an analysis of children's responses to listener feedback', *Child Development*, **51**, 1120–5.

Wilkinson, F.R. and Cargill, D.W. (1955) 'Repression elicited by story material based on the Oedipus complex', *Journal of Social Psychology*, **42**, 209–14.

Williams, J.E. and Best, D.L. (1990) *Measuring Sex Stereotypes: A Multination Study* (Newbury Park, Calif.: Sage).

Wimmer, H. and Perner, J. (1983) 'Beliefs about beliefs: representations and constraining function of wrong beliefs in young children's understanding of deception', *Cognition*, **13**, 103–28.

Wiseman, R. (1975) 'Crisis theory and the process of divorce', *Social Casework*, **56**, 205–12.

Wiseman, S. (1964) *Education and Environment* (Manchester: Manchester University Press).

Wood, D.J. (1988) *How Children Think and Learn* (Oxford: Blackwell).

Wood, D.J., Bruner, J.S. and Ross, G. (1976) 'The role of tutoring in problem-solving', *Journal of Child Psychology and Psychiatry*, **117**, 89–100.

Wortman, C.B. and Silver, R.C. (1990) 'Successful mastery of bereavement and widowhood: a life-course perspective', in P.B. Baltes and M.M. Baltes (eds), *Successful Aging: Perspectives from the Behavioral Sciences* (New York: Cambridge University Press).

Wright, E.O., Shire, K., Hwang, S.L., Dolan, M. and Baxter, J. (1992) 'The non-effects of class in the gender division of labor in the home: a comparative study of Sweden and the United States', *Gender and Society*, **6**, 252–82.

Yarrow, L. (1973) 'The relationship between nutritive sucking experiences in infancy and non-nutritive sucking in childhood', in H.J. Eysenck and G.D. Wilson (eds), *The Experimental Study of Freudian Theories* (London: Methuen).

Yarrow, L.J. (1964) 'Separation from parents during early childhood', in M.L. Hoffman and L.W. Hoffman (eds), *Review of Child Development Research*, Vol. 1 (New York: Russell Sage Foundation).

Youngblade, L.M. and Belsky, J. (1992) 'Parent–child antecedents of 5-year-olds' close friendships: a longitudinal study', *Developmental Psychology*, **28**, 700–13.

Zigler, E. and Berman, W. (1983) 'Discerning the future of early childhood intervention', *American Psychologist*, **38**, 894–906.

Index